山东省高校人文社会科学研究计划项目"新媒体时代著作权制度的应对与变革研究"（FL15G7）

数字网络技术背景下著作权法的
困境与出路

姜福晓 ◎ 著

知识产权出版社
全国百佳图书出版单位

图书在版编目（CIP）数据

数字网络技术背景下著作权法的困境与出路/姜福晓著. —北京：知识产权出版社，2017.8
ISBN 978-7-5130-5088-3

Ⅰ.①数… Ⅱ.①姜… Ⅲ.①著作权法—研究—中国 Ⅳ.①D923.414

中国版本图书馆 CIP 数据核字（2017）第 212864 号

责任编辑：高　超　　　　　　　责任校对：王　岩
封面设计：品　序　　　　　　　责任出版：刘译文

数字网络技术背景下著作权法的困境与出路
姜福晓　著

出版发行	知识产权出版社 有限责任公司	网　　址	http://www.ipph.cn
社　　址	北京市海淀区气象路 50 号院	邮　　编	100081
责编电话	010-82000860 转 8383	责编邮箱	morninghere@126.com
发行电话	010-82000860 转 8101/8102	发行传真	010-82000893/82005070/82000270
印　　刷	北京科信印刷有限公司	经　　销	各大网上书店、新华书店及相关专业书店
开　　本	720mm×1000mm　1/16	印　　张	14.5
版　　次	2017 年 8 月第 1 版	印　　次	2017 年 8 月第 1 次印刷
字　　数	250 千字	定　　价	48.00 元
ISBN 978-7-5130-5088-3			

出版权专有　侵权必究
如有印装质量问题，本社负责调换。

前 言

在所有的法律领域中,著作权法是对技术发展最敏感、也对技术发展会产生最直接影响的法律领域之一。从世界范围内的著作权法发展史来看,著作权法的发展与技术的发展总是相互交织在一起。印刷术、照相术、电影技术、录音录像技术、广播技术、复印技术都曾对著作权制度的产生和发展轨迹产生了直接的影响,而著作权法针对这些技术作出的回应也影响着这些技术的发展。无论是著作权产业,还是新技术产业,都是资本密集型行业。因此,除上述的技术因素外,市场力量也是影响著作权制度发展的关键因素。可以说,著作权法律制度的发展历史,就是法律、技术和市场这三个因素交织发展的历史。产生于20世纪后期的数字网络技术,在著作权法领域内掀起了轩然大波,引发了人们对著作权法律制度能否适应以及如何适应数字网络技术的讨论,甚至有人怀疑数字网络技术时代著作权法存在的必要性。著作权法如何应对数字网络技术的发展已成为世界性的讨论话题。

笔者对数字网络环境下的著作权法问题的兴趣始于攻读博士期间。笔者自2010年开始在对外经济贸易大学大学法学院攻读民商法学博士学位,期间对互联网环境下的著作权法律问题产生了浓厚的兴趣。2011年受国家留学基金委联合培养博士项目资助,赴美国范德堡大学法学院在Daniel Gervais教授的指导下对网络环境下著作权的保护以及著作权集体管理制度进行了为期14个月的研究。2012年回国后,经与博士授业恩师梅夏英教授讨论,最后以"数字网络技术背景下著作权法的困境与出路"为题开始博士论文的写作。在博士论文的研究过程中,梅夏英教授对互联网法律问题方面的洞见以及Daniel Gervais教授在网络著作权领域的深刻理解,都使笔者深受启发。在此,真诚感谢两位恩师的教、育之恩。虽然有幸得到名师指导，但鉴于自己学力有限，书中可能存在谬误，希望读者不吝赐教。

本书就是在笔者博士论文的基础上形成的。该论文于2014年通过答辩，至今已有三年。这三年中，互联网产业一直在快速发展，互联网商业模式在不断演化，欧盟、美国等国家互联网著作权领域的立法也有了一定的进展。笔者对本书相关内容进行了必要更新，同时将美国《数字千禧年法案》的核心部分《在线著作权侵权责任限制法案》（1998）、欧盟的《信息社会版权与相关权指令》（2001）、《欧盟数字单一市场版权指令草案》（2016）作为附录，以供读者了解欧美国家相关立法现状和趋势。

最后，值得提出的是，本书的研究系从权利配置、权利保护、权利实现三个维度探讨著作权法如何应对数字网络技术的挑战。因此，限于研究重点，本书的研究主要是系统性和框架性的，无法对某些问题进行过于深入的研究。例如，网络平台的著作权侵权问题就是一个极具重要性和争议性而需要深入研究的难题，本书虽然在第三章以P2P网络服务提供者的侵权责任为例进行了研究，但无法囊括各种不同网络平台的著作权侵权问题。笔者目前正在对网络平台的知识产权侵权问题进行专门研究，待时机成熟再行专门结集出版。

数字网络技术正如一个移动的靶子，著作权法之箭很难一箭命中，虽然笔者认为本书中的主要观点和判断至今仍然基本符合当今的互联网发展现实，但数字网络技术发展的不可预测性决定了本书的研究必然是阶段性的。希望本书能为数字网络技术环境下著作权法律问题的研究起到抛砖引玉的作用。

摘　要

　　自 17 世纪晚期以来 300 多年的历史看，著作权法的发展很大程度上起因于作品复制和传播技术的发展。数字网络技术是活字印刷以来最强有力的复制和传播工具，主要从三个方面对传统著作权法提出了严峻挑战：打破了著作权法上的利益平衡格局；冲击了著作权法的理论预设和基础架构；给著作权的保护和实现带来挑战。

　　数字网络技术引起的著作权法律问题在法律、经济、社会和政治领域引起了广泛的讨论。如何应对数字网络技术给著作权法带来的挑战成为一个全球化的难题。本文将从权利配置、权利保护和权利实现三个角度研究著作权法在数字网络技术背景下面临的困境，并试图探寻著作权法应对新技术带来挑战的对策。

　　除导论和结论外，本文正文部分共分五章。

第一章　数字网络技术对著作权法的挑战

　　本章主要从宏观层面分析数字网络技术对著作权法的挑战，并对著作权法在新技术背景下的困境进行了分析和理论抽象。第一节从历史的视角对新技术影响下的著作权制度的产生和发展进行了系统梳理，为寻求数字网络技术背景下的著作权法的出路提供一定线索。第二节主要阐述了数字网络技术对传统著作权法的冲击和挑战。第三节对数字网络技术影响传统著作权法的机理进行了分析，并从著作权人与使用人之间行为博弈的角度对传统著作权法在数字网络环境下的困境进行理论分析和抽象，为寻求数字网络技术背景下的著作权法的出路提供理论起点。

第二章　权利配置：著作权法的基础架构及调整

　　本章在对著作权法基础架构进行分析和讨论的基础上，从权利配置的角度对几个关乎著作权法基础架构的重要问题进行分析研究。第一节首先对著作权的正当性理论进行了剖析，并提出了自己的看法；然后分析了著作权法的价值目标，在此基础上阐述了基于利益平衡的著作权法基础架构。第二至四节分别以临时复制、首次销售原则、合理使用制度这三个关乎著作权法基础架构的问题为例，分析著作权法在权利配置层面的困境和出路，对著作权如何应对数字网络技术的挑战提出了自己的见解。

第三章　权利保护之一：使用者行为的失范与规制

本章以著作权人与使用人之间行为博弈的视角，从使用人的角度，分析了传统著作权保护模式的困境，并对数字网络环境下著作权保护的新思路进行了探索。第一节主要从权利保护的层面对著作权保护面临的挑战进行了分析。第二节对传统的"闭锁型"著作权保护模式及其困境进行了分析。第三节对"开放型"著作权保护模式的必要性、实践及效果进行了研究。第四节以莱斯格的规制理论为基础，描绘了整体性著作权保护机制的大致框架。第五节对整体性著作权保护机制在云计算、大数据、3D打印技术背景下的可能作为进行了展望。

第四章　权利保护之二：权利人技术保护措施的保护与限制

本章以著作权人与使用人之间行为博弈的视角，从权利人的角度，对技术保护措施的保护和限制问题进行了研究。第一节介绍了技术保护措施的产生背景、概念和性质。第二节对域外技术保护措施的保护立法和司法实践进行了分析评价，并对我国的立法提出了建议。第三节主要从合理使用和反不正当竞争两个角度对技术保护措施的限制进行了研究。

第五章　权利实现：数字网络环境下的著作权市场机制

本章从著作权实现层面，对数字网络环境下著作权市场机制进行研究。第一节对著作权授权模式转型的必要性进行了分析。第二节则阐述了网络著作权授权信息系统的基本构造。第三节对如何完善我国的集体管理制度尤其是如何防止集体管理组织垄断地位的滥用问题提出建议。

关键词：数字网络技术，利益平衡，逐级响应机制，技术保护措施，著作权集体管理

Abstract

With a history of more than three hundred years from the late 17 th century, the development of copyright law can be attributed to the advance of technologies of replication and dissemination to a large degree. The digital network technology is the most powerful tool of replication and dissemi-nation after movable-type printing. It has broken the balance of interests within copyright law, shocked the theoretical presupposition and infrastructure, and presented great challenges to the protection and realization of copyright.

The legal issues in terms of copyright caused by digital network technology have triggered extensive discussion in the fields of law, economy, society and politics. It becomes a global puzzle for the copyright law to cope with the challenges brought by the technology of digital network. This research studied the dilemma of copyright law in the environment of digital network from three dimensions, which are configuration of copyrights, protection of copyrights and realization of copyrights, and tried to explore the measures to cope with the challenges caused by new technologies.

Besides the introduction and conclusion parts, this research includes five chapters.

Chapter One   The challenges to copyright law brought by digital network

This chapter made analysis of the challenges to copyright law by digital network technology from the macro level, and made an analysis and theoretical abstraction of the dilemma of copyright law in the environment of digital network. Section one made a historical study of the emergence and development of copyright law, providing some clues to the exploitation of the way out of the digital dilemma. Section two analyzed the challenges to the traditional copyright law brought by the digital network technology. Section three analyzed the mechanism of how the digital technology influenced copyright law, and made an analysis and theoretical abstraction of the dilemma of copyright law from a perspective of game behavior between the right holders and the users. This chapter serves as the starting point of the exploitation of this research.

Chapter Two Configuration of Rights: the framework of copyright law and its adjustment

This chapter studied some important issues relevant to the framework of copyright law from the perspective of configuration of rights. Section one analyzed the justification theories of copyright law and gave some opinions. Then this section made a concise analysis of the values and framework of copyright law. The next three sections studied the dilemmas of copyright law and the way out by addressing the issues of temporary copies, the first sale doctrine and the fair use doctrine, which are very important parts of copyright framework.

Chapter Three Protection of rights (Ⅰ): The deregulation and regulation of behavior of users

This chapter analyzed the dilemma of the traditional mode of copyright protection from the perspective of the game between the right holders and users, and explored the new mode of copyright protection. Section one made a brief introduction of the challenges to copyright protection. Section two reviewed the traditional mode of copyright protection, which is featured "lock up". The third section addressed the necessity, practice and effects of the "open license" protection mode. Section four depicted a basis structure of the integrated mode of copyright protection based on the regulation theory of Lessig. Section five made an outlook on the potential role of "open license" protection mode in the environment with cloud computing, big data and 3D printing.

Chapter Four Protection of rights (Ⅱ): The protection and restrictions of TPM

This chapter made a study of the protection and restrictions of TPM from the perspective of game theory in terms of right holder. Section one introduced the background, conception and nature of TPM. Section two analyzed the foreign legislation and judicial practice of the TPM, and then gave some suggestions to the improvement of Chinese copyright law. The third section studied the restrictions on TPM from the perspective of fair use and anti-unfair competition.

Chapter Five   Realization of rights: The copyright market mechanism in the environment of digital network

This chapter studied the copyright market mechanism in the environment of digital network. The first section analyzed the importance of the transition of the copyright licensing mode. Section two addressed the basic blocks of the information system for copyright licensing. The last section gave some suggestions on how to improve copyright collective management, especially how to prevent copyright collective societies from abusing the monopoly position.

Keywords: Digital Network Technology, Balance of Interests, Graduated Response, Technological Protection Measures, Copyright Collective Management

目　录

- 导　论 …………………………………………………… 1
  - 一、研究背景 / 1
  - 二、研究意义 / 3
  - 三、研究现状 / 4
  - 四、研究目标与研究思路 / 9
  - 五、研究方法 / 9

- 第一章　数字网络技术对著作权法的挑战 ……………… 11
  - ◎ 第一节　传统技术影响下著作权法的产生与发展 / 11
    - 一、印刷机时代著作权法的产生 / 11
    - 二、模拟技术时代著作权法的扩张 / 14
    - 三、著作权法的发展规律 / 19
  - ◎ 第二节　数字网络技术对著作权法的挑战 / 20
    - 一、数字网络技术的产生与发展 / 20
    - 二、数字网络技术的特征 / 21
    - 三、数字网络技术对著作权法的冲击 / 22
  - ◎ 第三节　数字网络技术背景下著作权法困境的行为学分析 / 25
    - 一、数字网络技术引起著作权法的不确定性 / 25
    - 二、著作权法不确定影响下权利人与使用人的行为博弈 / 27

第二章 权利配置：著作权法的基础架构及调整 …………………… 30

◎ 第一节 传统著作权法的基础架构 / 30
一、著作权的正当性基础 / 30
二、著作权法的价值目标和利益平衡 / 34
三、基于利益平衡的著作权法基础架构 / 36

◎ 第二节 临时复制问题 / 37
一、临时复制问题的提出 / 37
二、临时复制的域外立法司法实践 / 38
三、对我国第三次著作权法修改建议 / 41

◎ 第三节 数字网络环境下的首次销售原则适用问题 / 41
一、首次销售原则概述 / 41
二、首次销售原则在数字网络环境下适用的国外司法实践 / 42
三、数字网络环境影响下首次销售原则的发展趋势分析 / 48

◎ 第四节 数字网络技术影响下合理使用制度 / 51
一、合理使用制度概述 / 51
二、合理使用制度的立法模式 / 52
三、数字网络技术影响下合理使用制度的调整 / 53

第三章 权利保护之一：使用者行为的失范与规制 …………………… 54

◎ 第一节 数字与网络技术对著作权保护带来的挑战 / 54

◎ 第二节 传统"闭锁型"著作权保护模式及其困境 / 60
一、对 P2P 服务提供者的间接侵权责任诉讼：阻止传播工具 / 60
二、对个人使用者的直接侵权责任诉讼：禁止传播行为 / 63
三、"逐级响应"机制：限制网络接入 / 64
四、技术保护措施：限制作品获取 / 67

◎ 第三节 "开放型"著作权保护机制的兴起 / 70
一、"开放型"著作权保护机制的合理性和必然性 / 70
二、"开放型"著作权保护机制的实践 / 71

三、"开放型"著作权保护机制的成效显现 / 75

◎ 第四节　迈向一种整体性著作权实现机制 / 76
　　一、莱斯格的整体性规制理论 / 77
　　二、整体性著作权保护机制的大致框架 / 79

◎ 第五节　云计算、大数据、3D打印与整体性著作权保护机制的
　　　　　前景展望 / 80

第四章　权利保护之二：权利人技术保护措施的保护与限制 …………… 82

◎ 第一节　技术保护措施的背景 / 82
　　一、网络侵权催生技术保护措施 / 82
　　二、技术保护措施的概念 / 83
　　三、技术保护措施的性质 / 84

◎ 第二节　对技术保护措施的立法保护 / 85
　　一、国际条约关于技术保护措施的规定 / 85
　　二、美国对技术保护措施的保护 / 87
　　三、欧盟对技术保护措施的保护 / 89
　　四、我国的技术保护措施立法及建议 / 91

◎ 第三节　对技术保护措施的限制 / 92
　　一、技术保护措施的正当性之辨 / 93
　　二、技术保护措施与合理使用的冲突与解决 / 95
　　三、技术保护措施与反不正当竞争的冲突与协调 / 103

第五章　权利实现：数字网络环境下的著作权市场机制 ……………… 107

◎ 第一节　数字网络环境要求著作权授权模式转型 / 107
　　一、数字网络技术改变传统著作权市场生态 / 107
　　二、著作权权利的碎片化要求建立著作权授权信息系统 / 110
　　三、著作权地域性与网络全球性的冲突需要建立跨境授权机制 / 111
　　四、数字网络时代著作权授权的线上迁移 / 112

◎ 第二节　网络著作权授权信息系统的基本框架 / 113
　　一、网络著作权信息系统的国际实践 / 113
　　二、著作权信息系统的跨境整合 / 115
　　三、我国著作权信息系统存在的问题和完善建议 / 118
◎ 第三节　数字网络技术背景下的著作权集体管理制度 / 121
　　一、传统技术背景下的著作权集体管理 / 121
　　二、数字网络背景下著作权集体管理制度的可能作为 / 124
　　三、著作权集体管理制度对数字网络技术的因应之策 / 126

结　论 ··· 131

参考文献 ·· 134

附录 1 ··· 143

附录 2 ··· 156

附录 3 ··· 177

导　论

一、研究背景

现代著作权法的设计理念是通过授予作者对其作品一定时间的排他权以促进科学进步。[1] 从著作权法自17世纪晚期以降300年的历史看，其发展很大程度上起因于作品复制和传播技术的发展。这主要表现在三个方面：著作权的产生源于现代印刷机的发明，并随作品复制和存储技术的发展逐渐将保护扩展至照片、电影和录音；广播技术使远距离提供作品成为可能，从而为著作权提供了新的市场；数字技术则代表技术创新的第三次浪潮。

数字技术和互联网是活字印刷以来最强有力的复制和传播工具。数字技术出现之前，文字作品必须印刷在纸张上，音乐作品必须灌制在唱片中，电影则必须录制在胶片中，而后通过这些载体进行传播。数字技术突破了传统作品载体的限制，使作品能够以统一的数字格式存储在光盘、硬盘等载体中。网络技术则对作品的传播带来了革命性的变化。数字与网络技术的出现和发展给著作权法带来了前所未有的严峻挑战。

总结起来，数字和网络技术对著作权法的挑战至少有以下几个方面：

（1）数字与网络技术打破了著作权法上的利益平衡格局。

数字技术使对作品高保真、低成本且瞬时的复制成为可能。模拟制品（如磁带、唱片）复制件的保真度低于原件，如果连续复制，保真度还会递减。数字制品则可以被无限复制而质量无损。随着技术发展，复制设备的成本也逐渐低廉到普通民众可以承受的程度，对数字文件的复制只需轻点鼠标即可实现。传统复制方式需要时间，因此作品的原始出版者在这段时间内就无须面对来自盗版的竞争。而数字复制很短时间就可完成，这使得侵权的门槛大大降低，对出版者的威胁也随之大大增加，著作权法上的利益平衡格局被打破。

（2）数字与网络技术冲击了著作权法的理论预设和基础架构。

首先，著作权法是以复制权为起点展开的，复制权是著作权法体系构建的

---

[1] 在历史上，著作权法与版权法是两个不同的概念。著作权的英文是 Authors' right，而版权的英文是 Copyright。现在一般将这两个概念等同使用，我国的《著作权法》也将著作权与版权等同使用。本文为了表述统一，使用"著作权"的称谓，但对于一些习惯用法，如"国家版权局"，继续沿用。

· 1 ·

原点。对复制权的控制构成保护著作权的有效机制。在传统有形世界中，作品的使用和复制是截然分开的，这是著作权法的重要前提之一。新技术则扩张了作品的复制方式，如将作品固定在光盘和硬盘等新的介质中、将作品上传至网络服务器、将作品从网络服务器下载到本地计算机中、通过网络向其他用户发送作品等。然而，新技术也给著作权法带来了巨大挑战。其中临时复制问题对著作权法传统的"复制"概念带来了强烈的冲击。这一问题在国际上存在广泛争议，至今尚无统一意见。美国法院曾在 MAI 一案中判决临时复制构成侵权，即一旦计算机程序进入计算机内存中，就认定产生了著作权法意义上的复制（MAI System Corp. v. Peak Computer, Inc., 991 F. 2d 511, 9th Cir. 1993）。该案对其日后美国的著作权法理论和司法实践产生了重大影响。但由于该问题争议重大，美国《著作权法》至今对临时复制问题尚未作出明确规定。临时复制问题来自对数字作品的使用不可避免地要对作品进行复制，数字世界中作品使用对复制的依赖性动摇了传统著作权法中作品使用和复制截然分开的基本假定。可以预见，随着技术的不断发展，哪些临时复制构成复制行为至今仍然是一个开放性的问题。

其次，从历史的角度看，著作权从来就是针对作品的专业使用者设计的。这是因为传统技术背景下，个人使用者的复制能力有限，个人使用者的复制对著作权人的影响基本可以被忽略。因此，早期著作权法中，私人复制和个人使用不在复制权控制范围之内。随着技术的发展，个人使用者对作品的复制和传播能力大幅提高，使专业复制和私人复制的区分出现困难，私人复制问题逐渐成为著作权法上的重要问题。由于私人复制的广泛性和复杂性，判定私人复制是合理使用还是侵权至今仍然是一个广泛讨论的问题。

最后，传统著作权法中，作品都是固定在传统的有形载体中。发行权与作品载体所有权的冲突是著作权法中首次销售原则存在的根源。而在数字环境下，作品的固定可以摆脱有形介质的束缚，因而不存在发行权与所有权的冲突问题。这样，首次销售原则在数字环境下的适用问题成为一个新的问题。首次销售原则是否适用于数字环境在美国至今没有定论。

（3）数字和互联网技术对作品传播方式起到革命性作用，给著作权的保护和实现带来严峻挑战。

数字和网络技术使作品的创作和传播成本大大降低，每个人都可成为创作者和传播者。新技术打破了使用者和创作者之间的壁垒。数字制品可以存储在电脑中并可以进行其他操作。随着压缩技术的进步和硬盘容量的增大，作品尤其是娱乐作品的使用者可以非常容易且低成本地创建海量作品库。如果说数字技术对作品的存储和复制产生了革命性的影响，那么网络技术则对作品的传播方式起到了颠覆性作用。网络技术使信息传播摆脱了传统有形载体和交通方式的限制。这种进步使信息传递成本得到极大降低，使作品大规模传播成为可能。其中，P2P 技术的出现更是使作品传播技术发生了历史性变革。P2P 技术引起的作品大规模网上传播成为著作权法上的难题。P2P 分享被认为是互联网环境下著作权产业尤其是音乐产业的首要威胁。

数字与网络技术引起的著作权法律问题在法律、经济、社会和政治领域引起了广泛的讨论。如何应对数字和互联网技术给著作权法带来的挑战成为一个全球化的难题。

二、研究意义

（一）理论意义

数字和网络技术对传统复制和传播技术带来了革命性变革，彻底改变了著作权领域的生态。数字与网络技术动摇了传统著作权法的理论预设和基础架构，其中临时复制、私人复制问题以及首次销售原则在数字环境下的适用问题是著作权法面临挑战的重要体现。传统印刷时代形成的著作权制度的基本概念必须重新审视，与此相对应的具体制度也必须重新设计。这些问题一方面涉及著作权的专有权的配置问题，另一方面涉及著作权的例外制度。这两方面内容构成了著作权制度的主要框架。

因此，如何应对数字和网络技术给著作权法带来的挑战，是一项牵一发而动全身的理论命题。本课题对立法者而言，可以为著作权规则的修改和新规则的制定提供理论支持；对司法者而言，可以为解决新技术背景下出现的著作权法律纠纷的处理提供富有价值的参考。因此，深入研究著作权法在新技术背景下面临的困境，并探寻解决著作权法应对新技术挑战的出路，具有重大的理论价值。

（二）实践意义

成功的著作权制度通常会较好地处理以下几对利益关系：促进作品自由提供从而实现作品的可获得性和控制作品传播以使创作者获得经济利益之间的关系；作品生产者与消费者之间的关系；创作者个人与社会之间的关系；使用作品的短期满足和促进文化活力的长期目标之间的关系。现实表明，数字和互联网技术已经深刻改变了这些平衡，并将天平的一端偏向了作品的自由提供、消费者、社会利益以及作品使用的短期满足。数字和互联网技术给著作权法提出了这样的问题：对著作权人而言，如何应对新技术带来的挑战，保护和实现自己的权利；对著作权政策制定者而言，如何尽可能地保证作品对于公众的可获得性以维护使用者的利益和社会利益，同时给予作品创作者及其商业伙伴合理的回报以激励作品的创作。因此，研究著作权法如何应对新技术带来的挑战，如何重新实现著作权法上的利益平衡，对于鼓励作品的创作、推动著作权产业以及整个经济的发展，以及促进社会公共利益的实现，具有重要的实践价值和社会意义。

（三）战略意义

我国自2005年起开始构建并准备实施自己的知识产权战略，并计划在2020年把我国建设成创新型国家。为此制定了包括知识产权战略在内的一系列国家战略。著作权法是这一战略的核心组成部分之一。当今世界科技进步日新月异，知识经济迅猛发展，经济全球化步伐明显增快，知识产权已经成为国际经济和企业竞争的焦点，并在经济社会中发挥越来越重要的作用。著作权制度是知识产权制度的三大支柱之一，著作权制度不仅关系到著作权产业的发展，更影响整个经济乃至国家的竞争力。因此，研究新技术对著作权制度带来的影响并解决著作权法面临的问题，在经济全球化、国际竞争日益剧烈和新型技术不断变革的时代背景下，具有重要的战略意义。

美国、欧盟等具有相对成熟的著作权法律制度，其著作权法的发展对世界的影响不容忽视。我国目前正在对著作权法进行大规模的修订，在经济全球化步伐不断加快，中美、中欧贸易日益增长的背景下，考察美国、欧盟等其他国家和地区如何应对新技术给著作权法带来的挑战，总结其经验和教训，对于我国有重要的理论实践价值和战略意义。

三、研究现状

目前，国内外关于数字与网络技术背景下著作权法的困境与出路这一主题已有不少研究成果。这些成果的研究涉及著作权法与新技术的互动、数字与网络技术对著作权法的影响、著作权法在新技术背景下出现的具体问题、著作权法的改革和出路等主题。

（一）国外相关研究

关于著作权法与新技术互动发展的历史，Paul Goldstein 做出了比较系统的研究。[1] Lyman Ray Patterson 从历史角度对著作权法的发展进行了深入考察。[2]

---

[1] Goldstein, Paul. Copyright's highway: From Gutenberg to the celestial jukebox. Stanford Law & Politics, 2003.

[2] Patterson, Lyman Ray. Copyright in historical perspective. Vanderbilt University Press, 1968.

导　论

关于新技术对著作权法的影响，学者们从不同角度对此做出了卓有成效的研究。Kleinman 从宏观的角度考察了科学技术对整个社会以及知识产权的影响，与此同时，该学者阐述了科学技术的社会性和政治性，并对科学主义和技术进步论进行了深刻反思，从而在一定程度上消除了人们对科学技术影响社会进行理解和反思的思维障碍。❶ 具体到著作权法领域，Gervais 用"未充分发展技术"（Inchoate Technology）的概念解释了著作权法无法适应新兴网络技术的原因，认为"未充分发展技术"像一个不断移动的靶子，这使得无论被认为多么合意的规制手段都可能偏离预期的方向。❷ 同时，他还认为，传统著作权法的规制失败很大程度上源于著作权法的预设规制对象的错位。❸ Jonathan Zittrain 则用"创生性"（Generative Pattern）理论解释了网络环境下著作权保护失效的原因。在他的理论下，创生性是指"通过不加过滤地吸收广泛、多样的受众的贡献，而产生不可预测变化的系统能力"。他用这一理论解释了技术保护措施失败的原因，认为只要能够保持终端的创生性和互联网的接入，具有颠覆性思维的技术专家们就能够开发出突破网络封锁的程序。❹ Tim Wu 认为著作权保护的困境来源于一直以来对"守门人"机制（Gatekeeper Enforcement Mechanism）的依赖。❺

关于著作权法在新技术背景下出现的具体问题，相关的司法案例是最好的研究对象。关于临时复制问题，美国《著作权法》至今并无明确答案。标志性的案例有 MAI v. Peak、❻ Cartoon Network v. CSC Holdings。❼ 随后便有学者对这些案例进行讨论，如 Levin 对前者进行了讨论，❽ Kim 对后者进行了讨论。❾

---

❶ Kleiman, Daniel Lee. Science and technology in society: from biotechnology to the internet. Wiley-Blackwell, 2009.

❷ Gervais, Daniel J. "The Regulation of Inchoate Technologies." *Houston Law Review* 47, no. 3 (2010): 665-705.

❸ Gervais, Daniel J. Use of Copyright Content on the Internet: Considerations on Excludability and Collective Licensing. In the Public Interest: The Future of Canadian Copyright Law, Michael Geist Ed., Chapter 18, p. 545, Irwin Law, 2005.

❹ Zittrain, Jonathan. The Future of the Internet-And How to Stop It. Yale University Press, 2009.

❺ Wu, Tim. "When Code Isn't Law." Virginia Law Review 89 (2003).

❻ MAI System Corp. v. Peak Computer, Inc., 991 F. 2d 511, 9th Cir. 1993.

❼ Cartoon Network, LP v. CSC Holdings, Inc., 536 F. 3d 121 (2d Cir. 2008).

❽ Levin, Katrine. "Intellectual Property Law-MAI v. Peak: Should Loading Operating System Software Into RAM Constitute Copyright Infringement." Golden Gate UL Rev. 24 (1994): 649.

❾ Kim, Vivian I. "The Public Performance Right in the Digital Age: Cartoon Network LP v. CSC Holdings." Berkeley Tech. LJ 24 (2009): 263.

· 5 ·

关于私人复制问题，典型案例有 Sony v. Universal Studios、[1] American Geophysical Union v. Texaco、[2] 以及 Napster 案。[3] 关于首次销售原则在数字环境下的适用，较典型的案例为欧盟的 UsedSoft v. Oracle 案以及目前正处于上诉阶段的 Capitol records v. Redigi 案。[4]

关于以 P2P 为代表的网络技术对著作权保护的挑战和应对问题，大部分的著作权法学者都参与了探讨和研究，无法一一列举。在此领域的研究比较有代表性的学者有 Jane Ginsburg[5]、Mark Lemley[6]、Daniel Gervais[7]、Rebecca Giblin[8]、Peter Yu[9] 等。关于如何应对 P2P 技术引起的网络盗版问题，学者们提出了不同的解决方案。William Fisher 提出了税收化的方案[10]，Neal Netanel 提出了特别使用费方案，[11] Daniel Gervais 等许多学者则提出市场授权机制是解决问题的最好办法。[12]

关于数字和网络技术背景下著作权法的未来出路问题，学者们的观点归纳起来主要有三种：（1）现有著作权制度已无法适应数字和网络技术时代。这

---

[1] Sony Corp. of America v. Universal City Studios, Inc., 464 U. S. 417 (1984).

[2] American Geophysical Union v. Texaco Inc., 60 F. 3d 913 (2nd Cir. 1994).

[3] 关于案件详细进展及法院判决理由见：A&M Records, Inc. v. Napster, In c., 2000 WL 573136, 10 (N. D. Cal. 2000); A&M Records, Inc. v. Napster, Inc., 2000 WL 1009483, 8 (N. D. Cal. 2000); A&M Records, Inc. v. Napster, Inc., 2000 WL 1055915 (9th Cir. 2000); A&M Records, Inc. v. Napster, Inc., 114 F. Supp. 2d 896, 927 (N. D. Cal. 2000); A&M Records, Inc. v. Napster, Inc., 239 F. 3d 1004, 1027 (9th Cir. 2001); A&M Records, Inc. v. Napster, Inc., 2001 WL 227083 (N. D. Cal. 2001); A&M Records, Inc. v. Napster, In c., 284 F. 3d 1091, 1099 (9th Cir. 2002).

[4] Capitol Records, LLC v. ReDigi Inc., No. 12-0095, 2012 U. S. Dist.

[5] Ginsburg, Jane C. "Copyright and control over new technologies of dissemination." Colum. L. Rev. 101 (2001); Ginsburg, Jane C. "Exclusive Right to Their Writings: Copyright and Control in the Digital Age", (2002) Me. L. Rev. 54 195.

[6] Lemley, Mark A., and R. Anthony Reese. "Reducing digital copyright infringement without restricting innovation" 56 Stan. L. Rev. 1345.

[7] Gervais, Daniel J. "The Regulation of Inchoate Technologies." Houston Law Review 47, no. 3 (2010); Gervais, Daniel J. "The Price of Social Norms: Towards a Liability Regime for File-Sharing." J. of Intell. Prop. Law 12, no. 1 (2003).

[8] Rebecca Giblin, Code Wars: 10 Years of P2P Software Litigation (2011).

[9] Peter Yu, "P2P and the Future of Private Copying" University of Colorado Law Review 76 (2005).

[10] Fisher, William. Promises to keep: Technology, law, and the future of entertainment. Stanford Law and Politics, 2004.

[11] Neal Netanel, Impose a Noncommercial Use Levy to Allow Free Peer-to-Peer File Sharing, 17 HARV. J. L & TECH 1 (2003).

[12] Gervais, Daniel J., Use of Copyright Content on the Internet: Considerations on Excludability and Collective Licensing. In the Public Interest: The Future of Canadian Copyright Law, Michael Geist Ed., Chapter 18, p. 545, Irwin Law, 2005.

一观点以 Barlow 为代表。❶（2）现有著作权制度能够适应新技术的发展。这种观点的代表学者是 Bruce Lehman。❷（3）必须对著作权制度进行重新构建。Jessica Litman 认为传统的复制权丧失了继续存在的理由，主张构建一种"商业利用权"；❸ Jane Ginsburg 则主张建立一种全新的"接触控制权"。❹

新近，William Patry、Jason Mazzone、Daniel Gervais 等学者对著作权法的出路做出了代表性研究。Patry 主张对著作权法进行大规模的立法改革，主要内容包括缩短保护期、恢复著作权形式（Formalities）要求、以补偿获得权代替排他权。❺ 而 Mazzone 则认为著作权法本身没有太大问题，问题是著作权人滥用了著作权。因此，他主张对法定损害赔偿制度、合理使用制度等进行改革，对著作权滥用进行规制，并提出了建立针对著作权滥用的公益诉讼制度等新颖的主张。❻ Samuelson 则对上述两位学者的研究进行了富有卓见的评论，指出了上述两项研究的贡献和不足，在此基础上对著作权法改革的可能路径进行了研究，并提出了著作权法改革应遵循的若干基本原则。❼ Gervais 认为，在数字网络环境下，现有的著作权法律制度存在诸多不足，不能够实现其本身的目的。其认为应当在准确诊断现有著作权制度的基础上，对著作权法进行系统的改革。❽

（二）国内相关研究

国内关于数字网络技术背景下的著作权法问题越来越多。早期对该问题的研究主要是对国外尤其是美国的研究成果的简单介绍，逐渐发展到对国外研究成果进行比较深入的考察和分析。近年来，由于国内外学术交流的日益频繁以及该领域研究学者学术背景和知识结构的不断优化，在此领域不乏富有创见的研究成果。这些研究成果不仅对国外相关研究现状有较深刻的理解，又能基于

---

❶ Barlow, John Perry. "A Declaration of the Independence of Cyberspace (Feb. 8, 1996)." p.234-237.

❷ Lehman, Bruce A., and Ronald H. Brown. Intellectual Property and the National Information Infrastructure: A Preliminary Draft of the Report of the Working Group on Intellectual Property Rights, Chair, Bruce A. Lehman; Ronald H. Brown, Chair, Information Infrastructure Task Force. Information Infrastructure Task Force, 1994.

❸ Litman, Jessica. "Digital copyright." (2006).

❹ Ginsburg, Jane C. "Can Copyright become User-Friendly-Review: Jessica Litman, Digitcal Copyright (2001)." Colum. JL & Arts 25 (2001): 71.

❺ Patry, William. How to fix copyright. Oxford University Press, USA. (2011).

❻ Mazzone, Jason. Copyfraud and other abuses of intellectual property law. (2011).

❼ Samuelson, Pamela. "Is Copyright Reform Possible?." Harv. L. Rev. 126 (2013): 740-868.

❽ Gervais, Daniel, "(Re)structuring Copyright A Comprehensive Path to International Copyright Reform-A Comprehensive Path to International Copyright Reform", Edward Elgar Publishing. (2017).

我国具体情况对我国著作权法的完善提出富有创见的结论。❶ 但仔细考察这些成果，其大部分是关于这一领域的具体问题的研究，如著作权法上的技术保护措施、P2P技术、技术中立等具体问题。关于新技术对著作权法影响的整体性研究仍然比较欠缺。虽然有不少关于数字网络对著作权法影响的研究，但是这些研究大多是关于某一具体问题的论述。从宏观上分析数字网络技术下著作权法面临的困境，并从全盘的角度寻求著作权法如何解决这种困境的研究比较欠缺。不过，新近有不少学者对数字网络技术时代著作权法的改革进行了研究和评述。吴汉东对信息网络技术背景下的著作权利益格局进行了分析，并对著作权法制度的创新提出了建议。❷ 胡波讨论了数字网络技术背景下信息自由与著作权法的关系及著作权法的变革问题，❸ 万勇则对美国目前的著作权法改革方案进行了评述，并讨论了我国著作权法改革问题。❹

（三）对国内外文献的分析

关于数字和技术背景下著作权法的困境和出路问题，欧美国家有着比较丰富的研究成果。学者们对该问题从各个角度进行了有意义的探索，探寻著作权法改革的各种可能性，为立法和司法提供了非常有意义的参考，也为其他国家借鉴其经验和教训提供了良好的素材。然而，尽管美国关于该主题的研究非常丰富，但关于著作权法如何应对数字和网络技术带来的挑战、著作权法如何改革等根本问题，学者们仍然见仁见智观点不一。我国对新技术背景下出现的著作权法问题的研究日渐增多，该问题日渐凸显并受到重视。相关研究成果也从早期对国外状况的简单介绍到研究逐渐深入，但这些成果大部分是关于这一领域的具体问题的研究，关于新技术对著作权法影响的整体性研究仍然比较欠缺。

随着数字和网络技术发展速度的不断加快，著作权法上的新问题不断涌现。目前，虽然著作权制度非常发达的欧美国家有着非常丰富的研究成果，但关于著作权法如何应对新技术的发展这一课题仍然是一个开放性的问题。在这

---

❶ 这些成果包括但不限于：刘铁光.论著作权权项配置中兜底条款的废除——以著作权与传播技术发展的时间规律为中心[J].政治与法律，2012（8）；王迁.版权法保护技术措施的正当性[J].法学研究，2011（4）；王迁.新型P2P技术对传统版权间接侵权责任理论的挑战——Grokster案评述[J].电子知识产权，2011（10）；许超.新技术与国际著作权保护的发展趋势[J].电子知识产权，2011（10）.

❷ 吴汉东.网络版权的技术革命、产业变革与制度创新[J].中国版权，2016（6）.

❸ 胡波.信息自由与版权法的变革[J].现在法学，2016（6）.

❹ 万勇.美国版权法改革方案述评[J].知识产权，2014（1）.

一背景下,对新技术背景下的著作权法的困境和出路进行比较研究,总结国外先进国家的经验和教训,为我国著作权法应对新技术的发展提供理论依据和参考,就显得尤为重要。

四、研究目标与研究思路

本书研究著作权法在数字和网络技术背景下面临的困境,分析这种困境的根源,探寻著作权法应对新技术带来的挑战的出路和对策。本研究以权利配置、权利保护、权利实现这一结构作为研究的逻辑框架,研究著作权法在数字网络环境下的困境和出路。导论主要对研究背景、研究对象等问题进行介绍。第一章主要分析了数字网络技术对著作权法的挑战,并对著作权法在新技术背景下的困境从权利人与使用人博弈的角度进行了行为学分析。第二章主要研究权利配置问题。该章首先对传统著作权法的基础架构进行从价值到制度的分析,然后对临时复制、首次销售原则以及合理使用原则三个关乎著作权法基础架构的问题如何应对数字网络技术带来的挑战进行研究。第三章、第四章分别从使用人和权利人两个角度研究著作权保护的困境与出路。第五章从权利实现的角度对数字网络环境下著作权市场机制进行了研究。

五、研究方法

本书在写作过程中将采用如下几种研究方法:
第一,比较研究方法。
著作权法起源于英国,发达于美国。相比之下,我国缺乏著作权法的本土资源。在知识经济日渐重要和经济全球化的背景下,借鉴发达国家的著作权制度、提高国家的创新力,成为我国的必然选择。而且,数字与网络技术也主要产生于美国,最新发展趋势也大多由其引领。因此,研究著作权法如何应对数字与网络技术的挑战这一课题无法绕过美国的经验和教训。美国的问题或许就是我们今天或将来面临的问题。我国目前正在对著作权法进行大规模修订,考察美国如何应对新技术给著作权法带来的挑战,总结其经验和教训,对于我国有重要的意义。因此,比较法研究是本书的主要研究方法。该研究将主要从立法、司法、学术研究等方面对美国如何应对新技术给著作权法带来的挑战进行详细考察和深入分析,总结其经验和教训,为我国在数字和网络技术背景下如何完善著作权法提供参考和建议。比较法的研究方法还要求在对国外进行比较研究的同时,应充分考虑我国的国情,确定对国外经验教训借鉴的可能性和限度。

第二，历史研究方法。

著作权法在与技术的互动中而发展。从安娜法案到当今的著作权法经历了漫长的历史演化过程。考察这一历史过程，对于探寻新技术如何影响著作权法以及著作权法的发展规律，有着重要的学术意义。历史研究方法贯穿于本研究宏观和微观两个层次：从宏观的角度研究著作权与技术的互动史；从微观的角度研究具体著作权法案例的发展史。

第三，案例研究方法。

立法通常具有滞后性，新的法律问题的出现通常最先在司法层面得以反映。因此，研究最新的法律问题离不开对新出现的司法案例的研究和分析。尤其是在数字和网络技术领域，新技术犹如移动之靶，规制之箭很难射中。在这种情况下，研究最新案例有利于追踪技术和法律的最新发展动态，确定需要研究的法律问题，并探寻有效的解决方案。另外，案例法在美国法律体系中的重要地位也决定了以美国著作权法为主要研究对象的研究离不开对相关判例法的研究。该研究将采用案例研究方法，通过研究著作权法领域的重要案例和最新案例，从微观角度研究新技术对著作权法的影响及法律对新技术的应对，从而把握著作权法的发展规律，探寻著作权法在新技术背景下的困境之源和应对之策。

第四，实证研究方法。

著作权法具有很强的实践性，理论研究离不开对实践的把握。当前，著作权法面临数字和网络技术的挑战，新问题不断涌现，如果仅仅进行逻辑推演和理论推理，往往无法解决问题，甚至可能得出荒谬的结论。著作权制度的设计和完善，必须以实证经验和证据为基础，而不能单纯依靠理论推理。本研究对实证研究方法的采用主要体现在新技术背景下著作权的保护制度部分，该部分主要以美国为例，充分利用著作权法领域的经验材料和数据资源，对其当前的著作权保护策略进行考察和分析，为我国如何构建新技术背景下有效的著作权保护制度提供参考和建议，力求使本研究的结论是基于证据，而非仅仅基于理论推演。

第五，法社会学研究方法。

虽然著作权法主要是受新技术的影响而不断演化，但事实上，著作权法的发展还受到很多因素的影响。这些因素包括但不限于国际因素、政治因素、市场因素、社会规范因素。因此，本研究在以技术与著作权法的互动为研究主线的同时，采用社会学的研究方法，对著作权法发展的其他变量进行研究，以此保证研究结果的客观性和全面性。

第一章　数字网络技术对著作权法的挑战

第一节　传统技术影响下著作权法的产生与发展

著作权与技术之间的关系并非一个全新的话题，从 20 世纪末期数字网络技术逐渐普及以后，二者之间的关系更是成为著作权研究领域的重要课题。从历史来看，著作权法的产生和发展虽然是由多种因素促成，但技术在著作权法的发展中始终担当核心的角色。研究著作权法与技术发展之间的历史互动关系，不仅有助于我们理解著作权法从何处来，还有助于我们判断著作权法将向何处去，更重要的是有助于我们回答著作权法应向何处去的问题。

一、印刷机时代著作权法的产生

著作权法的某些观念在古希腊和罗马时期就已经存在。[1] 罗马诗人 Martial 就曾将未经其同意而叙说其作品的行为称为剽窃。但是这种关于著作权的道德主张在印刷机出现之前属于极其个别的情形。[2] 这是因为，在以手抄为主要复制方式的时代背景下，"盗版"几乎没有任何成本优势。因此，在前印刷机时代，对于书稿所有人而言，所有权已经足以保护他们的利益，根本不需要著作权法。

15 世纪上半叶，德国人古登堡发明了金属活字印刷机，并于 1455 年首次使用活字印刷技术印制出 180 本圣经。[3] 商人 William Caxton 于 1476 年在英国

---

[1] [美] 罗纳德·V. 贝蒂格. 版权文化——知识产权的政治经济学 [M]. 1 版. 沈国麟，韩绍伟，译. 北京：清华大学出版社，2009：12.

[2] [美] 保罗·戈斯汀. 著作权之道：从古登堡到数字点播机 [M]. 金海军，译. 北京：北京大学出版社，2008：32.

[3] 维基百科，网址：http://en.wikipedia.org/wiki/Johannes_Gutenberg，访问时间：2013 年 10 月 27 日。在此之前，修道院的僧侣很少能在一年之内抄完一本经书，当时整个欧洲只有大约 3 万册图书，而到 1500 年时各种图书猛增至 900 万册，可见印刷机在当时的革命性意义。黄海峰. 知识产权的话语与现实——版权、专利与商标史论 [M]. 1 版. 武汉：华中科技大学出版社，2011：6-7.

· 11 ·

设立了第一家印刷所。到 1500 年,印刷机出现在欧洲的 245 个城市。❶ 活字印刷机的出现对当时社会的改变是巨大的。一方面,印刷机的出现使书籍的大规模复制成为可能,印刷业作为一个产业开始出现。印刷业天然就是资本密集型的产业,印刷设备的购置、纸张及油墨的储存、雕版的制作以及工人的雇用都需要大量的资金投入,而且由于书籍的销售需要时间,成本的回收也需要一定的周期才能实现,这样就存在一个巨大的商业风险,即如果其他出版商也同时印刷同一本或者同一类书籍,那么出版商极有可能无法收回投资甚至亏损。在这一背景下,新兴的出版商必然需要对印刷产业进行规制,取得出版书籍的垄断权,以避免上述商业风险的发生。另一方面,图书出版业的发展必然要求更多的书稿以满足社会的需求,职业写者(writer)作为一个阶层出现了。不过,这时的写者与现代意义上的作者(author)截然不同,出版商只是给写者一定的报酬交换对其书稿的所有权,写者并不享有现代著作权法上的任何权利。❷在出版商眼里,写者与印刷工人以及装订工人并无二致,只是分工不同而已。但值得注意的是,当 17 世纪末写作逐渐成为写者的谋生之道,文学和艺术作品逐渐被商品化后,"所有权的个人主义开始塑造作者对于他们自己作品的态度。"❸ 这为后来"写者"成为"作者"埋下了重要伏笔。

　　15 世纪中期以后,机器印刷逐渐成为生产图书的主要方式,而同时文艺复兴与宗教改革运动也在整个欧洲如火如荼。由此印刷机对当时社会产生的另一个重要影响是,印刷技术的广泛应用使图书的数量以及传播范围越来越大,传播速度也越来越快,这对当时政府控制异端言论带来了巨大的挑战。对政府而言,他们非常需要对"异端邪说"进行控制从而维护他们的统治。因此,政府通过赋予经过精心挑选的出版商出版书籍的特权,借此控制哪些出版商可以出版什么书籍,从而达到控制思想的目的,而被授予特权的出版商而言,这种特权则可排除其他出版商的竞争。❹ 1557 年,菲利普和玛丽向书商公会(Stationers' Company)颁发特许状,赋予其在英格兰印刷和出版领域持续 150

---

❶ 易建雄. 技术发展与版权扩张 [M]. 北京:法律出版社,2009:8.
❷ 在 17 世纪,写作仍然被认为是那些受过良好教育的、经济独立的人们的消遣活动。17 世纪下半叶,出版商开始向写者支付一定的报酬换取手稿。[美] 罗纳德·V. 贝蒂格. 版权文化——知识产权的政治经济学 [M]. 1 版. 沈国麟,韩绍伟,译. 北京:清华大学出版社,2009:18.
❸ Elizabeth Eisenstein, The printing Press as an Agent of Change, Cambridge University Press, 1979, p. 121.
❹ 虽然之前也存在政府对言论和出版物的审查和控制,但这种基于利益上的契合而产生的出版特权则是印刷机出现之后的事情。Lyman Ray Patterson, Copyright in historical perspective, Vanderbilt University Press, 1968, p. 20–27.

年的垄断权。只有书商公会的成员才可以取得这样的许可,因此出版商的数量、出版书籍的种类都被政府严格限制了。书商公会设有一个登记机构,其下属成员可以在此登记经过审查的出版书目,以享有独家合法印刷这些书目的权利。[1] 出版商的这种权利就是现代著作权产生的序曲,[2] 其本质上并不是作者对作品的权利,而是出版商享有的印刷出版作品的权利。[3]

随着光荣革命的爆发以及权利法案的诞生,代表书商垄断和出版审查的《许可法案》(Licensing Act of 1662)于1695年被议会拒绝续展,这样自亨利八世开始的出版许可和审查制度走到了尽头。[4]《许可法案》失效后,反对言论控制和主张出版自由的政治力量逐渐占据上风,出版商在以各种理由试图恢复法案效力以恢复出版审查制度的努力失败后,不得不改变策略,寻找其他可以为当时政治力量所接受的理由来实现自己的利益。1707~1710年,出版商多次以保护公共利益和鼓励作者创作为由请求议会立法保护作者以及原稿购买者的文学产权,这最终促成了1710年《安妮法》的诞生,该法通常被认为是世界历史上第一部著作权法,因为该法首次以书面的形式确认了作者的权利。《安妮法》开篇即写到该法案是一部"在所规定时间内将已经印刷图书的复制件授予作者或复制件购买者以鼓励学术之法律"。但是,值得注意的是,《安妮法》保护的重点不是"作者",而是"复制件购买者"——出版商,保护作者权利只是出版商保护自己商业利益的一个幌子而已,作者只是名义上的主角。但是,也正是这样的规定,使作者群体在后来一步一步争取自己的权利成为可能,现代著作权法传统才得以最终形成。[5] 到18世纪晚期,著作权已不再是出版商的权利,而成为作者的权利。[6] 正如有学者所言,"到1774年,现

---

[1] [美]罗纳德·V. 贝蒂格. 版权文化——知识产权的政治经济学 [M]. 1版. 沈国麟,韩绍伟,译. 北京:清华大学出版社,2009:17-18;易建雄. 技术发展与版权扩张 [M]. 北京:法律出版社,2009:13.

[2] Copyright 一词直到1735年才首次出现,易建雄. 技术发展与版权扩张 [M]. 北京:法律出版社,2009:30.

[3] Lyman Ray Patterson, Copyright in historical perspective, Vanderbilt University Press, 1968, p. 55. 出版商的版权其实经历了从 a license to print 到 the ownership of copy,再到 the ownership of a book 这样一个演化的过程,由于这一过程并非本文叙述重点,故在此不予赘述。

[4] 易建雄. 技术发展与版权扩张 [M]. 北京:法律出版社,2009:25.

[5] 关于《安妮法》之后作者群体如何争取权利而促成现代著作权法形成过程的论述,参见易建雄. 技术发展与版权扩张 [M]. 北京:法律出版社,2009:48-74.

[6] See Lyman Ray Patterson, Copyright in historical perspective, Vanderbilt University Press, 1968, p. 179.

代英美著作权法的一切基本要素都已具备"。❶

总结上述著作权法产生的过程，印刷机的发明和使用是全部故事的起点。印刷机的使用促进了出版业的繁荣，而印刷机技术背景下的出版业的"资本密集型"特点以及资金回笼的周期性使出版商需要对其出版的书籍享有专有权。印刷机的应用同时使图书的数量急剧增加，这对统治者控制言论又是极为不利的，因此统治者需要对出版业进行控制。这样出版商与政府客观上的利益契合便造就了出版特许制度，并逐渐发展成了出版商的"版权"。与此同时，印刷机的发明在促进出版业繁荣的同时，也促成了"写者"阶层的产生和不断壮大，"写者"群体经过长期的争取最终成为"作者"，现代著作权制度得以产生。可以说，印刷机的发明对著作权法的形成起到了原始动力的作用，它不仅催生了一个新的印刷产业，而且促成了一个"写者"阶层的产生，这两个因素构成了现代著作权法产生的基本条件。

二、模拟技术时代著作权法的扩张

如果说印刷机的发明促成了现代著作权法的诞生，那么后来出现的现代技术则使著作权法逐步扩张。这些技术包括摄影术、自动钢琴、留声机、电影技术、远程传播技术、静电复印技术、录像技术等。著作权法在适应这些新技术的过程中逐渐得到完善。

（一）摄影术的发明与作品范围的扩大

法国人 Louis Daguerre 于 1839 年发明的摄影术首先对著作权法造成了冲击。在英国，摄影术被引进之初，照片由于其本身是纯粹的机械操作的产物因而并不被认为构成作品，所以不能受著作权法保护。但是不久之后立法就开始对这一新的技术进行回应。1862 年的英国《美术作品著作权法》将照片作为美术作品予以保护。在美国，随着 19 世纪 60 年代摄影术的商业化运营，美国于 1865 年修改《著作权法》将照片列为《著作权法》保护对象。后来，照片的可著作权性又经过了长时间的司法实践逐渐被认可。到 20 世纪初，"照片可以成为独创性作品"的观念已被广泛接受。

（二）自动钢琴与机械复制权的产生

如果说摄影术引起了人们对著作权法中独创性新的思考，自动钢琴（player-piano）的发明则使人们对复制产生了新的认识。1895 年第一台自动钢

---

❶ Mark Rose, Authors and Owners, Harvard University Press, 1993, p.132.

琴在美国底特律诞生，其最大特点是通过钢琴卷（piano roll）控制钢琴演奏音乐而不用人工演奏。这使音乐作家和音乐出版商的收入大大减少。于是音乐作家和音乐出版商开始寻求司法的保护。在美国 White-Smith Music Publishing Co. v. Apollo Co.（1908）一案中，法院认为，虽然以机械方式复制声音所得产物应属复制，但按照目前著作权法规定尚不能作此延伸，修改法律的任务应由国会完成，从而拒绝了原告的请求。不过，随后的1909年美国《著作权法》就明确规定了机械录音权，禁止未经授权对音乐作品进行机械复制。同时为防止音乐出版商的垄断，该法还用强制许可的方式对该权利进行了约束。❶ 自此，复制权的概念扩展到机械复制。

（三）播放技术的进步与公开表演权的扩张及展览权的创设

随着留声机、唱片等技术以及电影的陆续发明则使公开表演权（public performance）的范围逐步扩张。❷ 随后的无线电通信技术更是使公开表演权的范围扩展至声音广播和电视广播。通过一系列的技术发展，美国最终于1976年在《著作权法》中规定公开表演权包括现场表演和机械表演，其中机械表演是指"借助任何装置或方法向公众或在第（1）项规定的场所，播送或以其他方式传播或展示作品的行为，不论有能力受到播送内容或展示的公众是否同时或在同一地点接收到播送的内容"。❸ 这种规定能够涵盖包括无线广播、有线电视等一切机械表演形式。但值得注意的是，为了平衡无线电视和有线电视之间的利益平衡，美国《著作权法》规定了强制许可制度，允许有线电视在支付法定许可费用的前提下可以再传送无线广播节目。❹

另外特别值得一提的是，1976年的美国《著作权法》为了应对新技术的挑战，还为著作权人单独设立了一项新的权利——"展览权"（display right），指"作品为文字、音乐、戏剧、舞蹈、哑剧、绘画、图标和雕塑作品的，包括电影及其他视听作品的单幅图像，向公众展览该著作权作品"。❺ 美国版权局在向国会提交的报告中认为，至少在某些领域，展览将代替复制件而成为公

---

❶ 一旦著作权所有人授权给某一钢琴卷公司或唱片公司对音乐作品进行机械复制，任何其他公司就都可按照每张唱片2美分的价格制作录音唱片。[美] 保罗·戈斯汀. 著作权之道：从古登堡到数字点播机 [M]. 金海军，译. 北京：北京大学出版社，2008：55.
❷ 易建雄. 技术发展与版权扩张 [M]. 北京：法律出版社，2009：124-128.
❸ 17 U.S.C. § 101. 引文参见：美国版权法 [M]. 杜颖，张启晨，译. 北京：知识产权出版社，2013.
❹ 17 U.S.C. §111.
❺ 17 U.S.C. §106（5）.

众了解作品的途径,与复制、发行等传统权利相比,展览权极具潜在重要性,著作权法应当将公开展览权确认为一项新的基本权利。❶

(四) 复制设备的发明对作品复制权的挑战

新技术在引起作品范围的扩张、机械复制权和机械表演权的产生的同时,还对复制权提出了更为严峻的挑战。1938 年美国人 Chester Carlson 发明了静电复印技术,随后施乐公司于 1959 年将该技术商业化,推出了静电复印机。美国人 Bing Crosby 于 1945 年生产出世界上第一台盘式磁带录音机,到 20 世纪 70 年代末兼具录放功能的录音机即大量投放市场。20 世纪 50 年代电子录像机在英国诞生,20 世纪 60 年代初录像机开始进入美国市场,70 年代家用录像机问世。这些设备的使用范围十分广泛。据统计,1966 年静电复印机在美国产出了 140 亿页的复印件,到 1985 年则超过 7000 亿页。另一项调查表明,1978~1979 年,美国 10 岁以上受访者中有 20% 用录音机录制过歌曲,到 1987 年这一数字则上升至 40%,到 1990 年美国每个家庭平均拥有两台录音机;1987 年美国一半的家庭都在使用录像机,到 1991 年这一数字则上升为 71%。❷ 这些新技术的发明给复制权带来的最大挑战在于,私人复制行为变得日益普遍,这大大影响了作品的销售市场,危及了著作权人的经济利益。于是,权利人开始采取行动维护自己的利益。

1. 复印机与图书馆复制的限制：Williams & Wilkins Co. v. United States 案

Williams & Wilkins Co. v. United States 案发生时正值施乐公司的 914 复印机畅销。原告是一家专业医学杂志出版社,在得知政府所属的国家医学图书馆每年都复制无数自己出版社的医学论文后,于 1968 年将美国政府起诉至法院。1972 年一审法院根据合理使用的四要素判断法认为,"图书馆复印的复制件与期刊论文原本完全一致;复印的目的在于达到替代或与购买原始论文一样的目的;复印行为将使原始期刊的潜在市场受到影响",因此判定图书馆的复印行为不属于合理使用。❸ 但是二审法院推翻了一审判决,认为认定图书馆的复制行为构成侵权将阻碍医学研究,法院不应作出被告侵权之判决,调和科学研究需要与出版商及作者利益的任务应通过立法的方式解决。❹ 原告不服二审判决

---

❶ See Paul Goldstein, Copyright: Principles, Law and Practice (Volume 1), Little Brown Company, 1989, p. 697.

❷ 易建雄. 技术发展与版权扩张 [M]. 北京:法律出版社,2009:133-134.

❸ Williams & Wilkins Co. v. U. S., 1972 WL 17712, 172 U. S. P. Q. 670 (Ct. Cl. Feb 16, 1972).

❹ Williams & Wilkins Co. v. U. S., 203 Ct. Cl. 74, 487 F. 2d 1345, 21 A. L. R. Fed. 151, 180 U. S. P. Q. 49 (Ct. Cl. Nov 27, 1973).

向联邦最高法院上诉，最高法院最终于 1975 年维持了二审判决，且未附任何理由。❶ 这样，原告的诉求在司法上没有得到满足。但原告并未停止维护自己利益的努力，继而需求立法保护，请求国会修改著作权法，对危及出版商利益的私人复制行为进行规制。国会最终在修改著作权法时考虑了私人复制问题，并在 1976 年美国《著作权法》中对图书馆复制问题进行了规制，一方面允许图书馆在一定条件下对收藏的作品进行复制，另一方面又对图书馆的复制规定了若干限制。❷ 总体而言，这种规定是对著作权人利益和图书馆利益进行调和的结果，这样，著作权人的复制权在新技术的影响下又向前发展了一步。

另外值得一提的是，本案原告面对新技术对其权利造成冲击时采取了多种方式维护自己的利益。除了上述在司法和立法上寻求保护之外，原告还采取了自力救济的方式保护自己的利益。上述案件进行期间，由于案件形势并不明朗，原告担心最终败诉，还设计了一种防拷贝纸（special noisy paper），以使其出版的医学论文无法被复印机复印。❸ 这是权利人在相关规则不确定的情况下的一种正常反应，权利人的这种面对新技术的反应在以后的技术挑战中经常出现。

2. 磁带录音技术与录音制品制作者权利的设立

如果说自动钢琴等机械的发明将复制的概念扩展至机械复制领域的话，那么磁带录音技术则造就了一个新的利益群体——录音制品制作者。当磁带录音技术逐渐趋于成熟和普及后，其对录音制品制作者的利益造成了巨大威胁，因为无论是制作者的商业竞争对手还是私人都可以轻易低成本地复制录音制品。当时由于美国《著作权法》并无保护录音制品制作者的规定，因此各州只能通过盗窃、不正当竞争，或者颁布本州的法律对录音制品制作者进行保护。❹ 1971 年美国国会通过的《美国录音制品法案》（Sound Recording Act of 1971）对录音制品提供了联邦层面的法律保护。1976 年修改著作权法时又将录音制品作为一种独立的保护对象加以保护，但录音制品制作者对录音制品的权利仅限于复制、发行与演绎，保护程度低于传统作品。

3. 技术的发明与合理使用制度的发展

继静电复印机和磁带录音机之后走进美国普通家庭而对著作权法产生重大

---

❶ Williams & Wilkins Co. v. U. S., 420 U. S. 376, 95 S. Ct. 1344, 43 L. Ed. 2d 264, 184 U. S. P. Q. 705 (U. S. Ct. Cl. Feb 25, 1975).

❷ 17 U. S. C. § 108.

❸ 易建雄. 技术发展与版权扩张 [M]. 北京：法律出版社，2009：136.

❹ 李明德. 美国知识产权法 [M]. 北京：法律出版社，2003：156.

影响的另一项发明是家用录像机。在 Williams & Wilkins 案之后不到 10 年即 1983 年，美国拥有电视机的家庭中，有 9% 同时拥有录像机，到 1991 年这一比例达到了 71%。❶ 其实，国会在 1976 年通过法律对图书馆复制进行规制的时候已经注意到了家庭录像机的存在。家庭录像机使普通家庭对视频节目的便利录制成为可能，因此对电影业存在很大的潜在威胁。不过国会担心如果将家庭录像机纳入考虑范围，很有可能使就图书馆复制问题达成的利益妥协和平衡功亏一篑，因此当时拒绝了电影业的呼吁。可以说，为了确保 1976 年美国《著作权法》顺利通过，家庭录像机问题被立法者有意忽略了。❷

这样，电影业只能求助于法院，Sony 案就是电影业就家庭录像机问题向法院利益诉求的集中体现。索尼公司是一家生产销售家用录像设备的公司。20 世纪 70 年代开始，索尼公司开始在美国销售一种名为 Betamax 的家用录像机。该录像机有两个功能：一是可以通过与电视连接将正在播放的电视节目录制下来进行收藏；二是可以在主人不在家的时候将电视节目录制下来以便在方便的时间观看，即"移时"功能（Time-shifting）。环球公司（Universal Studios）拥有一些电视节目的著作权，因此于 1976 年向加州中区联邦地区法院提起诉讼，认为消费者使用索尼公司的录像机录制电视节目侵犯了其所有的著作权。而且索尼公司向消费者销售用于侵权的工具，其作为帮助侵权者应当承担间接侵权的责任。一审法院没有支持原告的请求，认为用户对无线播放的作品的非商业性录制属于合理使用，因此不构成侵权。原告提出上诉后，上诉法院第九联邦巡回上诉法院又作出了截然相反的判决，支持了原告的请求。于是索尼公司向联邦最高法院提出上诉。

该案主要有两个焦点问题：（1）个人用户使用家用录像机录制节目的行为是否构成侵权；（2）索尼公司向用户提供录像机的行为是否构成帮助侵权从而承担侵权者责任。1984 年 1 月 17 日，联邦最高法院推翻了第九联邦巡回上诉法院的判决。关于第一个焦点问题，联邦最高法院在判决中指出，个人为了改变观看节目的时间而将节目录制下来，并在观看后删除，构成了合理使用。关于第二个焦点问题，最高法院参照专利法中的"通用商品规则"，认为如果产品具有"实质性非侵权"用途，即使制造商或销售商知悉该产品可能被用于侵权用途，也不能推定其有帮助侵权的故意。法院认为索尼公司生产的

---

❶ [美] 保罗·戈斯汀. 著作权之道：从古登堡到数字点播机 [M]. 金海军，译. 北京：北京大学出版社，2008：107.

❷ 易建雄. 技术发展与版权扩张 [M]. 北京：法律出版社，2009：138-139.

Betamax 录像机具有合理改变时间观看电视节目的"实质性非侵权"用途，而该用户使用录像机的该用途构成合理使用，所以索尼公司也无须承担帮助侵权的责任。❶

索尼案确立的"实质性非侵权"规则第一次被用来在著作权法领域确定技术制造者的侵权责任，该规则为高科技产品的发展清除了法律障碍，对新兴技术的发展起到了鼓励和促进的作用，成为此后 20 年指导涉及新技术案件的最重要案例之一。然而，索尼案在著作权领域设立的"实质性非侵权"规则却存在潜在的缺陷。该规则将一种产品具有实质性非侵权用途作为产品制造商免责的充分要件，这就为产品制造商故意设计一种主要用途为侵权，但却具有合法用途的产品留下了可乘之机，索尼规则的这一潜在缺陷在 20 年后应对 P2P 技术时暴露无遗。

三、著作权法的发展规律

著作权法因新技术的发明而产生，缘新技术的进步而发展。回顾上述传统技术背景下著作权法的产生和发展历史，我们可以得出以下规律。

首先，新技术发展是著作权法发展的动力。印刷机的出现促使著作权制度初步形成。摄影术、自动钢琴、播放技术以及复制设备的发明推动了著作权法在保护客体、权利体系以及权利限制制度各方面的发展。

其次，著作权法的产生和发展路径具有一定的偶然性和复杂性。回顾著作权制度的产生和发展，其路径并不是一开始就非常清晰和确定的。印刷机的发明促进了印刷业的发展，而新兴的印刷业又促成了印刷商阶层崛起，另外也使"写者"作为一个阶层出现。控制商业风险的需要又使印刷商需要对出版进行垄断。与此同时，统治者为了加强自己的统治也有控制言论的需要，两种需要结合在一起产生了出版特许制度。如果一切都没有变化，这种出版特许制度可能会一直延续很长时期。但在光荣革命以及权利法案诞生的社会背景下，代表出版特许制度的《许可法案》被废除。出版商为了继续维护自己的利益，又以保护作者权利的道德外衣游说立法对作者的权利予以确认。逐渐发展壮大的"写者"阶层更是"将计就计"，经过长期斗争最终成为真正的作者，现代著作权制度得以诞生。可见，著作权法是经历了极其复杂的环节才得以产生，而且任一环节对其产生都不可或缺。因此，著作权法的产生具有偶然性和复杂性。同时我们还应注意到，虽然新技术对著作权法的产生起到原动力的作

---

❶ Sony Corp. of America v. Universal City Studios, Inc., 464 U. S. 417 (1984).

用,但其他因素(如社会思潮、政治需要)等也起到至关重要的作用。因此,在考察著作权法问题时,不仅应当考虑技术因素,也应对其他因素予以兼顾。

最后,著作权法通过自身的不断调整可以适应技术的发展并实现自我完善。上述著作权法的发展历史表明,每次在面临新技术的挑战时,著作权法都能做出相应调整适应技术的发展。而且,著作权法在这种适应技术的不断调整中通过调整客体范围、扩张原有权利、增加新的权利种类,以及对著作权进行限制等方式实现了其制度体系的自我完善。

第二节 数字网络技术对著作权法的挑战

一、数字网络技术的产生与发展

17世纪,德国数学家卢布尼茨创造出一种新的计算方法,该方法用两位数0和1代替原来的十位数。1946年2月14日,美国人Mauchly和Eckert以二进制计算方法为基础,发明了世界上第一台电子计算机。该计算机有18800个真空管,占地1500英尺,重量达30吨,每秒钟可进行5000次的加法运算。自此,计算机以惊人的速度不断发展,晶体管取代了电子管,微电子技术则使计算机处理器和存储器上的电子元件体积越来越小,数量越来越多,计算机的计算速度越来越快,数据存储能力越来越大。与六十多年之后的今日相比,当年的计算机还不如现在的一些袖珍计算器,但它毕竟标志着数字计算的诞生,人类社会走进了一个崭新的信息时代。

数字技术是与电子计算机相伴而生的科学技术,它可借助设备将图文声等各种信息转化为电子计算机能够识别的二进制数字0和1,对数字信号进行计算、加工、存储、传播、还原的技术。由于该技术须借助计算机对信息进行编码、解码,因此也被称为数码技术、计算机技术等。与数字技术相对应的是传统的模拟技术,模拟技术是依靠电流的大小或者电压的高低来表达信息含义,只要干扰信号影响到电流或电压,就会对表达的信号含义造成干扰。数字技术与模拟技术相比,具有抗干扰能力强、精度高、信号便于长期存储、通用性好等优势,大大提高了人类的计算能力和处理信息的能力。

网络技术则是以计算机技术为基础的现代通信技术，该技术是按照网络协议，将位置不同、功能独立的多个计算机系统相互连接，通过软件实现硬件、软件、资源共享的信息传递系统。如今互联网技术已经渗透到社会生活的每个角落，对人类的社会生活产生了巨大的影响。

自20世纪90年代以来，互联网开始飞速发展。在1995年12月全球有1 600万网络用户，占世界人口0.4%；2000年12月网民数量增长为3.61亿，占世界人口5.8%；2005年12月全球网民增长为10.18亿，占世界人口15.7%；2010年9月全球网民数量为19.71亿，占全球人口的28.8%；2016年12月全球网民数量为36.96亿，占全球人口49.5%。❶截至2017年6月，我国网民规模达到7.51亿，互联网普及率为54.3%。❷如今，互联网已经成为人们发布信息和获取信息的最重要入口。

二、数字网络技术的特征

数字网络技术发展到今天，其特征日趋明显。归纳起来，数字网络具有开放性、平等性以及全球性三个特点。

第一，开放性。互联网技术的奠基者们在发明互联网之初就将开放性嵌入其中。发明者们并没有将互联网的基础技术进行财产化。许多基础性互联网技术都是非专利保护或著作权开放许可的技术，从而保证互联网的开放性。互联网采取TCP/IP的架构，使用"点到点透明"的数据传输方式，使信息与信息通道相互分离，提供标准、开放的网络接口。每个终端节点都可以通过一个唯一的IP地址接入网络。在这样的技术架构下，只要网络地址数量充足，互联网就可以容纳无限量的终端接入。

第二，平等性。互联网的TCP/IP架构将信息与信息通道相互独立，这就使得网络节点之间的数据传输是平等的，而没有主次之分。这一技术特性决定了互联网所有终端的平等性。终端之间可以按照协议相互进行数据和信息的交换。互联网这种信息交换的双向性就决定了每个人既可能是信息的创造者，也有可能是信息的使用者和传播者。P2P程序的应用就是对这种平等性的最好体现。

第三，全球性。互联网是由无数个局域网通过通信协议联系起来的全球性

---

❶ See Internet World Stats, http://www.internetworldstats.com/emarketing.htm.
❷ 参见中国互联网信息中心：《第40次中国互联网发展状况统计报告》第2页。网址：http://www.cnnic.cn/hlwfzyj/hlwxzbg/。

网络，本身具有一种分布式、去中心化的拓扑结构。互联网的连接可以超越任何地域、国家。与互联网的全球性不同，著作权是具有地域性的。这样，网络的全球性和著作权的地域性存在一定冲突。跨境著作权保护与跨境著作权交易构成数字网络背景下突出的法律问题。

三、数字网络技术对著作权法的冲击

数字技术和互联网是活字印刷以来最强有力的复制和传播工具。数字网络技术至少在五个方面对著作权法产生了深刻的影响。

第一，数字网络技术对作品的创作产生了深刻影响。在数字网络技术环境下，每个人都可成为创作者和传播者。以音乐作品为例，以往一件音乐作品从创作到最终经过艺术家表演而成为唱片需要复杂的程序和昂贵的成本。现在歌手则可以自己低成本且高质量地录制作品并通过网络发布。数字网络技术打破了作品使用者与创作者的壁垒，使每个人都可以成为作者。可以说，数字网络技术成就了一个"人人创作"的时代。

第二，数字技术给作品带来了全新的载体。数字技术出现之前，文字作品必须印刷在纸张上，音乐作品必须灌制在唱片上，电影则必须录制在胶片上，而后通过这些载体进行传播。数字技术突破了传统作品载体的限制，使作品能够以统一的数字格式存储在光盘、硬盘等载体上。

第三，数字技术带来了作品复制和存储的革命性进步，使对作品高保真、低成本且瞬时的复制成为可能。模拟制品（如磁带、唱片）复制件的保真度则要低于原件，如果连续复制，保真度还会递减。数字制品则可以被无限复制而质量无损。随着技术发展，复制设备的成本也逐渐低廉到普通民众可以承受的程度，对数字文件的复制只需轻点鼠标即可。传统复制方式需要时间，因此作品的原始出版者在这段时间内就无须面对来自盗版的竞争。[1] 而数字复制很短时间就可完成，这使得数字复制对出版者的威胁大大增加。数字化后的作品还可以存储在电脑中并进行其他操作。随着压缩技术的进步和硬盘容量的增大，作品尤其是娱乐作品的使用者可以非常容易且低成本地创建海量作品库。[2]

---

[1] [美] 威廉·M. 兰德斯，理查德·A. 波斯纳. 知识产权法的经济结构 [M]. 金海军，译. 北京：北京大学出版社，2005：53.

[2] Fisher, William. Promises to keep: Technology, law, and the future of entertainment. Stanford Law and Politics, 2004, p.14–15. See also Giblin, Rebecca. Code Wars: 10 Years of P2P Software Litigation. Edward Elgar Pub, 2011, p.12.

第四，数字和互联网技术使作品的传播成本大大降低。如果说数字技术对作品的存储和复制产生了革命性的影响，那么网络技术则对作品的传播方式起到了颠覆性作用。网络技术使信息传播摆脱了传统有形载体和交通方式的限制，这种进步使信息传递成本极大降低，使作品大规模传播成为可能。这一方面减少了作品发行者发行作品的成本，另一方面也减少了侵权者的侵权成本。

第五，数字网络技术使权利人对作品使用和传播的控制更为容易。对于数字作品而言，权利人可以使用权利管理措施（DRM）对其使用和传播进行控制，权利人还可以为作品的使用和利用设定特定的条款。利用这些技术，权利人可以设定使用者"进入"（Access）作品的条件，以及作品可以被复制多少次。❶ 在数字网络环境下，权利人第一次可以如此容易地与终端的作品使用者通过互联网连接起来，并设定作品的使用条款。权利管理措施一方面增强了权利人保护自己著作权的技术能力，另一方面也产生了权利人滥用技术保护措施，以致与合理使用原则相冲突，并侵犯公共领域的情况，破坏了著作权法的利益平衡。

数字网络技术在作品的创作、载体、复制和传播等方面的上述特点，给著作权法的基本架构带来了巨大的冲击。

首先，数字网络技术对传统著作权制度中的复制概念带来了挑战。数字技术对作品的复制带来了革命性的影响。一方面，数字技术可以实现对数字作品的无损复制；另一方面，数字环境下使用作品几乎都离不开对作品的复制。这就提出一个问题，临时复制是否构成著作权法上的复制？如果构成著作权法上的复制，那么这种复制是否应当完全由权利人控制？这些问题虽然在其他国家有相应的讨论或相关制度，但至今并无定论或存在争议。其次，数字网络技术对传统著作权制度的首次销售原则带来了挑战。数字网络技术的出现使网络环境下对作品进行传播和销售成为作品经济利用的重要方式。按照传统著作权制度，虽然著作权人享有对作品的发行权，但一旦作品的复制件由著作权人或经著作权人许可向公众转移所有权后，著作权人便无权对作品复制件的后续流转进行控制，合法取得作品复制件的所有者可不经著作权人同意而将其再销售、出租或者以其他方式处分。❷ 这样就提出一个问题：在数字网络环境中，网络

---

❶ See Yuko Noguchi. Toward better-balanced copyright regulations in the digital and network era: law, technology, and the market in the U. S. and Japan, Stanford University Doctoral Dissertation, 2006, p.13-14.

❷ 王迁. 论网络环境中的"首次销售原则"[J]. 法学杂志，2006（3）.

用户在购买音乐或者电影文件后，是否有权在自己不保留备份的情况下将自己购买的文件转售给第三人？换言之，首次销售原则能否适用于数字网络环境中？表面看这一问题仅仅是一个理论问题，但事实上涉及不同利益主体的不同利益。一方面，如果允许首次销售原则适用于数字网络环境，则权利人的利益将受到极大冲击；另一方面，如果不允许这一原则的适用，则会阻碍网络用户处分自己不再需要的音乐文件，阻碍图书馆利用数字网络建立数字图书馆，或者影响网络服务提供商运行对作品的数字化利用的商业模式（如 Google 数字图书馆）。正因为如此，首次销售原则在数字网络环境下的适用问题成为新技术背景下著作权法面临的又一个难题，数字网络技术对传统著作权的合理使用制度带来了冲击。

　　如上所述，数字网络技术为著作权人使用技术保护措施对著作权进行保护提供了技术上的可能性。但是，技术保护措施在保护著作权人权利的同时，时常会阻碍使用人对作品的合理使用，甚至将技术保护的触角延伸到公共领域。如何协调权利人使用技术保护措施保护著作权与合理使用制度之间的关系，成为数字网络技术给著作权法带来的又一大难题。

　　上述数字网络技术给传统著作权法带来的挑战引起的一个重要的结果就是：传统著作权法的很多基本规则已无法处理数字网络技术引起的新的法律问题，从而出现了著作权法在数字网络背景下的不确定性问题。在法律不确定的背景下，权利人与使用人就著作权的保护与作品的使用展开了利益博弈。对于权利人而言，其一方面利用技术保护措施对著作权进行保护，另一方面通过合同条款确定与作品使用者的权利义务边界。但是，在权利人对著作权进行自我保护的同时，经常会出现权利人的著作权滥用行为。权利人的著作权滥用主要体现在权利人利用技术保护措施以及合同条款对合理使用制度的侵犯及对公共领域的侵犯。对于使用者而言，他们可能对规则的不确定性产生两个极端反应。一方面，在规则不明确的情况下，使用者为了避免承担责任，可能选择尊重权利人的技术保护措施，接受权利人设定的合同条款，从而出现"过度守法"的现象；另一方面，使用者也可能由于规则的不明确而选择"冒险行为"，从而造成网络环境大规模侵权的现象。

第三节　数字网络技术背景下
著作权法困境的行为学分析

数字网络技术大大方便了对作品的复制和传播，从而导致了大规模网上侵权的发生。尽管权利人使用了包括诉讼、技术保护措施等手段阻止网络环境中的著作权侵权行为，但到目前为止，网络环境中未经授权对作品进行大规模使用的局面并未得到扭转，著作权法陷入了危机。著作权人惊呼"谁动了我的蛋糕"，他们主张著作权法应当加强对著作权的保护以应对新技术带来的危机，否则著作权产业就无法生存，著作权法就真的"死"了。而使用人为"技术带来的盛宴"欢呼，他们认为新的技术给人类思想的交流带来了前所未有的机遇，法律不应阻碍进步技术的发展，不应减损新技术给作品使用者乃至整个社会带来的福利。在数字网络技术的冲击下，"传统著作权法应何去何从"成为一个没有标准答案的难题。

以往，每当新的技术带来新的作品复制和传播方式时，就会出现如何重新划定著作权的边界的问题。著作权法发展的历史经验表明，在面对新技术挑战时，著作权法通过不断地调整著作权的边界以适应新技术的发展，并在这种适应过程中实现了自己的逐步完善。然而，关于新技术对著作权法的影响，虽然已有学者对著作权法与技术之间的互动进行了详尽的事实梳理，❶ 但我们对于新技术影响著作权法的内在机理的理论认识还远远不够深入。下面将从人类行为学以及博弈论的角度对数字网络技术如何对著作权法产生影响进行理论上的分析。

一、数字网络技术引起著作权法的不确定性

在数字网络时代，新技术以惊人的速度发展，即使新技术的发明者也无法准确预测这一新技术最终会带来什么样的影响。

新技术发展的迅速性和不可预测性使著作权法始终在技术的后面拼命追赶，但始终无法追上，这使著作权法与其他领域法律相比有更大的滞后性和不确定性。著作权法在适应新技术方面的滞后性和不确定性主要由以下因素

---

❶　对著作权法与新技术之间互动的历史进行深入研究的代表性成果当属易建雄的著作：《技术发展与版权扩张》。

造成。

第一，新技术发展的不可预测性使立法者无法准确预测技术发展的趋势，从而无法制定相应的规则以适用未来可能出现的变化。也就是说，技术的发展具有非常强的跳跃性，以致立法者根本无法根据现有技术预测下一步会出现哪些新技术。20世纪80年代配置低劣的个人计算机进入市场之初，人们根本无法想象如今个人计算机的速度和功能，也无法想象平板电脑与手机客户端的普及。当人们还在为静电复印机给复制技术带来的革命性变化而沾沾自喜的时候，他们也无法想象鼠标轻轻点击即可实现电子拷贝。当人们还在惊叹现代出版体系以及物流体系的发达给作品的传播带来的极大便利时，更想象不到一个小小的P2P程序就会使作品可以迅速传播到世界每一个连接互联网的角落。而这些新的技术都对著作权法产生了深刻的影响，当立法者注意到这些新技术的影响时，法律已经迟延多时了。

第二，新规则的制定本身需要一定的时间。法律的制定需要经过一套漫长复杂的程序。但是，新技术很多情况下却并非渐进性地出现。尤其是在数字网络时代，很多技术创新并不需要昂贵的投资和漫长的研发，一些技术的发明甚至就在一夜之间。这样，新技术与法律之间的鸿沟就会变得越来越大。

第三，著作权产业对新技术的影响评估不足在一定程度上也造成了法律的滞后性。从著作权法的发展历史看，著作权法的发展很大程度上来自于著作权产业向立法机关的呼吁。因此，著作权产业对新技术的反应速度很大程度上影响着著作权法对新技术的反应速度。如果一种新技术引起的著作权侵权没有从根本上撼动著作权产业的利益，著作权产业一般会对这些侵权予以容忍。一旦著作权产业觉察到新技术所带来的威胁时，影响往往已经非常严重。因此，在新技术出现到著作权产业开始采取行动应对新技术的挑战之间形成一段没有相关法律调整的真空地带。

有美国学者对著作权法应对新技术的滞后性进行了观察，其结论为：法律对新出现的进行定性和判断需要的平均时间为七年零两个月。（参见表1-1）[1]

---

[1] Depoorter, Ben. Technology and Uncertainty: The Shaping Effect on Copyright Law. University of Pennsylvania Law Review (2009): 1831-1868.

表 1-1 法律对于新技术规制的滞后性

技术	发明时间	法律规制	解决时间	滞后时间
Audio Cassette	1963	Sound Recording Amendment of 1971	1971	8
VCR	1972	Sony Corp. of America v. Universal City Studios, Inc.	1984	12
CD	1982	Audio Home Recording Act of 1992	1992	10
DAT	1986	Audio Home Recording Act of 1992	1992	6
DVD	1996	DVD Copy Control Ass'n v. Bunner	2004	8
BBS Boards	1979	Playboy Enterprises, Inc. v. Frena	1993	14
MP3 Format	1993	UMG Recordings, Inc. v. MP3.com, Inc.	2000	7
Diamond Rio	1998	Recording Industry Ass'n of America v. Diamond Multimedia Systems	1999	1
Napster	1999	A&M Records, Inc. v. Napster, Inc.	2001	2
Grokster	2001	Metro-Goldwyn-Mayer Studios Inc. v. Grokster, Ltd.	2005	4

二、著作权法不确定影响下权利人与使用人的行为博弈

正如上文所述，大多数革命性的技术进步出现后都会存在一段法律调整上的真空期或模糊期。在这段时期内，新技术的法律后果很难确定。这种不确定性对作品使用者以及著作权权利人的行为有着重要的影响。

著作权法的不确定性对作品使用者的行为可能产生两个相反方向的影响。对于一些使用者而言，风险规避对他们来说非常重要。以电影制片者为例，在使用作品行为的法律后果不明确的情况下，即使可能是合法使用，他们通常也会选择设法获取授权，而不是冒险使用。❶ 因为一旦侵权成立，其将会承担与其收益不相符的法律责任。除导致使用者的上述过度守法行为外，法律的不确定性还可能导致使用者的冒险行为。当使用作品的行为是否构成侵权并不明确

---

❶ James Gibson. Risk Aversion and Rights Accretion in Intellectual Property Law. 116 YALE L. J. 882, 884, 896-899 (2007).

时，有的使用者则会假设自己的使用行为并不构成侵权。这一方面是因为法律的不确定性本身就会导致冒险行为的发生，❶另一方面是由于在著作权法领域法律规则的日渐复杂化和专业化而引起的普通大众对法律理解的自我解释偏差。心理学领域的研究成果也为法律不确定性引起的使用者的冒险行为提供了解释。认知心理学认为，行为主体往往倾向于按照自己的理解去解释事实。❷例如，在网络上使用P2P软件免费下载音乐所带来的利益会使网络用户倾向于认为他们自己的下载行为应该是合法的。也就是说，行为主体会按照有利于自己的方式去理解和解释不确定的规则，从而调整自己的行为规范。其典型思维模式为，"我想下载音乐，因此我认为禁止使用P2P软件下载音乐是不公平的"。❸然后，使用者会用自己的观念影响其他使用者，以获得更广泛的支持。❹这样，一种"反著作权"的行为规范就逐渐产生，并逐步内化为使用者的行为规范。而且，一旦著作权法开始对先前使用者认为"合法"的行为进行规制，就会遭到使用者的抵制。这是因为，同样一件东西，得到后再失去比从来没有得到给个体带来的损失感往往会更强。这样，在法律明确之前，"反著作权"的行为逐渐扩散，并会内化为使用人的行为规范，影响法律的规制和著作权的实现。

当新技术使著作权法出现不确定性，并导致上述使用人的冒险行为时，依靠法律保护著作权会变得越来越困难。权利人为保护自己的权利，除了采取诉讼、游说立法等手段外，往往会采取法律之外的自我保护措施。在著作权法领域，这种自我保护集中体现为依靠技术保护措施保护自己的权利。按照目的的不同，权利人所采取的技术保护措施可以分为四类：（1）保护专有权利的技术保护措施；（2）控制接触作品的技术保护措施；（3）标记和识别作品的技术保护措施；（4）权利管理的保护措施。但从狭义上讲，法律上的技术保护

---

❶ Howard Latin, "Good" Warnings, Bad Products, and Cognitive Limitations, 41 UCLA L. REV. 1193, 1240 (1994); John E. Calfee & Richard Craswell, Some Effects of Uncertainty on Compliance with Legal Standards, 70 VA. L. REV. 965, 965 (1984).

❷ Dan M. Kahan & Donald Braman, More Statistics, Less Persuasion: A Cultural Theory of Gun-Risk Perceptions, 151 U. PA. L. REV. 1291, 1314-1315 (2003).

❸ Daniel S. Nagin & Greg Porgarsky, An Experimental Investigation of Deterrence: Cheating, Self-Serving Bias, and Impulsivity, 41 CRIMINOLOGY 167, 171 (2003).

❹ Michael Wenzel, Motivation or Rationalisation? Causal Relations Between Ethics, Norms, and Tax Compliance, 26 J. ECON. PSYCHOL. 491 (2005).

措施主要指保护专有权利的技术保护措施和控制接触作品的技术保护措施。❶美国著名网络法学者 Laurence Lessig 对技术保护措施评价时说,"在网络空间中,代码能够取代法律成为保护知识产权的主要武器,而且它的作用越来越大。这是一种私人的防护,而非国家法律的保护"。❷虽然这些由代码建立起来的数字围墙对保护著作权起到了重要的作用,但新技术同样也赋予了使用者突破这些数字围墙的能力。当权利人使用一种技术措施后,不久就会出现相应的破解技术,而且对技术的破解通常用该技术本身实现的。❸

这样,在权利人与使用者之间就技术保护措施救护就会展开"军备竞赛"。❹这一方面导致了著作权保护难题,另一方面增加了权利人和使用人双方的成本。著作权法在数字网络背景下应当何去何从,成为我们不得不认真思考的一个问题。著作权法要成功应对数字网络技术的挑战,主要应解决以下三个方面的问题:首先,在数字网络背景下,著作权法应如何调整对权利的初始配置;其次,在著作权的保护方面,传统的著作权保护途径是否能够适应新技术的发展,在新技术背景下应当如何对著作权进行保护,权利人技术保护措施如何与合理使用制度相协调;最后,新技术背景下,如何更好地促进著作权价值的实现。本书下面将对这三个方面的问题依次进行阐述。

---

❶ 吴伟光. 数字技术环境下的版权法危机与对策 [M]. 北京:知识产权出版社,2008:147. See Severine Dusollier, Yves Poullet, Mireille Buydens. Copyright and access to information in the digital environment. COPYRIGHT BULLETIN 34, no. 4 (2000): 4-36.

❷ 劳伦斯·莱斯格. 代码 [M]. 李旭,译. 北京:中信出版社,2004:156.

❸ See Competition, Innovation and Public Policy in the Digital Age: Is the MarketplaceWorking to Protect Digital Creative Works? Hearing Before the S. Comm. on the Judiciary, 107th Cong. 89-92 (2002) 见 Edward W. Felten 的作证发言。

❹ 值得注意的是,在这一"军备竞赛"中,规避技术保护措施的技术很多情况下不是由个体的使用者自己开发的,而是由技术提供者提供,美国的 DCMA 法案禁止提供规避技术的行为。

第二章　权利配置：著作权法的基础架构及调整

第一节　传统著作权法的基础架构

为什么会有著作权制度的出现？著作权制度的正当性在哪里？这是研究著作权法首先应当考虑的问题。数字网络技术对传统著作权法产生了剧烈的冲击，这使我们不得不思考著作权法如何走出新技术引发的困境。虽然本书的主题不在于研究著作权法的理论基础。然而，想探寻我们要向哪里去，必须先回答我们从哪里来的问题。

著作权同其他财产权一样，是人类社会发展到一定的程度后才出现的现象。印刷机的发明促进了出版业的发展，从而使出版商产生了对书籍出版的专有权。出版商的需求与当时统治者控制言论的需要正好产生契合。出版特许制度由此，并逐渐发展出"版权"概念。可以说，最初的"版权"概念与现今的版权概念截然不同。但在出版业发展的同时，写者阶层也不断发展，这一群体经过与出版商长期的斗争，最终促成了现代版权制度的产生。从这一意义上讲，现代著作权的制度的产生是必然性与偶然性相结合的产物。由于著作权制度产生背景和原因的复杂性，各国在引进或者建立自己的著作权制度时遇到的第一个问题就是为什么著作权制度是必要的？权利人是基于何种理由而享有著作权的？著作权到底是一种人类固有的自然权利，还是只是一种人为的安排？对这些问题的不同回答，不仅影响到著作权的具体制度构建，也影响到具体的案件处理。更重要的是，这一问题构成我们寻求著作权法未来方向的起点。

一、著作权的正当性基础

关于著作权法的正当性的讨论，从著作权法产生之初就开始了，至今这一讨论仍在进行，不同流派提出了不同的学说论证著作权的正当性。归纳起来，著作权的正当性理论主要分为自然权利理论和功利主义理论。

（一）自然权利理论

自然法理论源远流长，最早可追溯到古希腊时代。总体而言，自然法是指宇宙中最高主宰所指定的规则，这种规则适用于一切人，区别于国家制定的实在法。经由古希腊罗马时期和中世纪时期的发展，近代的格劳修斯、洛克、霍布斯、卢梭等将自然法思想发展到了一个新的高度。罗马教会权力的式微、新教以及人文主义、自然科学的兴起对这一时期的自然法思想产生了重要的影响。这一时期自然法的特点是将人从中世纪的神权中解放出来，强调自然法是来自人的理性，并分析了自然状态、自然权利。在近代自然法思想家中，洛克的思想对著作权的正当性提供了理论基础。

在洛克看来，人生来就享有生命权和财产权。洛克理论的基础来自于《圣经》，他认为，上帝将土地上的一切都赐予人类。土地上生产的果实和生活的兽类都归全人类所有。但是，这些自然状态下的东西需要以某种方式分配给个人。对此，洛克提出了财产劳动学说。在他看来，每个人都对自己的身体享有所有权，因此他所从事的劳动也是属于他的。只要他的劳动使东西从自然状态中脱离出来，那么该东西就属于他的财产。❶ 可见，洛克的自然权利理论是将财产权的正当性建立在个人劳动基础之上。他的理论最初只是作为有形财产权正当性的证成，后来成为知识产权正当性的重要理论基础。

自然权利理论关注的主要是作者个人的权利。在该理论下，创作作品的作者应当享有作品之上的经济利益和精神利益，并对作品所有形式的使用享有专有权利。❷ 自然权利理论对法国、德国等大陆法系国家的著作权法产生了深刻的影响。这种影响最明显的体现就是以大陆法国家为核心的《伯尔尼公约》。公约的前言明确规定了公约的目的是各成员国尽可能有效、一致地保护作者对其文学艺术作品的权利。❸ 从《伯尔尼公约》的这一规定我们可以看出大陆法国家的著作权法将保护作者的权利放在第一位，为作者权利的保护提供了坚实的理论基础。

然而，自然权利理论存在明显的缺陷。该理论无法解释的一个问题就是：既然著作权是权利人固有的自然权利，为何还要对其进行限制。也就是说，在

---

❶ 洛克. 政府论两篇 [M]. 赵伯英，译. 西安：陕西人民出版社，2004：145.

❷ 吴伟光. 著作权法研究——国际条约、中国立法与司法实践 [M]. 北京：清华大学出版社，2013：6.

❸ 《伯尔尼公约》前言。

自然权利理论那里并没有著作权制度中的期限限制、合理使用、法定许可等著作权的例外制度的空间。面对这些问题，人们开始向功利主义寻求答案。

（二）功利主义

功利主义理论来自于古典功利主义思想。休谟、边沁等人是这一理论的代表性人物。休谟认为，人类活动的最大目的就是尽可能追求快乐而逃避痛苦。他根据快乐与痛苦的原理，对人类行为的原动力进行分析，将人类的一切需求还原、化约成为一种对"幸福"的计算，不同的快乐可以根据一定的数量测算而进行衡量，从而决定对功利的取舍。❶ 因此法律并非建立在理性的基础上，对自己利益和公共利益的关切才是确立正义的法则。他认为，法律的正当性根源在于人类追求最大快乐的本性，私人所有权规则只能建立在功利基础之上。❷ 边沁提出了功利主义思想开创了一种新的理论体系。边沁之前，法律的正当性是通过自然法来证成，而边沁认为"自然法""天然秩序"这些措辞是在故弄玄虚，应当用新的标准替代这些空洞的字眼，这一新的标准就是"功利"。

后来，学者们把边沁的上述理论用来证明著作权法的正当性。他们认为著作权制度的主要目的是为最大多数人提供最大的益处，即通过鼓励作品的创作和传播从而促进社会公共利益。一般认为，美国的著作权法是这种功利主义的代表。

美国《宪法》中明确"保障作家和发明家对其作品和发明在一定期限内的专有权，以促进科学和实用艺术的发展"。❸ 因此，在美国宪法看来，著作权法的最终目的是促进科学和实用艺术的发展，保障作者的著作权只是实现这一目的的工具，对作者的保护只是第二层面的价值。功利主义在美国著作权立法过程中一直占据着主导地位。例如，1909 年美国众议院司法委员会在其对著作权法的修订报告中指出，国会依据宪法作出的著作权立法，不是基于任何作者对其作品享有的自然权利，而是基于公共福利的增进和科学以及实用艺术的进步。❹

这种功利主义还体现在国际公约中。《世界版权公约》中明确指出，公约的目的是："所有国家保证对文学、科学、艺术作品的著作权进行保护；确信

---

❶ 丹尼斯·劳埃德. M. D. A. 弗里曼修订. 法理学 [M]. 许章润, 译. 北京：法律出版社, 2007：105.
❷ 彭学龙. 知识产权：自然权利抑或法定权利 [J]. 电子知识产权, 2007（8）.
❸ 美国《宪法》第 1 条第 8 款。
❹ Sony Corp. of America v. Universal City Studios, 464 U. S. 417 (1984). Footnote 10.

适用于世界各国并以公约形式确定下来的著作权保护制度有利而无损于现行各种国际制度，并将确保尊重个人权利，促进文学、科学和艺术的发展；相信这种国际著作权保护制度将会促进人类精神产品的广泛传播和增进各国的相互了解"。❶《世界版权公约》关于公约目的的规定与《伯尔尼公约》明显不同。《伯尔尼公约》中保护作者的权利是公约目的，而《世界版权公约》的目的则是促进文学、科学和艺术的发展，保护著作权只是实现这一目标的工具。《世界版权公约》与《伯尔尼公约》的另一个明显不同是，它未规定对著作权人的精神权利的保护。两个公约有如此明显的区别，主要是因为《伯尔尼公约》是欧洲大陆法系国家主导的国际条约，而美国又想取得国际著作权立法的主导权，于是另辟蹊径，主导成立了《世界版权公约》，而新公约规则的制定也当然体现着美国对著作权制度的功利主义价值观。同样，TRIPs也规定："知识产权的保护和实施应当有利于促进技术创新、转让和传播，以有利于社会经济福利的方式促进知识和技术的生产者和使用者的相互利益，保护和实施的方式应有利于社会和经济福利，促进权利和义务的平衡。"❷ 这从一方面反映了当前美国在整个世界知识产权政策上的影响和主导地位。

这样，以两种理论基础作为依据的不同制度形成了两种著作权文化：欧洲的立法者属于著作权的乐观派，他们把著作权制度视为半满的水杯，为了保护作者的权利，可以将权利扩展到具有经济价值的任何方面；而美国的立法者则被认为是著作权的悲观派，他们把著作权制度视为半空的水杯，不愿将权利扩展到作品使用的新领域，除非这种权利的扩展对于激励创作来说是必要的。❸

（三）对两种理论的评价

通过上述分析可以看出，两种对著作权正当性的证成理论有着截然的区别：自然权利理论强调对作者权利的保护，而功利主义理论则强调对公共利益的促进，对著作权的保护只是实现这一目的的工具。著作权究竟是一种自然权利还是一种法定权利？究竟保护的是著作权人的利益，还是保护社会公共利益？这两种理论表面上看似乎相互矛盾，但二者并不存在根本的冲突。本书认为，这两种理论看似有着相反的主张，但实际上二者正如硬币的两面，各从一个侧面解释了著作权的正当性基础，只不过是不同的历史阶段，法律的诉求有

---

❶ 《世界版权公约》(1971年7月24日巴黎修订本)。
❷ TRIPs协议第7条。
❸ [美] 保罗·戈斯汀. 著作权之道：从古登堡到数字点播机 [M]. 金海军, 译. 北京大学出版社, 2008: 139.

着不同的侧重点。在著作权制度早期，为了使著作权摆脱封建特许制度的束缚，理论家们便以自然权利理论当作战斗口号，最终促成了著作权制度的产生。而美国制定自己著作权法时，著作权观念在欧洲已经确立，于是人们的关注重点就转向文化艺术的传播、社会公共利益等更高层次的价值。正如有学者所言，尽管著作权合理性的证成很大程度上归功于自然权利理论，但其又没有完全沿着自然权利的理论轨迹发展，由功利主义对其进行了修正和完善。❶ 可见，自然权利理论与功利主义理论并不冲突，二者公共铸造了当今的著作权制度。一个良好的著作权制度应当兼顾保护作者的利益和促进公共利益两个目标，并在二者之间保持适当的平衡。

事实上，自从 20 世纪 80 年代以来，随着经济全球化进程的不断加快和著作权贸易的国际化发展，两大法系的著作权法理念开始逐渐融合。美国于 1989 加入了代表自然权利理念的《伯尔尼公约》。而在法国和德国这样的自然权利主义的国家，著作权法应当实现作者利益和使用者之间的利益平衡也成为广为认可的理念。

二、著作权法的价值目标和利益平衡

著作权法以保护作者及其他权利人的利益为基础，但是著作权法并非仅仅保护著作权人利益。著作权法通过保护权利人的利益，最终达到促进学习、促进科学文化进步和促进公共利益的实现。著作权法的目的在大陆法系和英美法系有不同的侧重。大陆法系十分看重著作权的财产权属性，重视对作者权利的保护。在大陆法系中，著作权包含精神权利和经济权利，而且精神权利被视为作者人格的延伸。因此，著作权法的首要目的是充分保护作者的权利。在英美法系，虽然也有学者主张对精神权利的保护，❷ 但更加注重作者的经济权利。而且英美法系似乎更加注重对其他利益主体以及社会公共利益的保障。以美国为例，其宪法中的知识产权条款规定："为了促进科学和使用技术的发展，国会有权保障作者和发明者在有限期间内对他们的作品和发明享有专有权利。"❸ 英美法系学者普遍认为，制定著作权法的主要目的就是刺激创作，促进文学艺术的发展和进步。因此，著作权法主要有两个目的：一是保护作者的利益；二

---

❶ 李扬. 知识产权法定义及其适用 [J]. 法学研究，2006（2）.

❷ Liemer, S. (2005). How We Lost Our Moral Rights and the Door Closed on Non-Economic Values in Copyright. John Marshall Review of Intellectual Property Law, 5（1）.

❸ 美国《宪法》第 1 条第 8 款。

是促进知识使用和传播的公共利益。

如上所述，保护作者的利益与促进公共利益这两个目标之间并不矛盾。保护作者的利益是著作权法的基础价值目标，而促进公共利益的实现则是更高层面的价值。

（一）保护作者的利益是著作权法的基础价值目标

著作权法的实质是对利益关系进行调整协调的制度安排。著作权法对作者的利益进行保护，主要是为了鼓励作品的创作，为社会提供足够的知识产品。著作权法必须以保护作者利益为基础。著作权法的历史发展表明了作者在著作权法中的主导地位。1886年诞生的《伯尔尼公约》和1952年诞生的《世界版权公约》都确认著作权首先是作者的权利。美国康涅狄格州第一部著作权法的前沿也有"保障每一个作者能够获取出售其作品所获得的利润十分合乎自然的公正和公平原则"的论述。[1] 著作权法的根本作用就在于对作者的作品专有权利进行法律上的确认和保护，从而鼓励作者积极创作，促进人类文明进步。

（二）保护公共利益是著作权法更高层次的价值目标

著作权法除保护作者的利益之外，更重要的是促进公共利益的实现。美国《宪法》中的知识产权条款非常明确地阐明，赋予作者在有限时间内的专有权，其目的是促进科学和有用艺术的进步。著作权法的公共利益价值目标在很多司法案例中有集中的体现。Twentieth Century Music Corp. 一案的判决指出：著作权法的直接效果是作者从创造性劳动中取得公正报酬，但其最终目的是通过激励促进公共利益。[2]

（三）利益平衡是著作权法的基本原则和设计基础

著作权法不仅要保护作者的利益，还要在保护作者利益的基础上，通过激励作品的创作促进公共利益的实现。这就需要著作权法在不同利益主体之间建立一种利益平衡机制。这种平衡机制是各种相互冲突的不同因素处于相互协调之中的和谐状态，它包括著作权人权利义务的平衡，创作者、传播者和使用者之间利益的平衡，以及个人利益和公共利益之间的平衡。[3] 这就需要著作权法对著作权的保护维持在一个适当的水平，既不能保护不足，也不能过度保护。

---

[1] 冯晓青. 知识产权法利益平衡理论 [M]. 北京：中国政法大学出版社，2006：93-94.
[2] Twentieth Century Music Corp. v. Aiken, 422 U.S. 151 (1975).
[3] 吴汉东. 著作权合理使用制度研究 [M]. 2版. 北京：中国政法大学出版社，2005：18.

如果保护不足，创作者就会不愿意投入金钱、时间和精力进行作品创作。如果保护过度，公众对作品的使用就会受到限制，将不利于公共利益。实现利益平衡的关键是合理确定著作权这一法定垄断权的适当界限。为此，著作权法的整个体系都是基于利益平衡的目的进行构建的。

三、基于利益平衡的著作权法基础架构

著作权法通过一系列的制度建构保证作者权利的保护与公共利益之间的利益平衡。一方面，著作权法赋予权利人一定范围内的排他权，以实现激励作者进行创作的目的；另一方面，著作权法又对著作权进行限制，以促进公共利益的实现。

从著作权法的发展历史来看，著作权法对排他权的设置是以复制权为原点展开的。随着新技术的不断发展，新的作品形式以及对作品新的使用方式不断出现，为了满足创作者的利益需求，著作权的客体、权能以及期限不断扩张，逐渐形成如今的著作权法体系。❶ 在整个著作权法的权利体系中，复制权在著作权保护中处于核心地位，是著作权体系中的核心权利，其他权利都是以复制权为基点和核心构建的。世界上第一部著作权法《安妮法》诞生以来，复制权所控制的复制行为一直是作品使用的最基本的方式，其他使用方式都是以此为基础。发行权、展览权、表演权等权利的实现也都是以复制权为基础的。

著作权法在赋予著作权人一系列著作权专有权利的同时，通过对这些专有权的限制来实现权利人和公共利益之间的平衡，从而实现著作权法的目的。正如美国法官 Alex Kozinsiki 所说，过度的保护与保护不足同样有害。❷ 各个国家对著作权都有一定限制，有的国家将对著作权的限制称为"限制"，有的国家则称为"例外"。例如，《伯尔尼公约》将对著作权的限制称为"例外"，而美国《著作权法》则使用"合理使用"这一术语。但无论是"例外"还是"合理使用"都是对著作权的限制，故本书采用"限制"这一术语。❸ 著作权制度通常从两大方面对著作权进行限制：第一，对著作权的客体进行限制，将某些

---

❶ 关于著作权的扩张，冯晓青. 著作权扩张及其缘由透视 [J]. 政法论坛，2006（6）；李雨峰. 版权扩张：一种合法性的反思 [J]. 现代法学，2001（5）.

❷ See White v. Samsung Electronics America, Inc, 989 F. 2d 1512, 1993 U. S. App.

❸ 对著作权的限制可以分为外部限制和内部限制。外部限制是指著作权法之外的法律对著作权的限制，如宪法、反垄断法等法律对著作权的限制。内部的限制则是指著作权法自身对著作权的限制。基于本文的目的，这里仅指著作权法内部对著作权的限制。吴伟光. 著作权法研究——国际条约、中国立法与司法实践 [M]. 北京：清华大学出版社，2013.

对象排除在著作权保护之外。思想表达二分法就是对保护客体进行限制的理论工具。第二，对著作权人的权能进行限制，如首次销售原则、合理使用原则及法定许可等。

数字网络技术对著作权法基础架构带来了很大的冲击。首先，数字网络技术给著作权法中的复制权提出了挑战。临时复制问题的出现使我们不得不对复制权概念重新审视，对原有的理论和制度作出调整以适应新技术的发展。其次，数字网络技术对著作权的首次销售原则与合理使用制度产生了冲击。以下将依次对临时复制、首次销售原则及合理使用制度进行研究，探索著作权法如何对这几个关乎基本架构的问题进行调整以应对新技术提出的挑战。

第二节　临时复制问题

一、临时复制问题的提出

复制权是著作权权利系统中最根本的权利，很多其他权利都以复制权为基础。在数字网络空间中，由于每一个对作品的传输和使用都不可避免地要发生一系列对作品的复制，因此复制权在网络环境下的重要性更是不言而喻。

当网络用户浏览互联网页面时，出于技术上的需要，很多数据只是被临时复制在随机存储器（RAM）上，该信息可能被随时刷新，一旦电脑关机或运行其他的程序后，这些信息就会就会从内存中消失。临时复制在软件的使用中以及流媒体服务中非常普遍，因为复制缓存（Buffer Copies）对于网络内容传输是必不可少的技术环节。按照不同标准，临时复制可以分为多种类型。根据存储位置的不同，临时复制可以分为网络服务器上的临时复制、路由器上的临时复制以及浏览器上的临时复制等；根据作品传输阶段的不同，临时复制可分为网络服务器之间的临时复制、从网络服务器到终端计算机之间的临时复制和计算机终端到计算机屏幕上的临时复制等类型。临时复制还可根据临时复制的不同作用分为技术性临时复制和非技术性临时复制。其中前者是为了完成某项技术过程而必然要产生的复制，后者是技术过程之外产生的临时复制。❶

尽管临时复制只是短暂的、附带的，但是由于其对网络环境下的作品传输和使用非常重要，因此对著作权法有重要的影响。对于著作权人而言，他们希

---

❶ 向任东，焦泉．网络临时复制法律问题研究［J］．南京邮电大学学报（社会科学版），2008（2）．

望法律赋予他们控制临时复制的权利。这样,网络用户在计算机上使用盗版作品的行为就是未经许可的复制作品的侵权行为。相反,如果著作权人有权控制临时复制,就意味着使用者在很多情况下会失去获取信息的机会。如何对待临时复制问题,是关系到著作权法能否在数字网络环境下保持利益平衡的重要问题。

二、临时复制的域外立法司法实践

(一) 国际组织层面的立法

解决复制问题的关键在于如何界定临时复制与复制权之间的关系。为解决数字网络技术的发展给著作权带来的问题,世界知识产权组织于1996年12月著作权与邻接权外交会议上通过了《世界知识产权组织版权条约》(WCT)和《世界知识产权组织表演、录音制品条约》(WPPT)。临时复制问题是两个条约通过的协商过程中最有争议的问题之一。根据这两个条约,《伯尔尼公约》第9条中关于复制权及其例外的规定完全适用于数字环境,在电子媒体中以数字形式存储受著作权保护的作品构成复制。[1] 这两个条约对临时复制的法律定位并无硬性要求,并不要求成员国承担保护临时复制的义务。

(二) 美国立法及司法实践

根据美国法律,复制权并不限于制作永久物理复制件。[2]《美国版权法》对"复制件"的定义为:"不同于录音制品的物质载体,作品被现在已知或者后来开发的方法固定于该物质载体中,直接或间接借助于机器装置可以感知、复制或者传播物质载体中的作品"。[3] 对"以有形形式固定作品"的定义为:"作者本人或者经由作者授权后,作品被相对持久或稳定地包含在复制件或者录音制品内,足以对作品进行感知、复制或者不仅仅是短暂性质的传播。"

上述立法中的观点在司法判决中得到了体现。1993年,第九联邦巡回上诉法院在 MAI Systems Corp. v. Peak Computer, Inc. 一案中将上述立法中的定义应用到判决中,认为当一个程序载入 RAM 时,复制行为就已经发生了,从而

---

[1] WCT 第1条(4) 的议定声明;WPPT 第7条及议定声明(6)。

[2] See Final Report of the National Commission on New Technological Uses of Copyrighted Works note 18 at 12-13, 22.

[3] 17 U.S.C. §101 中关于"复制件"的定义。

第二章 权利配置：著作权法的基础架构及调整 ◎

构成侵权。❶ 事实上，原告的软件是在被告启动计算机时自动加载进内存的，而非人为进行。在一份2001年的报告中，美国版权局认为，"尽管在理论上存在这样一种可能性，即信息被存入RAM的时间很短暂，因而不能被提取、展示、复制或传播，但在实践中这种情况不太可能发生。"❷

在坚持上述立法观点的同时，美国法院又在司法中对一个复制行为在何种情形下由于太过短暂而不至于被认定为复制的标准进行了精细化。在Cartoon Network LP v. CSC Holdings, Inc. 一案中，法院认为存在时间不超过1.2秒的缓存复制不属于"固定"，因而不是著作权法意义上的复制。❸ 在另一个案中，法院认为网络服务提供商（ISP）作为使用者获取作品的渠道并没有参与复制行为，因为复制件被固定的时间过于短暂。❹

当然美国法律也规定了临时复制不构成侵权的情形。这些情形包括：为了使计算机正常使用或者维修计算机而进行的临时复制；❺ 为了再广播目的的临时复制；❻ 非交互性音频服务中的短暂录制；❼ 某些情形下的合理使用。❽ 美国版权局还认为，"在流媒体传输过程中产生的缓冲复制应当属于合理使用。因为，尽管这种使用并非转换性的（Transformative），而且是出于商业目的，但是这种复制只是为了促成已获授权的表演（licensed performance）的发生，促进已经存在的合法流媒体服务市场而已。"❾ 另外，美国版权局在上述报告中还建议在音乐流媒体服务领域增加临时缓存复制的法定例外情形。❿

---

❶ 991 F. 2d 511 (9th Cir. 1993).

❷ U.S. Copyright Office, A Report of the Register of Copyrights Pursuant to § 104 of the Digtial Millennium Copyright Act, 108 (2001), available at: http://www.copyright.gov/reports/studies/dmca/sec-104-report-vol-1.pdf.

❸ Cartoon Network LP v. CSC Holdings, Inc., 536 F. 3d 121, 129-30 (2d Cir. 2008), cert denied, 557 U.S. 946 (2009).

❹ CoStar Grp., Inc. v. LoopNet, Inc., , 373 F. 3d 544, 551 (4th Cir. 2004).

❺ 17 U.S.C. § 117 (c).

❻ 17 U.S.C. § 112 (a).

❼ 17 U.S.C. § 112 (e).

❽ See Perfect 10 v. Google, Inc., 416 F. Supp. 2d 828 (C.D. Cal. 2006), aff'd sub nom, Perfect 10 v. Amazon.com, Inc., 508 F. 3d 1146, 1169 (9th Cir. 2007); Field v. Goole, 412 F. Supp. 2d 1106, 1118 (D. Nev. 2006). see also 4 M. NIMMER & D. NIMMER, NIMMER ON COPYRIGHT § 13.05 [G], at 13-280.

❾ U.S. Copyright Office, A Report of the Register of Copyrights Pursuant to § 104 of the Digtial Millennium Copyright Act, 133-140, (2001), available at: http://www.copyright.gov/reports/studies/dmca/sec-104-report-vol-1.pdf.

❿ Id, 141-146.

（三）欧盟的相关立法

为了履行 WIPO 两个互联网条约，欧盟成员国在 2001 年《关于协调信息社会中著作权和相关权若干方面的指令》中第 2 条规定复制权覆盖"任何方式和任何形式的、直接或间接的、临时性或永久性的、全部或部分"的复制行为。❶ 这样，欧盟指令中的复制权涵盖了几乎所有的复制行为。

但是，该指令也包含了临时复制的例外规定。根据指令第 5 条第 1 款规定，在特殊情况下的临时复制不适用于第 2 条的规定。这种"特殊情况"的临时复制应符合三个条件：（1）从性质上看，该临时复制行为是短暂的或者是偶然的，是技术过程中不可分割的必要组成部分；（2）从目的上看，其唯一目的是使作品或其他客体在网络中通过中间服务商在第三方之间传输成为可能，或者使对作品或其他客体的合法使用成为可能；（3）从经济价值上看，该临时复制行为不具有独立的经济意义。❷ 这些条件是累积性的，即如果不符合其中任一条件，则复制行为就不能得到豁免。

另外，指令第 5 条第 5 款还规定第 1 款中规定的例外和限制应只适用于某些不与作品或其他客体的正常利用相抵触、也不会不合理地损害权利人合法利益的特殊情况。❸ 这一规定其实是为了使欧盟成员国对复制权例外的规定符合《伯尔尼公约》中的国际义务，即该条约第 9 条所规定的三步检验法。

事实上，欧盟法院在司法实践中也贯彻了这一规定。在其于 2017 年 4 月 26 日作出的 Stichting Brein 一案❹的裁决中，欧盟法院认为，销售能够通过网络非法获取电影并在电视屏幕上自由观看的多媒体播放设备的行为构成"向公众传播作品"的行为❺；同时，多媒体播放设备以流媒体形式提供版权作品的行为属于临时复制，但它并不属于法律豁免的情形。其在裁决中裁决："《指令》第 5（1）、（5）条所指之临时复制行为必须解释为：本案中被告在多媒体播放设备上对受著作权保护作品进行临时复制，而被临时复制的作品系通过流媒体技术从未经著作权持有人同意而提供作品的第三方网站获取，它不符合上述条款规定的条件。"简言之，根据欧盟法院的裁决，从非法来源处采用流媒体技术

---

❶ Directive 2001/29/EC, art. 2.
❷ Id, art. 5 (1).
❸ Id, art. 5 (5).
❹ Case C-527/15.
❺ 事实上，销售能够通过网络非法获取电影并在电视屏幕上自由观看的多媒体播放设备的行为是否属于"向公众传播作品"的行为是有待讨论的。但该问题并非此处研究重点，故不对其进行详细讨论。

（streaming）获取作品的行为不属于指令第5条中的"合法使用"。

三、对我国第三次著作权法修改建议

从美国和欧盟研究中可以看出，对临时复制是否属于著作权中的复制、什么样的临时复制侵犯著作权存在分歧。要解决这种分歧，就需要界定临时复制的法律性质，将临时复制与著作权法中一般意义上的复制区分开来。著作权法中的复制应该是在人的主观意识控制下所进行的有目的的行为。临时复制是由计算机自动产生的一种客观的技术现象，并不体现复制者的主观意识，不应将技术性临时复制认定为著作权法中的复制行为。❶ 不过，如果临时复制除了必要的技术性目的外还可有其他目的，而且有独立的经济意义，那么这种临时复制就会对著作权人的利益产生影响，则应考虑纳入著作权法中的复制权范围。

我国目前的著作权法没有关于临时复制的规定，这在互联网日益普及的背景下不能不说是一个法律漏洞。建议我国第三次著作权法修订应对临时复制问题予以充分考虑。在立法模式上，我国可以借鉴欧盟指令的做法，在对复制权范围进行界定的前提下，明确临时复制的法律性质，并根据临时复制的性质、目的以及经济价值等因素设置一定的例外规定。至于哪些情况应当设置临时复制的例外，可以参考美国、欧盟相关立法和司法案例中的问题，结合我国的实际情况进行规定。我国于2014年6月公布的《著作权法修订草案（送审稿）》❷对此并未予明确规定，这应该说是一个缺憾。

第三节　数字网络环境下的首次销售原则适用问题

一、首次销售原则概述

首次销售原则，又称为权利用尽原则。根据这一原则，著作权人在作品复制件首次销售之后，即失去对该复制件的控制权，该复制件的受让人可以不经原著作权人的同意对其进行再次销售、租赁或以其他方式处分。该制度的目的是通过对著作权人的发行权的限制确保公众对著作权产品的后续使用不受原著

---

❶ 王迁. 网络环境中的著作权保护研究[M]. 北京：法律出版社，2011：65.
❷ 《中华人民共和国著作权法（修订草案送审稿）》，网址：http://www.gov.cn/xinwen/2014-06/10/content_2697701.htm.

作权人限制。❶

　　在数字网络技术出现以前，作品在公众之间流通是以物理载体的转移为基础的。物理载体数量的有限性使作品不会像在网络环境下一样大规模传播。首次销售原则在作品载体的所有权与著作权发行权之间划出了一道清晰的界线，限定了著作权发行权的行使限度。正是因为这种对发行权的限制使图书馆、档案馆和博物馆等公益机构可以行使传播科学文化、服务社会公众的职能。在传统技术背景下，公众只能通过书店、音像商店等实体机构购买著作权产品。而在互联网环境下，人们可以通过服务商提供的服务下载以数字形式存在的著作权产品。对于通过网络空间合法取得的作品复制件，所有者是否可以按照首次销售原则不经著作权人许可而对该数字形式的作品复制件进行转让？对于这一现实问题的回答实际上是需要解决首次销售原则是否适用于网络环境的问题。根据传统的首次销售原则，著作权人无权对他人处分合法获得的作品复制件进行限制。因此，著作权人在通过网络提供服务时往往通过一定的技术保护措施限制用户对作品文件进行转让的能力。例如，一些数字图书馆要求用户将特定计算机与客户端进行"捆绑"。通过这些技术手段，用户就无法在不需要这些数字化作品后将其转让给他人。在这种情况下，如果首次销售原则适用于网络环境下通过合法途径取得的作品复制件，则著作权人就无权对作品复制件的拥有者的后续转让进行限制。反之，著作权人则有权对著作权产品的后续转让进行限制。

　　随着数字网络技术和数字版权产业的发展，首次销售原则能否适用于数字网络环境这一问题成为著作权法不可回避的重要问题。本节以欧盟和美国的两个新近案例为切入点，分析首次销售原则在数字网络环境下的适用问题。

二、首次销售原则在数字网络环境下适用的国外司法实践

（一）欧盟 UsedSoft v. Oracle 案❷

1. 案件事实

　　原告甲骨文公司（Oracle）是一家计算机软件公司。在该案中，原告主要通过网络下载的方式向客户销售自己开发的数据库软件。该软件是客户机—服务器软件（client-server-software）。客户可以将软件永久存储在服务器上，并

---

❶ See Melvile B. Nimmer & David Nimmer, Nimmer on Copyright, Matthew Bender & Company, Inc, Chapter 8. 11 (A) (2003).

❷ UsedSoft GmbH v. Oracle International Corp., Case C-128/11 (CJEU July 3, 2012).

允许一定数量的终端用户通过将软件下载到工作站计算机主存而使用软件。根据用户使用授权协议，客户在一次性付费后，有权非排他性地永久使用原告的软件，但客户不可转让对软件的使用权。根据单独的维护协议，客户还可以从甲骨文公司下载软件的更新和补丁。被告 UsedSoft 是一家经营二手软件许可的公司。为了实现经营目的，被告从原告的客户处获取软件许可协议，然后公开出售原告公司提供的软件许可协议，并声称原授权持有者与原告之间的维护协议仍然有效，购买者可以继续从原告网站下载更新和补丁。

2. 判决理由

原告起诉到慕尼黑第一地区法院，要求被告停止上述经营活动，法院支持了原告的请求。被告在上诉被驳回后最终上诉到联邦法院。联邦法院在判决前提请欧盟法院基于计算机软件保护指令（Directive 2009/24/EC，以下称"指令"）对三个问题进行初步裁决（Preliminary Ruling）。这三个问题分别为：❶

第一，在指令 Article 5（1）下，依据计算机软件发行权用尽而非用户使用协议对软件进行使用的人（即 UsedSoft 的客户）是否属于合法获得者（Lawful Acquirer）？第二，如果对第一个问题的回答是肯定的，那么根据指令 Article 4（2）前半句，软件发行权在获得者经权利所有者同意而从网络上下载软件从而产生新的复制件的情况下是否用尽？第三，如果对第二个问题的回答也是肯定的，那么在初始获得者删除并不再使用该软件后，后续获得者可否也依据权利用尽原则对软件进行使用？

第一个问题和第三个问题实际上是要解决二手使用协议的获得者能否以及在何种条件下被视为"合法获得者"的问题，从而可以不经权利所有者许可，基于使用的目的对计算机软件进行复制。欧盟法院根据指令的规定对这两个问题均作出了肯定的回答。第二个问题则涉及本案的核心问题，即原告的发行权是否用尽的问题。根据指令 Article 4（2）前半句，权利持有者实施或者经其同意实施的首次销售后，计算机软件的发行权即告用尽。因此，确定权利是否用尽的前提性问题就是本案原告与其客户之间的交易是否构成"首次销售"

---

❶ Directive 2009/24/EC 中相关的条款为：Article 4（Restricted acts）……2. The first sale in the Community of a copy of a program by the rightholder or with his consent shall exhaust the distribution right within the Community of that copy, with the exception of the right to control further rental of the program or a copy thereof. Article 5（Exceptions to the restricted acts）1. In the absence of specific contractual provisions, the acts referred to in points (a) and (b) of Article 4 (1) shall not require authorisation by the rightholder where they are necessary for the use of the computer program by the lawful acquirer in accordance with its intended purpose, including for error correction……Available at：http：//eur-lex. europa. eu/LexUriServ/LexUriServ. do? uri = OJ：L：2009：111：0016：0022：EN：PDF.

(First Sale)，即发行权是否已经用尽取决于是否存在软件销售行为。欧盟法院认为，虽然指令的条文并未明确规定"销售"这一词语的含义，但根据公认观点，"销售"是指一方将其所有的有形或无形财产转让给另一方而获得对价的行为。也就是说，一项使发行权用尽的交易必须涉及复制件所有权的转让。

原告认为其并未出售本案中的计算机软件，而是免费供客户从其网址上下载。如果客户要使用其免费下载的软件，则必须与原告签订许可使用协议。该协议使客户获得非排他的、不可转让的对软件永久使用的权利。原告主张无论是向客户免费提供软件还是许可使用协议都不涉及软件复制件所有权的转让。欧盟法院则认为，如果不能使用软件，则客户下载该软件毫无意义，因此应当将软件的下载和使用视为不可分割的整体。如果著作权人在用户一次性支付合理费用后，便可以从互联网上下载软件，并拥有永久使用权，那么这种交易就构成销售行为，则发行权即告用尽。如果不对"销售"这样解释，Article 4 (2) 的规定就会被架空，因为原告只要将许可协议表述为"License"而不是"Sale"，就可以规避权利用尽规则。在此基础上，欧盟法院还认为，由于互联网上下载的软件是销售标的物，原告的发行权已经用尽，无权禁止合法获得者的后续转售行为。只要原用户转售后自己不再使用已转售的软件并彻底从自己计算机中删除，就会受到首次销售原则的保护。鉴于确定原用户在转售后是否删除软件的困难性，法院认为原告可以通过技术保护措施保护自己利益不受侵害。

欧盟法院在判决中还讨论了首次销售原则是否仅适用于有形客体。原告认为首次销售原则不适用于从网络上下载的无形的计算机软件复制件。法院认为，指令 Article 4 (2) 并未规定首次销售原则仅限于固定在有形载体中的计算机软件。相反，该条通过"sale…of a copy of a program"的措辞并未对有形载体和无形载体做出区分。尽管综合 Directive 2001/29 中 Article 4 (2) 及其序言的内容，可以确定 2001 年指令规定首次销售原则仅适用于有形载体，但这并不影响对 2009 年指令 Article 4 (2) 的解释，因为 2009 年指令是关于计算机软件保护的特别法。

值得注意的是，欧盟法院对首次销售原则是否应当适用于无形客体进行了补充解释，认为：从经济学的角度，通过 DVD 有形载体与通过网络下载销售计算软件并无不同。以在线传输的方式销售软件是通过物质载体的方式销售软件的功能替代品（Functional Equivalent）。如果首次销售原则不适用于以在线传输方式销售的软件，那么著作权所有人就可能控制软件的后续转让，并就每个新的销售要求更多的补偿。

3. 小结

在上述案件中，法院就首次销售原则在数字网络环境下适用问题上的态度主要可归纳为如下两个方面：（1）首次销售原则不仅适用于对固定在有形载体中的计算机软件的销售，也适用于数字网络环境中通过网络传输对软件的销售；（2）判断双方之间的交易是否构成销售应当依据双方之间法律关系的实质内容判断，而不是协议表面形式。值得注意的是，根据欧盟的法律，首次销售原则在数字网络环境中的适用目前仅局限于计算机软件领域。

（二）美国 Capitol Records v. ReDigi 案[1]

1. 案件事实

与上述 UsedSoft 案不同，ReDigi 案中的被告不是销售二手计算机软件许可，而是提供二手数字音乐交易的市场服务。被告 ReDigi 从 2011 年 10 月开始运营一个在线市场网站，用户可以通过该网站买卖经验证为合法取得的音乐文件。用户要使用被告提供的在线市场服务，必须在被告网站上注册账户，下载并安装一个客户端。该客户端会对用户计算机进行分析并建立一个可出售的音乐文件的列表。只有从 iTunes 或者其他 ReDigi 用户处购买的音乐文件才可以在该系统中出售。用户可以将自己不需要的"二手"音乐文件出售。一旦出售成功，系统就会自动使卖方无法再收听该音乐。然而，客户端无法探测到存储在电脑其他位置的音乐文件。一旦不合法的文件被探测到，客户端就会提示用户删除该文件，但文件不会被自动或强制删除。ReDigi 对数字音乐文件的出售价定为 59~79 美分，当用户购买音乐文件时，售价的 20% 被分配给卖方，20% 投入到艺术家托管基金，ReDigi 则收取其余的 60%。

被告声称其服务的最大特色就是可以规避著作权法的规定，而无须涉及侵犯复制权的问题。其规避法律的原理主要分为两步：第一步需要出售方将其音乐文件上传到其个人云存储柜（Personal Cloud Locker）中，然后音乐文件会自动从出售方电脑中删除。尽管音乐文件的上传会产生新的复制，但 ReDigi 认为该复制属于基于个人消费目的的"空间转换"（Space-shift），应当属于合理使用，从而不会侵犯权利人的复制权。第二步则是二手音乐文件交易的处理。ReDigi 认为交易发生时并不存在新的复制行为，只涉及"文件指针"（File Pointer）[2] 的改变，买方在交易完成后可以将音乐文件下载到自己电脑中，虽然该下载行为

---

[1] Capitol Records, LLC v. ReDigi Inc., No. 12 Civ. 95 (RJS) (S. D. N. Y. Mar. 30, 2013).

[2] "文件指针"技术使 ReDigi 可以记录其服务器上的音乐文件的所有者，而无须为用户单独创造一个复制件。

会产生新的复制，但与上传行为一样，应当属于合理使用。

2012年年初，原告认为被告构建的商业模式未经取得授权而复制音乐文件，侵害了其复制权、发行权等著作权，以直接侵权（Direct Copyright Infringement）、帮助侵权（Contributory Copyright Infringement）、替代侵权（Vicarious Copyright Infringement）、引诱侵权（Inducement of Copyright Infringement）等诉因起诉被告，要求被告承担责任。被告则以合理使用对抗复制权侵权、以首次销售原则对抗发行权侵权。2013年3月30日，美国纽约南区地方法院对此案进行判决，支持了原告的诉讼请求。

2. 判决理由

关于被告对复制权侵权的合理使用抗辩，法院认为，复制权是一种排他的在新载体上再现作品的权利。从逻辑上讲，同一个物质载体（Material Object）不可能通过网络传输。客户对音乐文件的上传和下载都会产生新的复制件。❶ 因此，当用户下载音乐文件（数字序列）到硬盘时，不论原有复制件是否被删除，都构成复制行为。法院同时认为被告为音乐文件的交易提供方便并从中获利，使用的是整个音乐文件而非部分，对原告的市场有可能产生有害影响，从而驳回了被告关于复制权侵权的合理使用抗辩。

关于被告的首次销售抗辩，法院认为，首次销售原则只保护特定复制件所有者的销售行为。而在该案中，ReDigi的用户将音乐文件下载到硬盘，其拥有的是新的而非原来的复制件。被告认为，技术发展使著作权法原有的条文变得含糊，著作权法必须考虑其基本目的，即激励作品的创作、促进作品对社会公众的可获得性，拒绝将首次销售原则适用到该案将使原告的著作权得到扩张，而这种扩张与著作权法政策相悖。❷ 法院认为：首先，技术发展并未使著作权法变得模糊，著作权法明确规定首次销售原则仅适用于特定复制件的合法拥有者；其次，法院作为司法机关无权考虑其修改著作权法的建议。

法院在判决中还对被告的"法院对著作权法首次销售条款的解释会将数字作品排除在外"的观点进行了回应，认为被告的观点并不成立。法院认为，首次销售原则并非不保护数字作品，只是作品需固定在硬盘、iPod或者其他存储设备中一同出售；这种要求虽然可能比要求作品固定在磁带、CD中还要苛刻，但却并非不合理，因为人们在创设首次销售原则时无法想象当今数据传输的速度和容易性。至于这种要求是否已经过时则应当由国会考量。

---

❶ London-Sire Records, Inc. v. John Doe 1, 542 F. Supp. 2d 153 (D. Mass. 2008).
❷ Twentieth Century Music Corp. v. Aiken, 422 U.S. 151, 156 (1975).

3. 小结

总结上述案件的判决，美国法院就首次销售原则在数字网络环境下适用问题上的态度主要可归纳为如下：(1) 当用户下载音乐文件到硬盘时，都会产生新的复制件，不论原有复制件是否被删除，都不构成合理使用；(2) 著作权法只保护合法制作的特定复制件的拥有者对该特定复制件的处分，而在数字网络环境下转让音乐作品，"二手"音乐的卖方上传后的文件以及买方使用的文件已不再是"合法制作的特定复制件"❶，因此首次销售原则不适用于该案。

（三）对欧盟、美国两个案例的比较分析

对比上述两个案例，其相同之处在于，二者都涉及数字作品在网络环境下的传输，且在传输过程中都发生了复制行为。其不同之处在于，欧盟法院在案例中肯定了首次销售原则在数字网络环境下的适用，而美国法院则否认了首次销售原则的适用。两个案件判决结果的迥然不同可以从两个法域的相关立法中找到原因。

欧盟关于首次销售原则的立法主要体现在 Directive 2001/29 和 Directive 2009/24 这两个指令中。根据 2001 年指令序言（28）、（29）及第 4 条，该指令规定的著作权保护包括控制发行以有形物体现的作品的专有权；经权利人授权或同意，在共同体内首次销售作品原件或复制件将穷尽其对再次销售该物品的控制权；服务——特别是在线服务不存在权利穷竭问题，与知识产权附着于有形载体上不同，每次在线服务均应获得提供著作权或相关权利授权的行为。❷ 因此，按照 2001 年指令，首次销售原则并不适用于数字网络环境。但是，根据 2009 年指令第 1 条规定，该指令中的保护适用于以任何形式表达的计算机程序。第 4 条中对首次销售原则的规定也没有对有形载体和无形载体进行区分，规定"著作权人或者经其同意的计算机程序复制件的首次销售将在欧盟范围内穷尽该复制件的发行权。"这样，在 2009 年指令下，关于计算机程序的首次销售适用于数字网络环境。欧盟法院在上述案件的判决中认为 2009 年指令相对于 2001 年指令是特殊法，在计算机程序的领域内应当以 2009 年指令为判决依据。

美国关于首次销售原则的基本规定为著作权法第 109 条。根据该条规定，首次销售原则仅适用于"根据本法合法制作的特定复制件或录音制品的拥有者或

---

❶ 17 U. S. C. § 109 (a).

❷ 王迁．[荷兰] Lucie Guibault. 中欧网络版权保护比较研究 [M]. 法律出版社，2008：160-161, 169.

经其授权的人"。根据美国著作权法权威学者尼莫的总结，首次销售原则的使用须满足四个要件：复制件必须是经著作权人授权而制作；复制件的转让须经著作权人授权；复制件被转让前须为合法的所有者占有；该复制件为合法的著作权人所发行。他认为，数字作品的传输无法满足第四个要件，因为作品传输的同时发生了复制行为，并不是作品的发行行为。❶ 可以看出，虽然美国《著作权法》中的首次销售原则条款未明确区分有形载体和无形载体，但 ReDigi 案中的商业模式由于无法满足适用首次销售原则的要件而无法受到该原则的保护。

对比欧盟和美国关于首次销售原则的规定我们可以看出：欧盟立法强调的是"首次销售"，而美国立法则强调复制件的"特定性"和"合法性"。两个判决的法院也相应地分别把重点放在"销售"的认定和"特定性""合法性"的分析上。两个法院在自由裁量权运用程度上也有所不同。欧盟法院在认定"销售"时强调交易的经济本质，而美国法院在分析"特定性"和"合法性"时则注重对法律条文的字面解释，并严格恪守司法权与立法权之间的边界。这在一定程度上也构成上述两个案件判决结果不同的重要原因。

三、数字网络环境影响下首次销售原则的发展趋势分析

（一）数字网络环境下适用首次销售原则在现阶段存在一定法律和技术障碍

从上述两个案件看，无论是欧盟法律对于计算机程序的网络传输，还是美国法律对于数字音乐的网络传输，都没有明确否定首次销售的适用。这确实给首次销售原则在数字网络环境下适用提供了可能性。然而，在现阶段法律框架和技术条件下，在数字网络环境下适用首次销售原则存在一定障碍。

从欧盟案例来看，虽然法院最终肯定了首次销售原则的适用。但应当注意到，该案的判决仅说明法院有限度地肯定了首次销售原则在数字网络环境下的适用。首先，首次销售原则仅适用于计算机程序的网络传输。如上所述，2001年指令明确规定首次销售原则仅适用于固定于有形载体的作品。法院之所以在判决中肯定首次销售原则的适用是因为 2009 年指令这一特别法对计算机程序保护的单独规定。其次，即使在计算机程序领域，首次销售原则的适用也应当以双方之间的交易构成"销售"为前提，不构成"销售"的在线服务也不适用首次销售原则。因此，如果上述欧盟案例中涉及的是美国案例中的数字音乐，或者仅仅是不转移所有权的使用授权，则很可能出现相反的判决结果。

---

❶ Melville B. Nimmer & David Nimmer, Nimmer on Copyright § 8.12 (2013).

第二章 权利配置：著作权法的基础架构及调整

从美国案例来看，法院不支持首次销售原则在数字网络环境下的适用主要是因为该案中涉及的数字作品传输产生了新的复制件，从而无法满足"特定性"和"合法性"的要求。这是因为，第109条禁止作品发行过程中未经授权的复制行为，而数字作品的所有者无法做到传输作品过程中不对作品进行复制。正如尼莫所述，首次销售原则无法适用于数字网络环境部分是由当前技术的限制导致。❶ 另外，在传统技术条件下，作品的有形载体随着时间推移其品质会不断降低，这在一定程度上缓冲了首次销售之后的后续转让对著作权人利益的影响，从而使著作权与所有权之间可以达到平衡。而在数字网络环境下，目前的技术尚无法完全使数字作品具备有形载体的上述特征。在这种情况下，将首次销售原则适用于数字网络环境，可能打破原有的利益平衡。

因此，将首次销售原则适用于数字网络环境既存在法律上的障碍，也存在技术上的障碍。进而言之，这种法律上的障碍很大程度上是由于目前的技术条件使数字作品的网络传输无法满足法定的首次销售原则的适用要件。

（二）技术的发展将使首次销售原则在数字网络环境下适用成为可能

著作权法的精髓就在于通过一系列制度安排实现各方主体的利益平衡，首次销售原则也是如此。该原则通过在作品发行权和复制件所有权之间设定界限从而实现著作权人与复制件所有人之间的利益平衡。美国版权局根据DMCA的规定于2001年作出的一份报告认为，将首次销售原则限定在离线世界有很多原因，其中两项重要原因是书籍和模拟作品（与数字作品相对）随着时间推移品质不断降低，并且其运输受地理限制。这些天然的"刹车阀"缓冲了二手市场对权利人市场的影响。❷ 因此，在传统技术条件下，首次销售原则可以基本实现著作权人与复制件所有人利益的平衡。

同样，首次销售原则是否应当适用于数字网络环境也取决于其能否实现利益的平衡。在数字网络环境下，数字作品的品质并不随时间降低，且"二手"复制件与原件品质上没有丝毫不同。在数字网络空间，数字作品的复制和传输不再受时间、空间以及成本的限制。这样，数字网络环境下的二手市场对一手市场就会产生非常大的负面影响。这构成了现有技术条件对首次销售原则适用

---

❶ Ibid.
❷ DMCA第104条要求版权局对著作权法修订对电子商务以及技术发展的影响进行评估，并向国会报告。该报告就是美国版权局根据该规定就著作权法与技术发展之间的相互影响（包括技术发展与首次销售原则之间的关系）作出。See U. S. Copyright Office, DMCA Section 104 Report 92 n. 301 (2001), available at http: //www.copyright.gov/reports/studies/dmca/sec-104-report-vol-1.pdf.

· 49 ·

的限制。不过，如果以逆向思维思考，假如技术条件能够模拟传统技术条件下作品复制件的特定属性，使著作权人与复制件所有人的利益实现平衡，那么首次销售原则在数字网络环境下的适用就不应当是问题。

事实上，新近已经出现了一些技术，使首次销售原则在数字网络环境下适用成为可能。IBM 公司于 2011 年 11 月提交一项专利申请，该专利描述的系统可以使数字文件像普通的纸张或者照片一样逐渐老化。该系统可以设置外部温度、老化速度、作品载体的种类等参数，使数字文件的老化与非数字文件的老化过程相似。❶ 2013 年 1 月，亚马逊公司在美国获得了一项数字作品二级市场的专利。按照该专利的内容说明，该专利有如下特点：首先，用户从原始提供者购买的电子书、计算机软件等数字作品被存储到用户的个人数据存储空间。用户可以通过对作品进行移动、下载使用作品。当用户将自己拥有的数字文件转让给其他用户时，便可以将数字作品移动到其他用户的个人数据存储空间，并且系统将会把该文件从原用户的存储空间中删除。其次，当对数字作品的移动或下载达到一定次数时，则系统不再允许对该数字作品进行移动。❷ 就在亚马逊获得上述专利一个月之后，苹果公司于 2013 年 3 月也提交了一份专利申请。❸ 与亚马逊的专利功能相似，该专利可以使用户转让自己不需要的数字作品。按照该专利的描述，苹果公司将在每一个文件的技术保护措施中植入用户的信息。当该文件被转让给新的用户时，该文件的所有权信息将会变成新的用户，原来的用户便无法再使用该文件，只有新用户可以使用该文件。按照这一设计原理，该专利的这一设计原理有望避免 ReDigi 商业模式中文件上传和下载均会侵犯复制权的问题。该专利还可以将部分的转售收入支付给出版商或创作者，以及数字作品的最初出售者。❹

这些技术虽然各有特点，但其共同之处是从不同角度为首次销售原则在数字网络环境下的适用减少了障碍：IBM 的专利使数字作品具备了有形载体随时间推移而老化的特征，从而模拟首次销售原则在传统技术背景下适用的条件；亚马逊的专利则对数字作品可以无限复制的特点进行限制，从另一个角度模拟

---

❶ Aging File System, U. S. Patent No. 20110282838（filed Nov. 17, 2011）. Available at：http：//appft1. uspto. gov/netacgi/nph‐Parser？ Sect1 = PTO2&Sect2 = HITOFF&p = 1&u =% 2Fnetahtml% 2FPTO% 2Fsearch‐bool. html&r = 1&f = G&l = 50&co1 = AND&d = PG01&s1 = 20110282838. PGNR. &OS = DN/20110282838RS = DN/20110282838.

❷ U. S. Patent No. 8, 364, 595（filed May. 5, 2009）（issued Jan. 29, 2013）.

❸ U. S. Patent Application No. 20130060616（filed Mar. 7, 2013）.

❹ Jacqui Cheng, Apple follows Amazon with patent for resale of e‐books, music. Available at：http：//arstechnica. com/apple/2013/03/apple‐follows‐amazon‐with‐patent‐for‐resale‐of‐e‐books‐music/.

了传统技术条件下首次销售原则适用的环境；苹果公司的专利一方面可以避免ReDigi 商业模式下的复制侵权问题，解决了适用首次销售原则一个很大的法律障碍，另一方面还从收益分配的角度促进不同主体之间的利益平衡。虽然上述新兴技术可能尚有待改进和完善，其商业模式的实施也可能遇到困难，但这些技术通过模拟首次销售原则在传统技术环境下适用的条件以及调整不同主体之间的利益分配，促进新的利益平衡，大大增加了首次销售原则在数字网络环境下适用的可能性和现实性。可以预见，随着新技术的飞速创新发展和商业模式的不断演进，首次销售原则适用于数字网络环境下将成为发展趋势。

著作权法的发展很大程度上来源于新技术的发展，过去几十年数字网络技术的发展对著作权法的发展和演进产生了重要的影响。随着互联网技术的不断进步和互联网产业的不断发展，数字著作权市场的重要性将日益凸显。二手数字著作权市场是数字著作权市场的重要组成部分，会对著作权发行市场产生重要的影响，进而影响著作权法上的利益平衡。我国作为互联网产业大国，在鼓励技术创新的同时，应注重根据技术的发展对法律制度进行相应调整和创新，为商业模式的创新和发展提供制度保障。我国目前正在对著作权法进行第三次大规模修订，鉴于首次销售原则对数字著作权市场的重要性，有必要在修订过程中就新技术对著作权法的影响进行充分评估，并对首次销售原则在数字网络环境下的适用问题进行仔细考量。

第四节　数字网络技术影响下合理使用制度

一、合理使用制度概述

著作权法中的合理使用制度最先起源于英国判例法。1740 年 Gyles 诉Wilcox 一案是英国关于合理使用最早的司法判决。在本案中，法院认为被告未经原作者允许而在自己作品中使用原作 275 页中 35 页。根据当时的《安娜法》，只要是具有新创作的作品，那么就受法律保护。[1] 此后直到 1839 年的近一百年内，英国通过司法实践逐渐意识到只有在重新创作的情况下诚信使用他人作品才可以不经允许而合理使用他人作品。[2]

---

[1] 吴汉东. 著作权合理使用制度研究 [M]. 北京：中国政法大学出版社，2005：19.
[2] 于玉. 著作权合理使用制度研究——应对数字网络环境挑战 [M]. 济南：山东大学出版社，2007：5.

合理使用制度在美国判例法中得到进一步理论化、系统化。1841年法官Joseph Story在审理Folsom v. Marsh一案中，集以往判例法形成的合理使用规则之大成，系统阐述了合理使用制度的基本框架，即判断合理使用应考虑以下三要素：使用作品的性质和目的、使用作品的数量和价值、使用作品对原作市场销售存在的价值。此后，法院又通过判例对此原则继续深化，形成了判断合理使用的四要素原则，即使用的目的、被使用作品的性质、使用的程度、对被使用作品潜在市场价值所产生的影响。❶上述在判例法中形成的规则最终被美国成文法所采用，成为1976年美国《版权法》最重要的内容之一。随后，合理使用这一制度逐渐形成并得到进一步的完善，并对世界各国的著作权法产生了影响。如今，合理使用原则成为保持著作权法上利益平衡的重要工具。

二、合理使用制度的立法模式

合理使用制度主要有三种立法模式，即开放、半开放和封闭模式。

第一种是美国法上的"fair use"模式。美国《版权法》第107条规定，为诸如批评、评论、新闻报道、教学、学术或研究的目的合理使用有著作权的作品，不侵害著作权。此条对目的的限定使用了"诸如"（such as）一词，表明上述列举的目的并非是穷尽的。同时，第107条还规定了判定合理使用的四个要素，即使用的目的与特点，包括该使用行为属于商业性质还是非营利的教育目的；被使用作品的类型；相对于被使用的作品的整体，所使用部分的比例；使用行为对作品潜在市场或价值所造成的影响。该条中使用了"shall include"的措辞，表明这四个要件并非穷尽性的。该模式的最大优点是保持足够的开放性，法官可以在基本原则的限度之内，根据案件的实际情况对作品的使用是否属于合理使用。

第二种立法模式是所谓的fair dealing模式。该模式对合理使用行为进行了目的限制。例如，英国《著作权法》第29条和第30条规定基于研究或个人学习、批评或评论、时事报道三种目的可构成合理利用。该模式虽然明确规定了三种合理使用的目的，就限定目的的数量而言是封闭式的规定。但是，由于该模式仅仅规定使用的目的，目的以外的因素则完全留给法官在个案中判断。在实践中，法官要综合判断作品是否已发表、获取作品的手段、使用的量、使用

---

❶ 于玉. 著作权合理使用制度研究——应对数字网络环境挑战[M]. 北京：知识产权出版社，2012：2-3.

的方式、使用的动机、使用的结果、使用的目的可否通过其他方式实现等因素。❶

第三种立法模式是"exception of copyright"模式。在立法模式下,享有著作权是常态,而"例外"则是一种非正常状态,因此合理使用要受到严格限制。该种立法模式在立法技术上采用完全封闭的规范技术,通过法律规定穷尽式列举构成例外的具体情形。相应地,在解释上也采用狭义解释原则,只要法律无明确规定,法官就不得认定例外情形。有德国学者认为,"甚至不允许类推——只要存在原则/例外关系。"❷

总结而言,由于不同的历史传统,英美法系国家更倾向于采用以原则规定为特点的弹性立法模式,而大陆法系国家更倾向于采用以穷尽列举为特点的刚性立法模式。然而,这两种模式都有一定缺陷,对于弹性的立法模式而言,尽管其可以较好地适用社会生活的复杂性,但它也带来了法律适用上的不确定性。而列举式的规定虽然确定,但有时过于僵化,难以适应社会的发展变化。

三、数字网络技术影响下合理使用制度的调整

数字网络技术使作品的创作、传播和使用模式发生了本质的变革,使整个社会进入"人人"时代,这大大增加了在网络环境下使用作品的必要性和可能性。因此,在数字网络环境下,如何调整合理使用制度成为一个必须思考的问题。我国有必要在第三次著作权法修改过程中,重视数字网络技术对合理使用制度的影响,在结合各国立法例的基础上,建立适合我国国情和现实需求的合理使用制度。我国目前的立法模式主要是采用列举式的刚性规定,对合理使用的情形进行穷尽性的列举。这种立法模式已经无法适应数字网络技术引起的社会飞速发展。本书认为,我国应改变以往的列举式立法模式,采用刚性与弹性相结合的立法模式。这样,既可以对现有的应当纳入合理使用的情形予以法律确认,又可以对未来的不确定因素保持一定的开放性。可喜的是,我国第三次著作权法修订草案(送审稿)中已经作出了相应改变,一方面,对需要确认的合理使用情形进行列举;另一方面,又规定了三步检验法,使我国的合理使用制度保持充分的弹性,以应对未来社会的变化。❸

---

❶ Lionel Bently, Brad Sherman, Intellectual Property Law, Oxford University Press, 2001, p. 195-197.
❷ [德] M. 雷炳德. 著作权法 [M]. 张恩民,译. 北京:法律出版社,2005:297.
❸ 我国著作权法第三次修订《著作权法修订草案(送审稿)》第43条。

第三章　权利保护之一：使用者行为的失范与规制

第一节　数字与网络技术对著作权保护带来的挑战

现代著作权法的设计理念是通过授予作者对其作品一定时间的排他权来促进科学进步❶。著作权与新技术之间的互动并非全新话题。从著作权法自17世纪晚期以降三百年历史看，其发展很大程度上起因于作品复制和传播技术的发展。这主要表现在三个方面：著作权的产生源于现代印刷机的发明，并随作品复制和存储技术的发展逐渐将保护扩展至照片、电影和录音；广播技术使远距离提供作品成为可能，从而为著作权提供了新的市场；数字技术则代表技术创新的第三次浪潮❷。以美国为例，每一次重要技术进步都会带来著作权法的变动，尤其1976年形成现行著作权法之后，几乎每年都要对其进行修订，而这些修订几乎都是应对新技术带来挑战的结果。❸

数字技术和互联网是活字印刷以来最强有力的传播工具。数字技术出现之前，文字作品必须印刷在纸张上，音乐作品必须灌制在唱片中，电影则必须录制在胶片中，而后通过这些载体进行传播。数字技术突破了传统作品载体的限制，使作品能够以统一的数字格式存储在光盘、硬盘等载体中。数字技术至少有三个特点被证明对著作权法有重要影响。首先，数字技术使对作品高保真、低成本且瞬时的复制成为可能。模拟制品（如磁带、唱片）复制件的保真度则要低于原件，如果连续复制，保真度还会递减。数字制品则可以被无限复制

---

❶ 世界上绝大部分著作权法的宗旨都大同小异。关于著作权法宗旨最经典的论述可见美国《宪法》，U. S. Const. art. I, § 8, cl. 8；我国《著作权法》第1条对著作权的宗旨和目标也进行了类似的阐述。

❷ Menell, Peter S., Envisioning Copyright Law's Digital Future (September 3, 2002). N. Y. L. School Law Review, Vol. 46, p. 63, 2002–2003.

❸ See Paul Goldstein, Copyright's Highway: From Gutenberg to the Celestial Jukebox (1994); Jessica Litman, Copyright Legislation and Technological Change, 68 Or. L. Rev. 275, 353–354 (1989).

第三章 权利保护之一：使用者行为的失范与规制

而质量无损。随着技术发展，复制设备的成本也逐渐低廉到普通民众可以承受的程度，对数字文件的复制只需轻点鼠标即可。传统复制方式需要时间，因此作品的原始出版者在这段时间内就无须面对来自盗版的竞争。❶ 而数字复制很短时间就可完成，这使得数字复制对出版者的威胁大大增加。其次，数字和互联网技术使作品创作和传播成本大大降低，每个人都可成为创作者和传播者。以往一件音乐作品从创作到最终经过艺术家表演而成为唱片需要复杂的程序和昂贵的成本。现在歌手则可以自己低成本且高质量地录制作品并通过网络发布。新技术打破了使用者和创作者之间的壁垒。再次，数字制品可以存储在电脑中并可以进行其他操作。随着压缩技术的进步和硬盘容量的增大，作品尤其是娱乐作品的使用者可以非常容易且低成本地创建海量作品库。❷

如果说数字技术对作品的存储和复制产生了革命性的影响，那么网络技术则对作品的传播方式起到了颠覆性作用。网络技术使信息传播摆脱了传统有形载体和交通方式的限制。这种进步使信息传递成本得到极大降低，作品大规模传播成为可能。

虽然网络的出现使大规模传播作品成为可能，但这种可能性并不必然等同于现实。❸ 尽管早在1993年就有在网上传播音乐作品的尝试，但由于音乐文件非常大、CD刻录成本高昂、稀缺且非常慢的网络接入使人们认为对未经授权作品网上传播不会成为问题。因为以当时最理想的网速下载650M的CD需要一个月的时间，这远不如买一张CD光盘划算。然而这种状态在20世纪90年代后期发生了转变。性能强大的个人电脑价格便宜到商务和家用领域可以广泛采用的程度。万维网、搜索引擎的出现、网络接入费用的降低以及网速的提高，使互联网更加强大。同时，数据存储费用的大大降低和MP3压缩技术的出现使网上传播文件突破了文件大小限制。自此，网上大规模传播作品的基础条件都已具备。❹ 万事俱备，只欠东风。这种使网上大规模传播作品成为现实的"东风"就是大名鼎鼎的P2P技术。

自从1998年美国波士顿东北大学新生Shawn Fanning编写了小小的P2P应

---

❶ [美]威廉·M.兰德斯,理查德·A.波斯纳.知识产权法的经济结构[M].金海军,译.北京：北京大学出版社,2005：53.

❷ Fisher III, W. W. (2004). Promises to Keep: Technology, Law, and the Future of Entertainment, 14-15. See also Rebecca Giblin, Code Wars: 10 Years of P2P Software Litigation (2011), p.12.

❸ See Wu, Tim, Application-Centered Internet Analysis (March 15, 1999). Virginia Law Review, Vol. 85, No. 6, p. 1163-1204, 1999. Tim Wu 在该文中主张,在作法律上的分析时,应将互联网与应用程序分开讨论.

❹ See Rebecca Giblin, Code Wars: 10 Years of P2P Software Litigation (2011), p. 11-12.

用程序 Napster 那一刻起,作品传播技术发生了历史性改变。❶ 随后,与 Napster 类似的服务 Scour 和 Aimster 也相继问世。P2P 软件可以支持网络用户之间分享文件,用户可以用该程序大规模获取和分享流行音乐和电影,其中大多数作品未经著作权人任何授权。P2P 技术最大的特点是使用这一程序的每一个个人都是消费者,又是传播者。人们利用 P2P 技术可以将信息瞬间传递到世界每个角落。这使得作品传播绕开了传统传播者(图书出版商、唱片公司及电影公司等)的技术和资金壁垒。P2P 应用程序最终使作品大规模网上传播成为现实并构成著作权法的难题。著作权人们虽然以前经历了点唱机、收音机、影印机和录像机带来的挑战,但面对 P2P 技术还是产生了恐慌。于是他们本能地对 P2P 分享服务的提供者和使用者发起了著作权保卫战。❷ 著作权人的权利保卫运动一直没有终止,但 P2P 技术本身却未因此消亡,而且迅速发展至今,P2P 使用者也未因诉讼就停止使用。

著作权法的设计基础以及著作权保护机制的构建前提都是数字网络出现之前的技术,数字网络技术的出现彻底改变了著作权法的设计基础和保护机制的构建前提。数字网络技术对著作权的保护带来的挑战主要体现在以下三个方面:

(1) 著作权法规制对象发生错位。

从历史角度看,著作权主要是针对作品的专业使用者而设计的,个人使用者在很长一段时期内被忽略。首先,世界上第一部著作权法《安妮法》就是皇室赋予出版商禁止其他出版商再利用他们作品的特权。著作权起初就是一种专业人士对抗专业人士的"专业权"。其次,一直到 20 世纪 90 年代互联网出现之前,著作权法主要都是针对专业机构的。这些机构包括合法的广播公司、有线电视公司,以及非法的磁带、光盘生产商和销售商。数字网络技术则改变

---

❶ Rebecca Giblin, Code Wars: 10 Years of P2P Software Litigation (2011), p. 1.

❷ 著作权人先是依据美国著作权法上的间接侵权责任 (Secondary Liability) 是对 P2P 服务提供者提起诉讼,最后 Napster、Scour 和 Aimster 都由于败诉而无法继续提供它们的服务,从而迅速倒闭。上述三个服务败诉的关键原因是其"集中式"架构使得间接侵权得以成立。但故事并未就此结束,上述三个服务虽然倒闭,但迅即又出现了"分散式"P2P 分享软件。著作权人这次发现起诉分享技术提供者遇到了异地起诉以及间接侵权可能难以成立等困难。著作权人见势不妙,于 2003 年又发起了对文件分享服务使用者个人提起了诉讼攻击。See Fisher III, W. W. (2004). Promises to Keep: Technology. Law, and the Future of Entertainment, 110-127. 关于著作权人对第二代 P2P 服务提起的诉讼的具体分析见王迁. 网络环境中的著作权保护研究 [M]. 北京:法律出版社,2011:180-203. 关于著作权人对 P2P 使用者个人发起的诉讼,See Electronic Frontier Foundation (2008). RIAA v. The People: Five Years Later. Available at: https://www.eff.org/wp/riaa-v-people-five-years-later.

第三章　权利保护之一：使用者行为的失范与规制

了著作权产业的生态，每一网络用户既可以是作品使用者，又可以是作品传播者，非专业的网络用户成为网络环境中的新兴力量。而与此同时，过去专门用来规制专业商人之间的合同关系或对抗专业盗版的工具仍然被用来对付非专业的网络用户。这种状况导致一方面，权利所有者想通过上述策略阻止个人网络用户未经许可网上传播作品，并获取作品的使用费用；另一方面，在网络社会中，作品使用者都希望能够利用互联网技术给他们带来的巨大社会福利获取和传播信息。这样，在网络环境下就产生了强大的且日益增长的对作品进行使用的社会需求。数字网络技术其实已悄无声息地在权利所有人和终端使用者之间开通了市场之路，❶而权利所有者们却漠视这一千载难逢的市场机会，将数以亿计的使用者视为盗版者，从而将其推向著作权保护的对立面。

（2）传统"守门人"著作权保护机制失灵。

"守门人"（Gatekeeper）理论最早是由社会心理学家 Kurt Lewin 提出。该理论认为，信息传播是通过守门人进行的，只有符合一定规范或价值标准的信息才能被传播给听众。❷ 具体到著作权领域，"守门人"是图书出版商、唱片制作者、电影公司以及其他大规模生产作品的机构，这些机构主要是通过阻止购买侵权产品的渠道来预防侵权对法律的入侵。❸ 但"守门人"著作权保护机制的最大弱点就是对"守门人"专业性的依赖。基于作品复制行业的投资和技术门槛，它假定对作品的大规模复制行为并非任何人都可以胜任，这是保证"守门人"机制的有效性的前提。然而，新技术使这种机制逐渐走向崩溃。一方面，数字技术的出现使普通个人具备了无损、快速且低成本复制作品的能力，这使传统"守门人"的角色被大大弱化。网络的出现则使作品在网上大规模传播成为可能，从而放大了数字技术的效应，并使过去的"守门人"失去了在信息传播中的垄断权。另一方面，数字网络技术使"守门人"机制的有效性大为降低。网络使用者可自由上传下载文件导致了信息本身及其传播主

---

❶ 据统计，1999—2000 年期间的美国，大约有 8000 万至 9000 万的人能上网，而 Napster 拥有 6000 万注册用户。这就是说，Napster 覆盖了三分之二的潜在市场，这一数字是大多数营销专家遥不可及的。See Daniel J. Gervais, Use of Copyright Content on the Internet: Considerations on Excludability and Collective Licensing. In the Public Interest: The Future of Canadian Copyright Law, michael Geist ed., Chapter 18, p. 545, Irwin Law, 2005.

❷ See http://communicationtheory.org/gatekeeping-theory/.

❸ See Wu, Tim. "When Code Isn't Law." Virginia Law Review 89 (2003), p. 132-133; see also Kraakman, Reinier H. "Gatekeepers: the anatomy of a third-party enforcement strategy." JL Econ. & Org. 2 (1986): 53, p. 87-93.

体数量上的爆炸性增长。这样，在数字网络技术的影响下，传统"守门人"著作权保护机制逐渐失灵。

(3) 法律规范与社会道德规范脱节。

如果一项新技术已经被社会行为规范广为接受，而法律却规定这些行为是违法的，就会造成法律规范与社会道德规范脱节，这是导致著作权法对网络技术尤其是 P2P 技术规制失败的重要原因。当一项技术广为流行甚至足以造就新的社会道德规范时，法律想保持其有效性，就必须将自己保持在该社会道德规范的范围之内。在社会道德规范可接受的范围内，使网络用户的行为趋向一定的方向，或者将社会道德规范慢慢推向一定的方向是可能的。但如果法律超出社会道德规范的范围，通常就会失败，这是因为技术很可能对法律进行规避。❶ 有学者指出，美国音乐产业应当吸取的最大教训就是，产业界应当停止对 P2P 技术的法律战争，而应将精力转向市场，学会从 P2P 中获取作品使用费，顺应网络用户的市场需求，对 P2P 分享进行授权。❷ 另有学者总结，P2P 技术背景下既有的著作权保护措施失败的重要原因就是音乐产业没有向公众展示一个活生生的人的形象，因为公众不太可能去关心一个只会赚钱而没血没肉的唱片公司的感受。如果歌迷们知道他们付的钱会进入到艺术家兜里，他们将会愿意为他们的音乐下载付钱。❸

总结数字网络技术对著作权保护带来的挑战，究其根本原因是传统著作权保护方法将物理世界的规则应用到了虚拟世界。在物理世界中，人人都受物理规则约束，开发和散播传播工具的成本昂贵，传播作品的技术都是用来营利的，传播技术的开发者不会将技术秘密与消费者和竞争者分享。而虚拟世界的规则大为不同：以代码形式存在的传播技术开发成本可以非常低；传播技术开发者不一定有营利目的；开发者会公开技术秘密以促进技术改进。❹

---

❶ Gervais, Daniel J. "The Price of Social Norms: Towards a Liability Regime for File-Sharing." J. of Intell. Prop. Law 12, no. 1 (2003): 39-74, p. 54.

❷ Ibid, p. 62.

❸ Yu, Peter. "Digital Copyright and Confuzzling Rhetoric." Vanderbilt Journal of Entertainment and Technology Law 13 (2011): 881-939, p. 914.

❹ See Rebecca Giblin, Code Wars: 10 Years of P2P Software Litigation (2011), p. 6-11, 142-147.

第三章　权利保护之一：使用者行为的失范与规制 ◎

　　如今，P2P 分享被认为是互联网环境下著作权产业尤其是音乐产业的首要威胁。❶ P2P 技术的流行产生的数字盗版问题在法律、经济、社会和政治领域引起了广泛的讨论。❷ 如何应对数字和互联网技术，尤其是 P2P 技术给著作权保护和实现带来的挑战，成为一个全球性的问题。

　　好的著作权制度通常会较好地处理以下几对利益关系：促进作品自由提供从而实现作品的广泛可获得性和控制作品传播以使创作者获得经济利益之间的关系；作品生产者与消费者之间的关系；创作者个人与社会之间的关系；使用作品的短期满足和促进文化活力的长期目标之间的关系。现实已经表明数字和互联网技术已经深刻改变了这些平衡，并将天平的一端偏向了作品的自由提供、消费者、社会利益以及作品使用的短期满足。❸

　　数字和互联网技术给著作权法提出这样的问题：对著作权人而言，如何应对新技术带来的挑战，保护自己的权利；对著作权政策制定者而言，如何尽可能保证作品对于公众的可获得性以维护使用者的利益和社会利益，同时给予作品创作者及其商业伙伴合理的回报以激励作品的创作。尽管数字网络技术对著作权的保护带来了上述挑战，并且有学者主张传统的著作权法已经无法适应数字网络社会，❹ 但迄今为止，对著作权予以保护仍然是促进科学进步的最有效途径。因此，当新技术的产生和发展对网络环境下著作权的保护带来挑战时，我们面临的最重要的问题就是：既有的网络著作权保护方式能否有效保护著作权？如果不能，那么在数字网络环境中应当采用何种保护方式保护著作权并促进著作权价值的实现？

　　本部分主要以美国为例，首先对数字和网络技术对著作权法带来的挑战进行了介绍；然后在对美国音乐产业应对新技术挑战而先后采用的两种策略——"闭锁型"著作权保护模式和"开放型"著作权保护模式——进行深入考察的基础上，得出"开放型"著作权保护模式是著作权法应对新技术的必然选择；

---

❶ See A&M Records v. Napster, Inc., 114 F. Supp. 2d 896, 909-911 (N. D. Cal. 2000). 该案对数个关于 Napster 经济影响的研究做了归纳。一项后来由经济学者 Stan Leibowitz 做出的研究表明，Napster 的影响并没有在 Napster 诉讼中被证明，但从长远来看 P2P 分享对于音乐是有伤害。See Stan Liebowitz, Policing Pirates in the Networked Age 14-15 (Cato Policy Analysis No. 438 May 15, 2002), available at: http://www.cato.org/pubs/pas/pa438.pdf

❷ Peter S. Menell, Envisioning Copyright Law's Digital Future (September 3, 2002). N. Y. L. School Law Review, Vol. 46, p. 35, 2002-2003. Available at SSRN: http://ssrn.com/abstract=328561.

❸ Dr. Francis Gurry, Dir. Gen., World Intellectual Prop. Org., The Annual Horace S. Manges Lecture at Columbia Law School (Apr. 6, 2011). Available at: http://www.law.columbia.edu/kernochan/manges.

❹ Barlow, John Perry. "A Declaration of the Independence of Cyberspace (Feb. 8, 1996)": 234-237.

最后对两种著作权保护模式的关系进行了简要分析,并尝试描绘了"开放型"著作权保护模式的大致框架。

第二节 传统"闭锁型"著作权保护模式及其困境

数字技术和互联网技术使网上大规模使用和传播作品成为现实。新技术虽然给著作权人带来了技术红利,但同时也影响了著作权人的经济利益,至少他们这样认为。❶ 面对作品的网上大规模使用和传播,摆在著作权人和政策制定者面前有两个选择:阻止或者允许。他们本能地选择了前者。实践中主要有四种策略被采用,这些策略是被目前大部分著作权法体系所采用的著作权保护的传统方式。

一、对 P2P 服务提供者的间接侵权责任诉讼:阻止传播工具

面对 Napster 对音乐产业产生的巨大威胁,大型唱片公司于 1999 年 12 月对 Napster 提起诉讼,依据著作权法上间接侵权责任(Secondary Liability)的规定要求 Napster 承担两项间接侵权责任:帮助侵权责任(Contributory Liability)和替代责任(Vicarious Liability)。案件经历了两年多的时间,法院最终认定两种间接侵权责任均成立,并要求 Napster 对非法作品进行屏蔽,且在百分之百过滤所有侵权内容前不得上线。这对 Napster 实际上是一个无法完成的任务。❷ 最终,Napster 于 2002 年 6 月 3 日提交破产申请。与 Napster 提供相似服务的 Scour 与 Aimster 也都难逃倒闭的命运。❸

---

❶ Gervais, Daniel J., Use of Copyright Content on the Internet: Considerations on Excludability and Collective Licensing. In the Public Interest: The Future of Canadian Copyright Law, Michael Geist ed., Chapter 18, p. 545, Irwin Law, 2005. Available at SSRN: http://ssrn.com/abstract=816964.

❷ 关于案件详细进展及法院判决理由见:A&M Records, Inc. v. Napster, In c., 2000 WL 573136, 10 (N. D. Cal. 2000); A&M Records, Inc. v. Napster, Inc., 2000 WL 1009483, 8 (N. D. Cal. 2000); A&M Records, Inc. v. Napster, Inc., 2000 WL 1055915 (9th Cir. 2000); A&M Records, Inc. v. Napster, Inc., 114 F. Supp. 2d 896, 927 (N. D. Cal. 2000); A&M Records, Inc. v. Napster, Inc., 239 F. 3d 1004, 1027 (9th Cir. 2001); A&M Records, Inc. v. Napster, Inc., 2001 WL 227083 (N. D. Cal. 2001); A&M Records, Inc. v. Napster, In c., 284 F. 3d 1091, 1099 (9th Cir. 2002).

❸ See Fisher III, W. W. (2004). Promises to Keep: Technology, Law, and the Future of Entertainment, 113-114.

第三章　权利保护之一：使用者行为的失范与规制

　　Napster 的败诉原因主要在于其"集中式"拓扑架构（Centralized Topology）❶。这种拓扑结构意味着：如果没有服务器的编目与检索服务，用户就无法通过网络下载和上传作品；Napster 如果发现侵权内容，有能力终止侵权账号。这让法院可以依据其拓扑结构得以曲解 Sony 案判决的精神而对认定合理使用的"非实质性侵权用途"❷规则做了解释性修改从而认定帮助侵权责任和替代责任成立。

　　但故事并未就此结束，上述三个服务虽然倒闭，但又出现了新一代 P2P 分享软件。这些 P2P 软件为规避法律，避免 Napster 的命运，采用"分散式"拓扑结构（Decentralized Topology）。这种架构摆脱了对服务器的依赖，用户可以直接搜索其他用户计算机中的分享内容。这种架构的雏形是产生于 2000 年的叫 Gnutella 的 P2P 网络。Gnutella 虽然是对"集中式"架构的突破，但也有规模限制、易受攻击以及搭便车等诸多问题。为克服这些问题，一套更好的文件分享协议 FastTrack 于 2000 年年末被开发出来。其开发者创建了一家叫 KaZaA 的公司，向用户提供免费接入，随后又许可另外两家公司 Morpheus 和 Grokster 接入其系统。❸ FastTrack 服务迅速流行。可以想见，他们迟早会坐上被告席。2001 年 10 月 2 日，Grokster、Morpheus 和 KaZaA 被 MGM（Metro-Goldwyn-Mayer）公司起诉。❹ 案件结果能否如程序开发站所愿避开法律责任？起初结果确实如其所愿：两级法院均依据 Sony 案的"实质性非侵权"规则判决 Grokster 不承担侵权责任。❺ 但原告将案件上诉到了最高法院。最高法院意识到仅适用"实质性非侵权"规则会导致不合理结果。最高法院认为产品具有实质性非侵权用途是免除侵权责任的充分条件的理解是错误的，并认为在销售一种同时具备合法和非法用途的产品时知悉使用者会使用该产品的非法用

---

❶　这种架构的工作原理是：所有用户上传的音乐文件索引和存放位置的信息通过一个中央索引服务器保存；当某一用户需要某个音乐文件时，必须先连接到中央索引服务器，由服务器检索，服务器返回存有该文件的用户信息，再由请求者直接连到文件的所有者传输文件。关于其技术分析参见 http：//www.intsci.ac.cn/users/luojw/P2P/ch02.html。关于其法律分析，See Rebecca Giblin, Code Wars: 10 Years of P2P Software Litigation（2011），p. 58-63.

❷　Sony Corp. of America v. Universal City Studios，464 U. S. 417（1984）.

❸　See Fisher III, W. W.（2004）. Promises to Keep: Technology, Law, and the Future of Entertainment, 122.

❹　See Metro-Goldwyn-Mayer Studios v. Grokster，2003 WL 186657（C.D. Cal. Jan. 9, 2003）（No. Civ. 01-08541）.

❺　See Metro-Goldwyn-Mayer Studios v. Grokster, Ltd., 259 F. Supp. 2d 1029（C. D. Cal. 2003）. 法官在判决中认为，服务提供者没有"为他人的侵权提供实质性帮助"（帮助侵权的要件）或者"具有监督侵权行为的权利和能力"（替代责任的要件）。二审维持一审判决，See Metro-Goldwyn-Mayer Studios v. Grokster, Ltd., F. 3d 1154, p. 1036-1039（9 th Cir. 2004）.

途，就可以从该行为本身推定销售者具有帮助他人侵权的意图。因此，最高院实质上是改变了 Sony 案的规则，给"实质性非侵权用途"规则附加了一个条件，即：被告要想免除责任，不仅要证明"实质性非侵权用途"，还要证明没有故意教唆和引诱他人侵权。最后法院认定被告的行为构成引诱侵权。❶

至此，著作权人完全取得了对 P2P 技术在诉讼上的优势，但著作权人却暂时停止了这种起诉技术提供者的策略。这种结果看似矛盾但却并非如此。因为著作权人认识到：诉讼上的胜利可以让一个 P2P 服务关闭，但无法阻止其他 P2P 软件的爆炸式增长。这种结果的看似矛盾性使探讨其形成原因成为必要。但相关研究比较缺乏。Tim Wu 认为这种结果主要由两个原因导致：(1) 著作权法长期依赖把门人机制（Gatekeeper Enforcement Mechanism）（为了法律的执行，国家对特定商品或服务的提供课加责任，提前消灭违法行为），而数字技术和互联网打破了这种机制，即 P2P 服务的提供者规避了法律的传统执行方式；(2) 这种法律的执行缺少道德支持。❷ Rebecca Giblin 则对 P2P 技术能够避开法律执行方式的深层原因进行了分析。她认为，这一结果出现的主要原因是将物质世界的规则应用到了网络世界。物质世界的规则有：人人都受物理世界规则的约束；开发和散播传播工具的成本昂贵；传播作品的技术是用来营利的；传播技术的开发者不会与消费者和竞争者分享技术秘密。而网络世界的规则大为不同：以代码形式存在的传播技术开发成本可以非常低；传播技术开发者不一定有营利的目的；开发者会公开技术秘密以促进技术改进。❸ 另外，Mark Lemley 和 Anthony Reese 认为起诉 P2P 服务提供者从社会层面看不是最优选择，因为这种诉讼混淆了合法行为和非法行为，使作品的合法传播失去了传播网络，要求服务提供者承担监管责任并不解决问题，且有损技术创新。❹

---

❶ Metro-Goldwyn-Mayer Studios Inc. V. Grokster, Ltd. (04-480) 545 U. S. 913 (2005); 380 F. 3d 1154. 该案在推翻原判决的同时将该案发回重审。重审判决对"引诱侵权"的规则进行了细化，成为日后认定相关案件的重要参考。该案件的具体分析，可参见王迁. 网络环境中的著作权保护研究 [M]. 北京：法律出版社，2011：180-194.

❷ See Wu, Tim, When Code Isn't Law. Virginia Law Review, Vol. 892003, p.132-133.

❸ See Rebecca Giblin, Code Wars: 10 Years of P2P Software Litigation (2011), p.6-11, 142-147.

❹ See Lemley, Mark A., and R. Anthony Reese. "Reducing digital copyright infringement without restricting innovation" 56 Stan. L. Rev. 1345, 1379-1389 (2004).

二、对个人使用者的直接侵权责任诉讼：禁止传播行为

唱片公司在采取保护著作权的策略时之所以首先以 P2P 服务提供者而非 P2P 个人使用者为目标，是因为它们清楚：起诉个人无异于"汤匙舀大海"；另外，起诉自己的客户也绝非正确商业策略。❶ 但残酷的事实（诉讼上的成功根本无法阻止 P2P 技术的传播和使用者大规模的网上分享）使唱片公司陷入恐慌，在无计可施的情况下尝试通过起诉 P2P 软件使用者个人发动诉讼以扭转局势，❷ 这次起诉的法律依据是著作权法上的直接责任。从 2003 年到 2007 年，唱片业对个人使用者发动了超过 30000 个诉讼。❸ 这些被随机选择的被告包括孩子、祖孙、失业的单身母亲、大学教授。❹ 这种诉讼很快陷入了公关危机。❺ 另外，这种诉讼也遇到了确认用户的真实身份的技术上的困难。❻

针对个人使用者提起诉讼的结果是：虽然判决获得胜诉，但却受到公众和

---

❶ Fisher III, W. W. (2004). Promises to Keep: Technology, Law, and the Future of Entertainment, p. 125.

❷ "Music Labels Declare War on File Swappers", PCWorld.com, September 8, 2003, http://www.pcworld.com/article/112364/article.html.

❸ David Kravets, "File Sharing Lawsuits at a Crossroads, After 5 years of RIAA Litigation," Sept. 8, 2008, available at: http://www.wired.com/threatlevel/2008/09/proving-file-sh/. 对比 2002 年全年美国在著作权方面的民事诉讼的数量可以说明这次针对个人的诉讼规模之巨大。2002 年全美著作权民事诉讼的数量是 2084 起。See Motivans, Mark. Intellectual property theft, 2002. US Department of Justice, Office of Justice Programs, Bureau of Justice Statistics, 2004, available at: http://bjs.ojp.usdoj.gov/content/pub/pdf/ipt02.pdf.

❹ See Electronic Frontier Foundation (2008). RIAA v. The People: Five Years Later. Available at: https://www.eff.org/wp/riaa-v-people-five-years-later.

❺ 一个典型的例子就是发生在密歇根的 Warner et al v. Scantlebury 案。该案中，被告在法院判决之前去世，而原告却仍旧不依不饶，对死者的孩子继续诉讼，虽然继续诉讼前死者家属被给予了 60 天的时间来悲伤。唱片业的这种行为饱受批评，慢慢失去了公众和社会的道德支持，开始怀疑唱片业的动机和商业模式。See "RIAA defendant dies, heirs given 60 days to grieve before depositions", available at: http://arstechnica.com/uncategorized/2006/08/7487/这样的例子还有很多。See Electronic Frontier Foundation (2008). RIAA v. The People: Five Years Later, p. 5. Available at: https://www.eff.org/wp/riaa-v-people-five-years-later.

❻ 原告起诉侵权用户前必须先确认潜在被告的身份。由于用户的注册名大部分是虚假的，因此必须通过 IP 地址确认网络用户真实身份，这就需要网络服务提供商（ISPs）帮助。大部分 ISP 并不愿意提供用户信息，因为这样会吓跑他们的客户。不过，根据千年数字著作权法案（DMCA）512（h）条规定，ISP 有义务披露涉嫌侵权人的身份信息。这样原告掌握了被告的身份信息后就可以开始诉讼。但是，这种确定被告身份的办法有一个弱点：只要用户能够藏自己的 IP 地址，就不会被找到。具有隐名功能的 Freenet 应运而生，与著作权人玩起猫捉老鼠的游戏。陈明涛. P2P 网络条件下的著作权责任研究（三）：从理念、技术、法律三层面之解读［EB/OL］. 中国知识产权研究网，网址：http://www.iprcn.com/IL_ Lwxc_ Show.aspx?News_ PI =1524.

社会的广泛质疑；更重要的是，P2P分享的数量仍然丝毫未减。❶针对P2P个人用户大规模诉讼的失败，直接原因主要有两个：（1）P2P用户太多，使起诉全部使用者变得不可能，即"法不责众"效应；（2）P2P软件隐名技术的发展使确定使用者身份非常困难，从而使P2P用户受到追诉的可能性大大降低；（3）很多用户并不认为P2P分享是违法行为。❷

三、"逐级响应"机制：限制网络接入

因为大规模起诉P2P用户也无法遏制P2P大规模侵权的增长，美国唱片业又转向其他办法。2008年年底，音乐产业突然宣布将放弃针对个人用户的大规模诉讼策略，声称找到了对付网络盗版的更好办法。这种办法就是依靠与网络服务提供商的合作来应对网络盗版问题。唱片业称他们已与网络服务提供商达成初步协议。按照这种协议，如网络用户非法分享音乐文件，网络服务提供商就会通知或者警告该客户。如果该客户仍然进行分享活动，他们就会收到一封或更多电子邮件并会受到降低网速的惩罚。最严重的后果可能是切断其网络服务。❸这种做法被称作"逐级响应"（Graduated Response）或"三振出局"（Three Strikes）。❹

实际上，虽然一些ISP愿意与著作权人合作，向用户发出侵权通知，但它们不愿采取对用户进行断网等更严格的措施，因为切断用户的服务不符合ISP本身利益。❺数年来，音乐产业及其他著作权产业一直都在说服ISP采取更为积极和配合的行动。直到2011年年中，音乐产业（RIAA）和电影产业（MPAA）才

---

❶ 到2007年，P2P分享软件比以往任何时候都多。虽然音乐文件分享增加并不明显，但瞬时链接数也达到了一千万。但是电影文件的分享变得流行起来，2006年5月有817588用户使用BitTorrent，一年后这一数字变为1357318，增长了66%。See Eric Bangeman, "P2P traffic shifts away from music, towards movies", available at: http://arstechnica.com/tech-policy/2007/07/P2P-traffic-shifts-away-from-music-towards-movies/但另一方面，代表音乐产业的RIAA在回应对其批评时坚持说他们起诉的目的已经达到了，因为他们从没期望终止盗版，这些诉讼的主要作用在于教育，使公众知道著作权法和违反的法律后果。See Paul, "The RIAA Says Suing Individuals Was an Effective Strategy", available at: http://www.digitalmusicnews.com/permalink/2011/111207riaa.

❷ Ginsburg, Jane C. "Exclusive Right to Their Writings: Copyright and Control in the Digital Age", (2002) Me. L. Rev. 54 195, p. 211-213.

❸ Sarah Mcbride and Ethan Smith, "Music Industry to Abandon Mass Suits", Wall Street Journal, available at: http://online.wsj.com/article/SB1229666038836021137.html.

❹ 事实上，这种机制在其他国家先前已经得到采用，如法国、英格兰、爱尔兰、新西兰、韩国等。关于"逐级响应"机制的详细介绍，请：//graduatedresponse.org/new/.

❺ Steven Seidenberg, The Record Business Blues, 96-JUN A. B. A. J. 54, 55-56 (2010).

第三章　权利保护之一：使用者行为的失范与规制

与主要的 ISP（AT&T，Comcast，Verizon 等）达成一项关于"逐级响应"机制的协议。❶ 按照该协议，协议方成立著作权信息中心（Center for Copyright Information，简称 CCI）负责"逐级响应"机制的执行。按照约定，该协议的有效日期为自协议生效之日起四年。从该协议的具体内容来看，其对非法文件分享的态度非常保守，需作出许多妥协，尤其对著作权人而言。❷ 随后，协议参加方公布了在这一协议的基础上形成的著作权警告系统（Copyright Alert System）。❸ 这一系统严格来说已不能称为"三振出局"，而应称为"六振出局"。因为这一著作权警告系统由六次警告构成。❹ 这种著作权警告机制是相对缓和的：一方面，这一机制由"三振出局"变为"六振出局"；即使了通过 ISP 六次警告后仍然从事侵权行为，用户也不会必然被切断网络服务。这一系统直到 2013 年 2 月 26 日才开始实施。❺

这种著作权警告机制与娱乐业先前采取的措施相比对用户具有更强的教育功能，且吸取了其他国家实施该制度的教训。但自其面世就受到了批评和质疑。这些质疑包括缺乏公共投入、媒体公司与 ISP 之间的激励倒错（Reverse Incentives）、缓和措施过于严厉以及举证负担的倒置等❻。由于这一机制在美国刚实施不久，其效果如何尚很难确定。2014 年 5 月 CCI 发布首个关于"逐级响应"机制运行情况的报告。该报告的结论认为：著作权警告系统（CAS）的第一年重点是确保该系统的成功运行，事实上这一目标已经达到；

---

❶ 协议详细内容见 http：//www.copyrightinformation.org/resources-faq/.

❷ David Moser & Cheryl Slay, Music Copyright Law, (2012), p.291.

❸ Brimmeier, Khristyn. Music, Film, TV, and Broadband Collaborate to Curb Online Content Theft, RIAA, July 2011. Available at: http://www.riaa.com/newsitem.php?content_selector=newsandviews&news_month_filter=7&news_year_filter=2011&id=2DDC3887-A4D5-8D41-649D-6E4F7C5225A5.

❹ 这种"六振出局"机制的内容如下：第一次和第二次警告通知网络用户其账户被用来著作权侵权并要求其对如何避免将来的侵权做出解释，并将用户导向合法内容网络；如果用户仍然进行侵权行为，ISP 将发出第三次和第四次警告，要求用户点击通知确认其已经收到来自 ISP 的警告；如果用户仍然我行我素，ISP 将发第五次警告，而且 ISP 可以采取一些缓和措施（Mitigation Measures），如降低网速，返回登录界面直至用户联系 ISP 对其侵权行为作出回应；如果第五次警告仍然无效，则 ISP 会在此发出第六次警告，并采取第五次警告中采取的缓和措施。这种机制假定，绝大部分用户在经历了六次警告后会停止侵权行为。See Nate Anderson, Major ISPs agree to "six strikes" copyright enforcement plan, July 7 2011. Available at：http://arstechnica.com/tech-policy/2011/07/major-isps-agree-to-six-strikes-copyright-enforcement-plan/.

❺ Cyrus Farivar, "Six strikes" enforcement policy debuts, Feb 26 2013. Available at: http://arstechnica.com/tech-policy/2013/02/six-strikes-enforcement-policy-debuts/.

❻ Masnick, Mike, Major US ISPs Agree to Five Strikes Plan, Rather Than Three, July 7 2011. Available at：http://www.techdirt.com/articles/20110707/10173014998/major-us-isps-agree-to-five-strikes-plan-rather-than-three.shtml.

作为美国首个此类项目，CAS 仍然处于早期阶段；从前十个月的数据看，该机制的效果是令人鼓舞的。❶

但值得注意的是，University of Rennes 研究人员的一项研究认为法国的"三振出局"机制不仅没有起到反盗版的作用，反而使盗版增加。❷ 另外，法国文化部长 Aurelie Filipetti 也在 2012 年的一个讲话中认为"三振出局"反盗版预算过高。他认为，总统萨科齐希望通过该机制能够证明惩罚文件分享是一种让人们回归到音乐和电影商店并远离未授权网站的办法，但现在与 HADOPI 有关的一切都不太好。❸ 另外，爱尔兰也于 2011 年出于保护隐私考虑废止了"三振出局"机制。❹ 到目前为止，在世界范围内尚未见有说服力的证据表明"逐级响应"机制减少了著作权侵权或者增加了合法使用。❺ 因此，尽管这一机制在美国刚刚实施不久，无法盖棺定论，但也不能对其预期效果过于乐观。

2017 年 1 月 27 日，CCI 发表声明宣布 CAS 经过四年的运行将完成其使命。该声明宣称：该项目表明，如果内容创作者、互联网创新者以及消费者联合起来，该项目取得实质进展是有可能的；CAS 在使人们知道合法内容的可获

---

❶ "the copyrightalert system：phase one and beyond"，网址：http：//www.copyrightinformation.org/wp-content/uploads/2014/05/Phase-One-And_ Beyond. pdf.

❷ 该研究发现：虽然 BitTorrent 的使用率从 17.1%下降到 14.6%，但停止使用 P2P 服务的这些用户转向了并未被 HADOPI 法案（打击网络非法下载行为的法案，该法案仅覆盖 P2P 分享）覆盖的流媒体服务和私人下载网站；另外，使用盗版的用户中有一半同时经常购买合法的正版内容，如果使用"三振出局"关闭他们的网络服务会影响正版内容的销售。See BBC, French pirates "dodge" tough laws, March 29 2010. Available at：http：//news.bbc.co.uk/2/hi/technology/8592444. stm.

❸ "Three Strikes Anti-Piracy Budget "Too Expensive to Justify" Says Minister". Available at：http：//torrentfreak.com/three-strikes-anti-piracy-budget-too-expensive-to-justify-says-minister-120603/.

❹ "File-Sharing 3 Strikes Killed in Ireland, Government Promises Site Blocking". Available at：http：//torrentfreak.com/file-sharing-3-strikes-killed-in-ireland-government-promises-site-blocking-111219/.

❺ 有新的研究认为法国的分级响应机制对法国境内苹果公司 iTune 渠道的销售有正面影响。See Brett Danaher et al, The Effect of Graduated Response Anti-Piracy Laws on Music Sales：Evidence from an Event Study in France（version as at March 2012）(2012) available at：http：//papers.ssrn.com/sol3/papers.cfm?abstract_ id=1989280 [Accessed at 6 March 2013]. 但是有研究对其提出了有力质疑。See Jeremiah and Baruch Leloup, Hadopi, the source of growth iTunes?（2012）, Le Monde. Available at：http：//www.lemonde.fr/technologies/article/2012/01/24/hadopi-source-de-la-croissance-d-itunes_ 1633919_ 651865. html>. 虽然国际唱片业协会（IFPI）2013 年数字音乐报告中称逐级响应机制使新西兰 P2P 服务使用率下降 16%，使韩国侵权网络存储平台用户数量下降 22%，但上述数据的可靠性同样受替代性非法服务存在状况的影响。另外，究竟是合法服务商业模式的兴起还是逐级响应机制使侵权服务用户数量下降，目前并未见相关实证研究。关于 IFPI2013 年数字音乐报告，见 http：//www.ifpi.org/content/library/dmr2013. pdf。

得性以及关于网络侵权方面，起到了良好的教育作用。❶ 但是，这并不意味着网络著作权侵权得到了有效控制，但机制的效果与作用仍然有待评估，产业界将采取何种新的实践保护著作权也仍然是值得持续关注和研究的问题。

四、技术保护措施：限制作品获取

数字和网络技术的出现使作品无损复制和大规模传播变得空前容易，这对著作权的影响非常严重，导致事后法律救济往往无济于事。在这种背景下，对著作权作品的技术保护措施应运而生。目前，已经使用的技术措施至少包括反复制设备、电子水印、数字签名或数字指纹技术、数字权利管理系统、追踪系统以及控制进入受保护作品的措施。❷

为应对数字式录音磁带（DAT）的发明，防止 DAT 录制者制作二代复制品或连环复制品，美国于 1992 年出台《家庭录音法》（Audio Home Recording Act），要求任何进口到美国、在美国生产或销售的数字录音设备和数字音频接入设备必须安装 SCMS（Serial Copy Management System）系统，并规定禁止或者篡改 SCMS 设备为非法行为。❸ 但这一法案存在致命缺陷：（1）制定得太晚。因为 DAT 技术早在六年前就出现了，在这六年中，实际发生或可能发生的诉讼已经使数字录音设备远离了消费者。❹ 立法的延迟导致了数字录音设备的商业上失败。（2）该法案针对的对象太过具体，这使该法案在技术飞速发展的背景下很快处于边缘地位。随着电脑在复制和传播领域发挥日益重要的作用，该法案日渐衰微。（3）该法案未对家庭录制音乐是否是合法态度含糊。这也为后来发生的 Napster 案埋下伏笔。❺

随着数字和网络技术发展，通过技术保护措施和著作权管理信息措施对在数字环境下传播的作品进行保护，并保证这些措施不被篡改或破解成为一种普遍需要。在此背景下，160 个国家于 1996 年 12 月在日内瓦成立《世界知识产权组织版权公约》（WCT）。根据该公约，著作权人可以选择对其作品进行反复制措施和权利管理信息的保护。但这种规定必须转化为国内法才能实施。鉴

---

❶ Internet Service Providers, Studios and Record Labels Call It Quits on Copyright Alert System, http：//variety.com/2017/digital/news/copyright-alerts-piracy-mpaa-comcast-att-1201971756/.
❷ 梁志文. 技术措施的著作权保护 [N]. 人民法院报，2002-06-23（3）.
❸ 17 USC 1002（c）.
❹ 这也是美国消费者很少拥有数字录音设备的重要原因。
❺ See Fisher III, W. W. (2004). Promises to Keep: Technology, Law, and the Future of Entertainment, 85-87.

于法律是否对作品提供保护以使其免于规避技术措施和权利管理信息的设备的侵害存在不确定性，加上履行国际公约义务以及利益团体的游说，美国最终在著作权法 Title 17 下新增一章，作为 1998 年《数字千年版权法案》（DMCA）的重要组成部分。❶ 按照 DMCA，技术保护措施分为"接触控制"措施和"权利控制"措施。"接触控制"即任何人都不得对使作品受接触控制保护的技术措施进行规避。❷ "权利控制"指任何人都不得对使作品受权利保护的技术措施进行规避。❸

技术保护措施对著作权的保护采用事前救济，以技术制衡技术的办法相比侵权法保护的事后救济有一定优势。但技术保护措施有"以子之矛攻子之盾"的问题，因为任何技术手段都可以被突破，各种规避或破坏技术保护措施的反技术措施几乎与技术措施相伴而生，❹ 这使得技术保护措施的效果大打折扣。其次，技术保护措施不利于对表达自由、隐私、竞争、学术研究和消费者的保护。❺ 另外，很多与技术保护措施的案件表明，技术保护措施不是被用来保护著作权，而是被用来限制竞争。❻ 更具有讽刺意味的是，很多游说对技术保护措施进行立法保护的产业界正在放弃使用技术保护措施。❼

技术保护措施立法作用的有限性，很大一方面是由于其事前调整的属性。❽ 因为旧技术所有者总是试图阻止他们看来有威胁的新技术，而不去寻找与新技术合作的路径。❾ 技术保护措施的立法正好迎合了旧技术所有者的这种

---

❶ Robert A. Gorman, Jane C. Ginsburg, and R. Anthony Reese, Copyright: cases and materials. Foundation Press, 2011, p. 1082-1083.

❷ DMCA, Section 1201 (a).

❸ DMCA, Section 1201 (b). 关于这两种技术保护措施的详细介绍，吴伟光. 数字技术环境下的著作权法：危机与对策 [M]. 北京：知识产权出版社，2008：161-168.

❹ 王迁. 知识产权法教程 [M]. 3 版. 北京：中国人民大学出版社，2011：242.

❺ Brown, Ian. "The evolution of anti-circumvention law", International Review of Law Computers & Technology 20.3 (2006): 240.

❻ Brown, Ian. "The evolution of anti-circumvention law", International Review of Law Computers & Technology 20.3 (2006): 249-250.

❼ Dizon, Michael Anthony C., Does Technology Trump Intellectual Property?: Re-Framing the Debate About Regulating New Technologies (August 17, 2011). SCRIPTed, Vol. 8, p. 132. Available at: http://ssrn.com/abstract=1940887.

❽ Ginsburg, Jane C. "Copyright and control over new technologies of dissemination." Colum. L. Rev. 101 (2001): 1631.

❾ Lucchi, Nicola, Intellectual Property Rights in Digital Media: A Comparative Analysis of Legal Protection, Technological Measures and New Business Models Under E. U. And U. S. Law. Buffalo Law Review, Vol. 53, No. 4, Fall 2005, p. 104, 106.

心态。立法仅仅是延迟了新技术带来的社会和经济变化，但不可能扭转这种趋势。

为更清楚地说明权利所有者及政策制定者为规制作品网上使用与传播所采取的各种策略，我们不妨进行一个思想实验，把用户网上获取和传播作品的过程比作水路货物运输。如果说作品是上游的货物，则权利所有人就是货主，用户就是下游目的地的客户。如果说网络接入服务是这条河流的河道，那么传播软件就是河流上运输货物的轮船。如上所述，面对数字和网络技术带来的挑战，为阻止网络用户未经授权使用和传播作品，权利所有者几乎穷尽了所有方法。这些方法包括：禁止船厂向客户提供轮船（对P2P服务提供者的诉讼）、禁止客户使用轮船运输货物（对个人用户的诉讼）、不断警告客户不准运输货物甚至限制河道通行（"逐级响应"机制），以及给货物上锁使客户无法打开货物，即使打开也无法使用。但事实证明所有这些方法均无法奏效。虽然上述权利人保护自己权利的方法各不相同，但却有明显的共同点，即都采用禁止的策略。我们把这种策略称为"闭锁型"权利保护模式。正如上所述，这种"闭锁型"权利保护模式在消灭大规模未授权网络传播上的失败是由于物质世界的规则被应用到了网络世界，从而造成了规制与规制对象之间的脱节。

从法律制度和政策层面讲，"闭锁型"权利保护模式的失败很大程度上源于著作权法本身。因为从历史的角度看，著作权从来就是针对作品的专业使用者设计的，而忽略了个人使用者。首先，世界上第一部著作权法《安妮法》就是皇室赋予作者和出版商禁止其他出版商再利用他们作品的特权。著作权起初就是一种专业人士对抗专业人士的"专业权"。其次，一直到20世纪90年代出现互联网之前，著作权法主要都是针对专业机构的。这些机构包括：合法的有广播公司、有线电视公司；非法的有非法磁带、光盘生产商和销售商。❶ 这也就是说，"闭锁型"权利保护方式是在使用过去专门用来规制专业商人之间的合同关系或对抗专业盗版的工具来对付网络终端个人使用者。一方面，权利所有者想通过上述策略阻止个人用户未经许可网上传播作品并获取使用费用。❷ 而另一方面，在网络社会中，每个个体都希望能够利用技术给他们带来

---

❶ Daniel J. Gervais, Use of Copyright Content on the Internet: Considerations on Excludability and Collective Licensing. In the Public Interest: The Future of Canadian Copyright Law, Michael Geist ed., Chapter 18, p. 519, Irwin Law, 2005.

❷ YouTube上90%的著作权人选择授权而不是禁止作品的使用，从而获得一定的经济回报。See Dr. Francis Gurry, Dir. Gen., World Intellectual Prop. Org., The Annual Horace S. Manges Lecture at Columbia Law School (Apr. 6, 2011). Available at: http://www.law.columbia.edu/kernochan/manges.

的最大社会福利（互联网）获取和传播信息，由此产生了强大的且日益增长的社会需求。❶ 数字和互联网技术已悄无声息地在权利所有人和终端使用者之间开通了市场之路❷，而权利所有者们不但没有利用好这一巨大的技术红利，却将数以亿计的使用者视为盗版者，从而将其推向对立面。正如学者所言，著作权从来都不是水坝，而是被用来疏通河道。❸ 换句话说，著作权的目的不是阻止市场，而是开发市场。这就意味着，权利所有者和著作权政策制定者应将"阻止"的思维定式转变为"许可"。❹ 我们把这种思维模式称之为"开放型"权利保护模式。

第三节 "开放型"著作权保护机制的兴起

一、"开放型"著作权保护机制的合理性和必然性

当权利人面对数字和网络技术带来的挑战时，他们有两个选择：禁止；许可。个人使用者也同样如此，他们在网上获得作品的途径有两个："免费"获得；合法购买。从经济理性角度，用户会选择成本较低的一种途径。这就涉及合法供给与"免费"的竞争。针对"免费"讨论成本似乎矛盾，但实际上并非如此，因为"免费"的背后隐藏着潜在的非金钱成本。这些非金钱成本可能包括在网上寻找文件所需的时间；下载文件的质量问题；下载文件与终端设备的兼容问题；搜寻（甚至购买）"翻墙"服务所需的成本；潜在被起诉的危

---

❶ 国际唱片业协会（IFPI）在澳大利亚、德国、英国、美国和加拿大开展的研究表明，从1997年到2002年，音乐消费的需求增长了30%。IFPI《2004年度在线音乐报告》第8页. 网址：http://www.ifpi.org/content/library/digital-music-report-2004.pdf.

❷ 据统计，1999—2000年期间的美国，大约有8000万至9000万的人能上网，而Napster拥有6000万注册用户。这就是说，Napster覆盖了三分之二的潜在市场。这一数字是大多数营销专家遥不可及的。See Daniel J. Gervais, Use of Copyright Content on the Internet: Considerations on Excludability and Collective Licensing. In the Public Interest: The Future of Canadian Copyright Law, Michael Geist ed., Chapter 18, p. 545, Irwin Law, 2005.

❸ Daniel J. Gervais, Use of Copyright Content on the Internet: Considerations on Excludability and Collective Licensing. In the Public Interest: The Future of Canadian Copyright Law, Michael Geist ed., Chapter 18, p. 526, Irwin Law, 2005.

❹ 但这并不意味着权利者可以拥有一切形式的商业开发。授权许可仍应受到合理使用以及法定许可等限制。See, Jane C. Ginsburg, "Copyright and control over new technologies of dissemination." Colum. L. Rev. 101 (2001), 1615-1616.

险；缺乏道德感，等等。因此，如果存在对"免费"获取的良好替代品，即合法取得在线文件的授权机制，那么网上大规模非法使用和传播作品的问题就会得到解决。正如 Pink Floyd 的第一任经理人 Peter Jenner 指出，我们用 19 世纪和 20 世纪的商业模式去应对 21 世纪的技术，我们现在处于一片混乱不足为奇。新技术使作品发行和获取回报有了新的选择，而整个产业界在对这种新的选择做出适当的回应方面是失败的，发达国家的大规模的网络盗版就是这种失败的一种反映。❶ 以 Napster 为代表的 P2P 技术之所以如此流行也正是因为它们为新出现的需要提供了一种市场解决方案。❷ 因此，最好的办法就是提供一种机制，既能满足用户巨大的市场需求，又可以使著作权人得到合理回报。这样，当用户面临两个选择时，一个是方便、价格合理的合法服务，一个是搜寻费时费力、有病毒感染危险的非法文件分享，他们会选择哪个就变得非常明显了。❸

二、"开放型"著作权保护机制的实践

由于上述各种形态"闭锁型"著作权保护方式的效果都没有达到令人满意的程度，人们开始反思这种模式，并考虑迎合市场的需求，对网上作品的大规模使用进行授权，希望以此使音乐产业走出窘境。在这一背景下，以授权为核心的"开放型"著作权保护机制开始兴起。目前，主要有以下几种类型的商业模式被实践或建议。

（一）数字音乐零售（Digital Retail）

苹果公司于 2003 年 4 月 28 日在美国推出了 iTune Store（当时叫 iTune Music Store），这是第一个广受媒体关注的线上音乐商店。苹果公司的这一授权模式成为数字零售这一商业模式的先驱。这种商业模式有两个显著特点：采用 iPod+iTune 软件与硬件相结合的营销策略；采用以单曲基本价格 0.99 $ 出售的定价方式。iTune Store 在 2008 年 4 月成为美国最受欢迎的音乐销售商，

---

❶ See Kot, Greg. "Ripped: How the wired generation revolutionized music", New York: Scribner (2009). 该书引用 Peter Jenner 的话 "我们在试将 19 世纪和 20 世纪的商业模式强加到 21 世纪科技上……我们现在乱成一团糟，这就不足为奇"。

❷ 但可惜的是，当时的唱片公司没有利用好这种新技术提供的巨大机会来开拓新的市场。Napster 高管曾多次向唱片公司提出其将引入收费增值服务，并愿意将收益的 80% 给唱片公司，但大多数公司最终拒绝和解。Fisher III, W. W. (2004). Promises to Keep: Technology, Law, and the Future of Entertainment, 115.

❸ Lemley, Mark A., and R. Anthony Reese. "Reducing digital copyright infringement without restricting innovation." Stan. L. Rev. 56 (2003), p. 1426.

2010年2月成为世界最受欢迎的音乐商店。❶到2012年10月10日，iTune占据了64%的在线音乐市场份额，并占据全世界音乐销售的29%。❷截止到2013年2月6日，iTune共卖出了250亿首歌曲。❸有证据表明在线音乐授权服务有助于使用户从P2P非法分享向合法服务转移。❹另外，线上音乐服务也使音乐创作者的收入增加。❺

类似的零售模式的数字音乐服务还有CD Baby、Amazon Music Store、Google Play等。

（二）订阅服务（Subscription Service）

（1）流媒体订阅。订阅服务的典型代表是2006年面世的Spotify。其盈利模式是一种"免费加增值"（Freemium）模式：向用户提供免费但含有广告的流媒体服务（Streaming Service）以便使用户试用；如需增值服务（去除广告、去除媒体流限制、更高的质音频量、可在iOS以及Android等移动设备上使用）则需交每月9.99美元服务费。Spotify还支持付费下载功能。Spotify既提供交互式服务，也提供非交互式服务。交互式服务是指用户可以在其个人选择的时间和地点获取作品。例如，用户可以在线欣赏或者下载自己想听的歌曲。而非交互式服务则是与交互式服务相对而言，最简单的例子就是广播电台提供的服务，只是Spotify提供的是网络电台服务。从技术上来说，这种服务是将P2P技术合法化，用插播广告的方式获得利益平衡的商业模式。❻到2012年8月，Spotify拥有四百万付费用户，月收入2000万欧元。到2012年12月6日，其在全球拥有2000万活跃用户，超过500万付费用户，其中包括100万美国用户。❼类似的流媒体订阅音乐服务还有Rhapsody、MOG、Rdio、Zune、Slacker等。

（2）下载订阅。这种服务模式的典型是eMusic。其盈利模式是：用户每

---

❶ See Wikipedia, iTune, http：//zh. wikipedia. org/wiki/ITunes.

❷ CEPro, "iTunes Dominates Download Market & Streaming Audio Grows". Available at：http：//www. cepro.com/article/itunes_ dominates_ download_ market_ streaming_ audio_ grows/.

❸ See Apple.com, "iTunes Store Sets New Record with 25 Billion Songs Sold", http：//www.apple.com/pr/library/2013/02/06iTunes-Store-Sets-New-Record-with-25-Billion-Songs-Sold.html.

❹ 美互联网用户正从P2P盗版网络向iTunes转移．［EB/OL］. http：//tech. sina. com. cn/i/2005-07-11/1048659274. shtml；另见http：//www. enet. com. cn/article/2005/0722/A20050722437253. shtml.

❺ Mark Sweney, "iTunes and Spotify boost UK songwriters' income". Available at：http：//www.guardian.co.uk/business/2012/apr/02/itunes-spotify-uk-songwriters.

❻ 关于其具体商业模式，http：//en. wikipedia. org/wiki/Spotify.

❼ http：//en. wikipedia. org/wiki/Spotify.

个月付费 11.99 美元可以下载 24 首单曲；31.99 美元可以下载 73 首。由于下载音乐的格式是 MP3，故该服务下载的音乐可在任何设备上播放。

（三）网络广播（Webcasting）

网络广播模式的典型是 Pandora，它可以提供自动音乐推荐服务。只要用户输入自己喜欢的歌曲或者艺术家，系统就可以播放相似的歌曲。这样用户就可以形成自己个性化的广播电台。用户有两种选择，一种是有广告的免费服务；另一种是每年 36 美元或者每月 3.99 美元，可以享受免除广告、高音质、个性皮肤、使用独立于浏览器的桌面应用的服务。❶ 类似的服务还有 Turntable.fm、Last.fm、Sirius XM Satellite Radio、Podcasts 等。

（四）"艺术家对歌迷"模式（Direct-To-Fan）

数字和网络技术出现之前，音乐的现场演出、广播授权以及发行一直都由唱片公司控制。新技术使艺术家可以相对独立地创作、发行自己的作品。"艺术家对歌迷"模式就是在这种背景下产生的。它是指艺术家绕开唱片公司控制，通过网上商店、社交网络等途径直接向歌迷出售自己的作品。例如，一个歌手可以将自己的新作品放在个人网站上，歌迷们则可直接在网站上购买歌曲。这种模式一方面可以使艺术家独立于唱片公司的控制，减少发行成本；另一方面还可以培养歌迷对艺术家的忠诚度，从而形成固定的歌迷群体，打造自己的品牌。Bandcamp 是这种商业模式的代表，这种服务可以为已有的乐队网址增加实体或数字音乐、商品（T恤衫、卫衣、海报等）销售选择，或者直接作为艺术家的网站。Bandcamp 能够提供快速、可靠的对艺术家作品的流媒体服务和下载服务；艺术家设定价格（当然也可以免费）。在这种模式下，艺术家可以得到 85% 以上的收益。❷ 类似的服务还有 Radiohead experiment、Nine Inch Nails experiment、Magnatune 等。

（五）自愿集体授权（Voluntary Collective Licensing）

电子前线基金（the Electronic Frontier Foundation）最早于 2004 年 4 月发布白皮书建议唱片业采纳像广播电台那样使用的自愿性集体授权模式。❸ 目前，该白皮书的最新版本是 2008 年的 2.1 版本。❹ 该白皮书在前言中写道："在对

---

❶ http://help.pandora.com/customer/portal/articles/84834-pandora-one.
❷ 见 Bandcamp 网页。网址：http://bandcamp.com/pricing.
❸ Peter Yu, "P2P and the Future of Private Copying" University of Colorado Law Review 76 (2005), p.712.
❹ Fred von Lohmann, "A Better Way Forward: Voluntary Collective Licensing of Music File Sharing". Available at: https://www.eff.org/wp/better-way-forward-voluntary-collective-licensing-music-file-sharing.

P2P 分享发起的法律战争中,谁都不是赢家。唱片公司销售继续下滑,数千万美国音乐分享者(歌迷)都感觉自己是罪犯。损害每天都在增加——隐私受到侵害,创新被阻碍,经济增长被压抑,还时不时有随机被挑选的个人被唱片公司起诉。同时,针对歌迷的诉讼没有使艺术家们得到一分钱。我们需要一个更好的出路。"❶ 该授权机制的主要内容是:音乐产业成立几个集体管理组织,使音乐消费者能够以合理价格使自己的文件分享行为变成合法行为,如每月五到十美元。只要用户付费后,就可以随意使用 P2P 软件分享音乐。集体管理组织根据音乐流行的程度将收入分配给权利人。这样,分享者越多,权利人得到的回报越多。在这一机制中,权利人可以选择参加上述集体管理组织并获得报酬,也可以选择不参加这种机制。这种机制的设计实质上是模仿美国表演权(Public Performance)集体管理组织 ASCAP、BMI 和 SESAC 的成立而成立新的集体管理组织对 P2P 进行授权。换言之,如今音乐产业看待 P2P 分享正如当初曲作者们如何看待新型的广播一样。❷ 因此他们认为,既然可以成立 ASCAP、BMI 和 SESAC 来对音乐作品公开表演进行授权,那么同样可以成立集体管理组织对 P2P 文件分享进行授权。

新近出现的与上述类似的授权机制是加拿大作曲家协会(SAC)设计的,旨在对利用 P2P 技术进行的非商业性音乐文件分享进行收费从而达到各方利益平衡的一种方案。该授权机制最终版本于 2011 年年底面世。其基本原理是:由作品创作者或权利人成立一个新的公司 Song-Share.ca,该公司与网络服务提供者(ISP)合作,向消费者提供音乐文件分享授权;该模式只对非商业性文件分享行为提供授权,商业性行为需按正常法律手续从权利人处取得授权;消费者可以用一切基于网络的工具进行文件分享,无须任何行为的改变;授权使用费将作为网络接入收费中的一项由 ISP 将账单发送给消费者;ISPs 从收取的授权费中扣除手续费用后转付给 Song-Share 公司。公司自己或使用第三方机构分析歌曲的使用次数并根据该数据将收入在表演者、作曲者和权利所有者之间分配,使用费的分配主要是通过相应的集体管理组织转付。❸ 该建议对商业模式的工作原理进行了介绍,还附加了很有说服力的可行性分析。有评论指出,"虽然这种商业模式并非尽善尽美,但却触碰到了问题的本质。音乐产业

---

❶ https://www.eff.org/wp/better-way-forward-voluntary-collective-licensing-music-file-sharing.

❷ https://www.eff.org/wp/better-way-forward-voluntary-collective-licensing-music-file-sharing.

❸ Songwriters Association of Canada, "S. A. C. Monetizing Music File Sharing: A New B2B Model", October 31, 2011. Available at: http://songwriters.wiredsolutions.ca/sacsurvey2011.aspx.

不应增加限制而应寻求能够使消费者通过支付合理费用从而能够使用全世界的音乐"。❶

另外，为应对 P2P 技术引起的网上大规模文件分享问题，还有税收化（Taxation）❷、特别使用费（Levy）❸ 等建议被提出。这些建议均须以法律的形式对市场进行干预，从本质上属于强制许可（Compulsory Licensing）。❹ 这些强制许可方案，虽然也可一定程度上解决 P2P 带来的问题并同时使权利者得到补偿，但其起码有以下问题：需要立法或对法律进行修改；如何确定分配方案非常困难；不一定能使权利者得到足够补偿；对所有用户征收同样的价格不公平；可能减损合理使用政策。这种法定许可模式最大的问题在于使权利所有者失去了控制并利用自己著作权的权利，从而无法在与使用者的授权谈判中最大程度实现自己的利益。因此，除少数例外需要，法律没有必要违背权利所有者意思代替其处分自己的权利，而应将问题交给市场机制解决。基于研究重点和篇幅限制，本书对此不作深入阐述。

三、"开放型"著作权保护机制的成效显现

如前所述，在线音乐的出现给传统音乐商业模式带来巨大挑战开始于 Napster 为代表的 P2P 服务。但由于唱片业开展的一系列的诉讼，在线音乐的发展始终没有明确方向。苹果公司于 2003 年推出的 iTune 打破了这种尴尬局面，它代表着"开放型"著作权保护模式的开始，构成网上音乐发展的里程碑。❺ 2003 年美国消费者可以购买歌曲的曲库有 40 万~50 万首，❻ 到 2004 年

---

❶ TorrentFreak, "Canadian Songwriters Want to Legalize File-Sharing". Available at: http://torrentfreak.com/canadian-songwriters-want-to-legalize-file-sharing-111206/.

❷ Fisher III, W. W. (2004). Promises to Keep: Technology, Law, and the Future of Entertainment, p. 199-258.

❸ Neal Netanel, Impose a Noncommercial Use Levy to Allow Free Peer-to-Peer File Sharing, 17 HARV. J. L & TECH 1 (2003).

❹ Peter Yu, "P2P and the Future of Private Copying" University of Colorado Law Review 76 (2005), p. 704.

❺ 洪春晖. 由 Apple iTunes 之成功看在线音乐经营模式的转变．[EB/OL]．[2004-04-29]．http: //tourism. pu. edu. tw/wang/ec2/Articals/%E7%B7%9A%E4%B8%8A%E9%9F%B3%E6%A8%82%E7%B6%93%E7%87%9F%E6%A8%A1%E5%BC%8F. pdf.

❻ IFPI Digital Music Report 2004, available at: http://www.ifpi.org/content/library/digital-music-report-2004.pdf.

这一数字就变为100万。❶ 2003年全球范围内提供的合法音乐服务少于50家，而到2009年则增长到400多家❷。

与此同时，国际唱片业协会的研究表明，2004年是在线音乐产业取得实质性利润的第一年。❸ 2003年下半年美国单曲销售下载量还只有1920万首，到2004年则增长为1.426亿❹，2005年达到3.53亿，2006年则为5.82亿，❺到2012年达到13.4亿。❻ 美国2004年数字音乐收入为4亿美元，2005年这一数字增加到11亿，到2007年则为29亿。❼ 2012年数字音乐的收入超过音乐产业总收入的一半，占55.9%。❽

上述数据虽然不甚完整，但已经可以呈现一个明显的事实，即数字音乐销售收入增长与数字音乐服务的增长呈明显的正相关关系。在其他条件没有明显改变的情况下，这说明"开放型"著作权保护机制的成效已经开始显现。有学者指出，随着合法在线音乐市场的持续增长和授权标准的不断发展，对合法音乐服务的挑战将逐渐消失。❾

第四节　迈向一种整体性著作权实现机制

从上述对两种著作权保护模式的产生与发展来看，"开放型"模式是在"闭锁型"模式无法达到预期目的的背景下兴起的。因此，二者在时间顺序上

---

❶ IFPI Digital Music Report 2005, available at: http://www.ifpi.org/content/library/digital-music-report-2005.pdf.

❷ IFPI Digital Music Report 2010, available at: http://www.ifpi.org/content/library/digital-music-report-2010.pdf.

❸ Supra note. 228.

❹ Id.

❺ IFPI Digital Music Report 2007, available at: http://www.ifpi.org/content/library/digital-music-report-2007.pdf.

❻ The Nielsen Company & Billboard's 2012 Music Industry Report, available at: http://www.businesswire.com/news/home/20130104005149/en/Nielsen-Company-Billboard%E2%80%99s-2012-Music-Industry-Report.

❼ IFPI Digital Music Report 2008, available at: http://www.ifpi.org/content/library/digital-music-report-2008.pdf.

❽ The Nielsen Company & Billboard's 2012 Music Industry Report, available at: http://www.businesswire.com/news/home/20130104005149/en/Nielsen-Company-Billboard%E2%80%99s-2012-Music-Industry-Report.

❾ David Moser & Cheryl Slay, Music Copyright Law, (2012), p.289.

有明显的先后关系。但是,"闭锁型"模式中的具体著作权保护手段并没有随"开放型"模式下的音乐授权商业模式的兴起而消失。相反,"闭锁型"权利实现模式下的著作权保护手段对于音乐授权商业模式起到重要辅助作用。为避免误解,有必要对两种著作权实现机制的关系进行澄清。

两种著作权实现模式的本质区别在于面对数字和网络技术带来的挑战时预设思维的不同。"闭锁型"模式的预设思维是"堵",以禁止为目的,采用各种方式对作品的网上使用进行"围追堵截"。"开放型"模式的预设思维在于"疏",以授权为目的,采用各种方式为作品的网上使用开通合法通道。美国音乐著作权保护的实践清楚地表明"闭锁型"权利保护模式无法实现阻止作品网上大规模使用的目的,而"开放型"保护模式则有效回应了新技术的发展和市场需求,使音乐产业逐渐适应了新的技术条件。

上文对"开放型"模式的阐述主要以音乐作品授权商业模式为重点,这样就容易造成授权商业模式就是"开放型"模式的全部的误解。事实上,商业模式是"开放型"著作权保护模式的核心内容,而"闭锁型"模式下的具体著作权保护方式构成授权商业模式的周边设施。这些周边设施通过促使使用者从未授权的非法服务转向合法的授权服务、遏制非法服务的发展来促进音乐作品授权商业模式的顺利运行。在这种关系中,授权商业模式是目的,而"闭锁型"模式下的著作权保护方式是促使这种目的实现的手段。因此,授权机制缺位下的"闭锁型"手段是没有意义的。换言之,运行良好的授权机制对"开放型"著作权保护模式起到画龙点睛的作用。

网络著作权与传统财产权、著作权的差异性、新技术发展的不可预测性以及来自盗版的竞争,决定了新技术背景下不能过于依赖既有的网络著作权保护方式,必须转向以授权为核心的开放型著作权保护模式。除了开放型著作权保护模式的市场路径外,由于新技术的不可预测性以及网络环境下法律规范与社会道德规范的脱节,又使得著作权的实现又必须充分考虑技术、社会道德规范等其他因素。而且,新技术条件下著作权的保护又涉及多方主体,所以需要协调多元利益的平衡。这一切都意味着在新技术背景下必须走向一种整体性的著作权保护模式。在这里,美国著名学者莱斯格的规制理论可以为我们提供一定启发。

一、莱斯格的整体性规制理论

按照莱斯格的规制理论,法律、社会道德规范、市场、架构共同构成对规制目标的规制要素。[1] 以网络空间中对作品的下载和分享为例：首先，法律通过侵害著作权的直接侵权责任和间接侵权责任对著作权侵权予以惩罚。其次，对作品的下载和分享还会受到社会道德规范的约束。在网络空间中，分享已经成为网民广为接受的行为规范，这对作品的下载和分享产生了很大的影响。再次，市场对规制作品的下载和分享也起到了至关重要的作用。如果市场能够提供具有足够竞争力的服务，网络用户很可能就会由非法的服务转向合法的服务，反之，网络著作权侵权行为就会更盛行。最后，技术也是重要的影响因素，上文提到的技术保护措施和分级响应机制虽然无法从根本上解决著作权网络侵权问题，但却是可以增加著作权侵权的难度。[2]

可见，各种规制要素对规制对象的规制方式各不相同：法律通过惩罚和责任、规范通过共同体施加的荣辱感、市场通过供应和价格、架构通过物理约束进行规制。同时，这些规制要素既相互依赖又互相制约。例如，技术规制可能增强，也可能减弱法律和社会道德规范的规制；而相反，法律也会影响到其他规制因素对规制对象的规制。单一的规制因素常常会影响到其他规制因素对规制对象的规制效果。在改变一个特定规制因素之前，必须充分考量这一改变对其他规制因素的影响以及其他因素对这一要素的反弹效应。因此，不同规制因素之间的这种关系决定了对规制对象的规制必须采取整体性的视角。在网络著作权保护领域，各种规制要素之间的关系要求必须综合考虑上述四个规制要素促进网络著作权的实现。

虽然根据莱斯格的理论四种规制要素是相互作用的，但在网络著作权实现这一具体领域中各要素的地位却是不同的。正如上所述，单纯的侵权诉讼效果并不理想，无法有效规制对作品的大规模网络侵权，而以市场授权为中心的开放型著作权保护模式则可以使网络用户从非法的服务转向合法的授权服务，从而促进著作权的实现。正如有学者所言，以严格的执法取代对数字作品的许可是一种错误的立场。[3] 在合法的在线作品服务的供给不足时，使用侵权诉讼、刑事惩罚等强制执法手段很可能导致传统著作权产业消除在线市场竞争，阻碍技术和新的商业模式的创新。[4] 因此，网络著作权的保护必须以开放型著作权

---

[1] See Lessig, Lawrence. Code: And Other Laws of Cyberspace, Version 2.0. Basic Books, 2006, p. 121–123.

[2] 在莱斯格的理论下，技术要素被称为架构（Architecture）。

[3] See Hargreaves, Ian. "Digital opportunity: a review of intellectual property and growth: an independent report." (2011).

[4] 李琛. 网络环境下著作权法与市场的互动 [J]. 中国版权，2012（4）.

保护模式为中心，兼顾其他规制因素。

二、整体性著作权保护机制的大致框架

根据上述整体性规制理论，我们尝试以开放型著作权保护模式为中心，兼顾法律、社会道德规范以及架构等其他规制要素，对网络著作权整体性保护机制的框架作大致描述。

首先，网络著作权的保护应当以作品授权为中心，通过开发行之有效的商业模式来组织市场，为使用者对作品的使用提供授权通道，同时使著作权的权利人获得激励，这是因为网络著作权价值的实现主要不在于能够减少多少侵权，而在于能够增加多少授权。

其次，使网络用户从非法服务转向合法授权服务是开放型著作权保护模式成功运行的必要条件，这可考虑从以下几方面着手：作品授权的商业模式必须能够为用户提供方便、优质的服务；适当运用技术保护措施增加使用非法服务的成本；与网络服务提供商合作，对用户进行侵权提醒，提高网络用户的著作权意识；完善著作权集体管理制度，一方面减少作品服务提供者取得授权的成本，另一方面发挥集体管理组织的维权功能，增加用户的违法成本。

最后，要使网络用户从非法服务转向合法授权服务，瓦解非法服务的商业模式是非常重要的一环。音乐产业可以采取与网络服务提供商、支付平台、搜索引擎、广告主等进行合作的方式瓦解非法服务的生存环境：（1）与网络服务提供商合作，利用"通知-取下"规则对非法内容进行删除，同时考虑采取逐级响应措施，促使用户停止使用非法服务，切断非法服务的客户源。（2）与搜索引擎合作，在搜索结果中将非法服务靠后或删除。（3）广告收入是非法服务得以运营和盈利的主要来源，因此促使广告主不在非法服务网站投放广告是瓦解非法服务的重要途径，可考虑由集体管理组织向广告主通知非法网站名单，并要求广告主撤下广告。制定行业规范也是促使广告主不与非法网站合作的可行途径。[1]（4）与支付服务商合作，使非法服务无法利用这些支付服务进行交易，切断非法服务的资金流动管道。这样，在法律、社会道德规范以及架构等不同规制因素的配合下，开放型著作权保护模式将在网络环境下对著作权的实现起到核心作用。

当然，上述对整体性著作权保护机制的描述只是框架性的，在具体制度设

---

[1] See Hugenholtz, p. Bernt. "Code Of Conduct And Copyright Enforcement In Cyberspace." Stanmatoudi, Irini. (ed.) COPYRIGHT ENFORCEMENT AND THE INTERNET (2010), p. 303–320.

计和运作中还需对各种规制因素在整个规制框架下的配置作进一步考量。这是因为著作权保护制度一方面涉及权利持有人、作品使用者、网络服务提供者、广告主等多方主体的利益，另一方面还需要促进新技术发展和保护社会公共利益。因此，一个好的著作权保护机制必须充分协调好上述多种利益之间的平衡。从这一意义上说，整体性著作权保护机制的设计更像是精密的钟表制造，而不是简单的木工活。

第五节　云计算、大数据、3D打印与整体性著作权保护机制的前景展望

在数字网络技术的冲击下，技术保护措施、侵权诉讼以及逐级响应机制等以减少侵权为目的的传统著作权保护方式无法实现著作权法的目的。网络著作权与传统财产权、著作权的差异性、新技术发展的不可预测性以及来自盗版产业的竞争使以授权机制为中心的整体性著作权保护机制在数字网络技术背景下成为必要，而且现有事实已经证明这种著作权保护机制已经出现成效。不仅如此，最新网络技术的发展也使我们有理由相信以授权核心的整体性著作权保护机制在未来将发挥越来越重要的作用。

首先，云计算技术的发展不仅可以从技术上保障授权商业模式的实施，而且更有利于控制侵权。云技术时代的来临将会使更多的终端设备接入云端，数据同步、云存储以及新的应用将大大提高授权商业模式的用户体验，这将进一步促进商业模式的不断发展。随着网络接入和终端设备的进一步普及，过去P2P时代的上传、下载、传播将逐渐减少甚至消失，这从客观上有利于控制大规模复制传播的侵权行为，瓦解非法服务，使更多用户转向合法的授权服务。

其次，大数据的价值挖掘使得作品授权商业模式在未来很长一段时期内以免费或非常低廉的价格向用户提供作品成为可能。对开放型商业模式来说，一个非常大的挑战在于其一旦收费，将会有很大一部分用户专享免费的非法服务。而大数据技术的迅猛发展使用户爱好、消费习惯等数据成为价值不可限量的金矿，这可以使授权商业模式一方面可以免费或以较低价格向用户提供音乐、影视等作品服务，另一面通过大数据价值挖掘弥补其取得著作权的成本。目前，我国消费者缺乏著作权意识，付费意愿不高，这使音乐产业对音乐服务进行全面收费在短期内非常困难。在这种背景下，大数据技术的发展可以为授

权商业模式争取用户、培养用户付费习惯提供宝贵的缓冲时间。

最后,3D打印领域很可能成为整体性著作权保护机制发挥作用的新领域。虽然3D打印技术目前仍然处于起步阶段,但随着打印材料技术的不断成熟,3D打印技术将对传统制造业起到颠覆性的影响。❶ 3D打印技术将使对著作权作品的大规模复制从虚拟网络世界扩张到现实世界。只要输入需要的材料,人们通过扫描或在网络上取得数据,可以利用3D打印机高质量、高效率地打印一切物品。可以预见,对三维作品的未经授权的复制在不远的将来很可能成为继P2P技术以来著作权保护的又一新的难题。❷ 如果将来仍然用传统的著作权保护思维去规制3D打印,那么对P2P技术规制失败的故事很有可能重新上演。我们有理由相信,整体性著作权保护机制在解决未来可能出现的3D打印领域的著作权问题方面将发挥重要的作用。

美国音乐产业解决大规模网上作品使用问题的教训和经验表明:既有的网络著作权保护方式无法应对新技术带来的挑战,以开放型著作权保护模式为中心的整体性著作权保护机制是数字网络技术背景下著作权实现的必然选择。我国网络著作权尤其在网络音乐著作权领域侵权纠纷不断,其根本原因在于网络著作权的授权渠道不畅造成❸。我国可以吸取美国的经验和教训,将网络著作权保护的重心放在以增加合法使用为中心的整体性著作权保护机制上,而不是单纯依靠强制执法去减少非法使用,这应当是应对数字网络技术对著作权保护和实现带来的挑战的理性思路。

---

❶ 有研究预测,到2016年,3D打印产业将达到31亿美元的规模。See Forbes,3D Printing Industry Will Reach ＄3.1 Billion Worldwide by 2016. Available at:http://www.forbes.com/sites/tjmccue/2012/03/27/3d-printing-industry-will-reach-3-1-billion-worldwide-by-2016/ (Feb 20, 2014)

❷ 据预测,3D打印将对现有的商业模式造成很大冲击,并对知识产权的保护构成很大威胁,到2018年3D打印引起的知识产权损失将达到每年1000亿美元的惊人规模。See Information Week,3D Printing to Ignite Major Debate Ethics Regulation by 2016:Gartner. Available at:http://www.informationweek.in/informationweek/news-analysis/287329/3d-printing-ignite-major-debate-ethics-regulation-2016-gartner. (Feb 20, 2014)

❸ 张洪波.加强著作权集体管理,完善作者授权通道 [J].传媒,2010 (8).

第四章　权利保护之二：权利人技术保护措施的保护与限制

技术的进步和发展一方面会造成大规模网上侵权的潜在风险，另一方面也赋予了权利人新的自我保护工具：技术保护措施（Technological Protection Measures）。权利人可以利用数字技术控制作品的使用方式。20世纪90年代在美国非常流行的一句话就是"机器问题的答案在于机器"。❶ 但是，仅有技术保护措施不足以保护权利人的权利，因为很多情况下，技术保护措施可以被很快地破解。为了避免技术保护措施使用者和破解者之间的"军备竞赛"造成的社会资源浪费以及对著作权造成的威胁，技术保护措施需要法律的确认和保护。但与此同时，在很多情况下，会发生权利保护措施与合理使用等对著作权的限制相冲突的问题，如何协调个人对自我权利的保护与使用者以及公共利益之间的利益平衡成为著作权法需要解决的一个重要问题。

第一节　技术保护措施的背景

一、网络侵权催生技术保护措施

数字网络技术使很多新的应用程序可以被设计用来规避现有法律的规制。例如，兴起于20世纪末直到现在仍被广泛使用的P2P应用软件。这些软件利用了现行法律对终端用户进行私人复制相关规定的模糊性以及对终端用户执法的欠缺，通过端对端去中心化的技术设计使终端用户可以在网上大量复制和传播数字作品，而无须或承担非常小的违法成本。由于技术发展的迅速性和不可预测性，使得法律在一定程度和时间内无法对新技术做出有效的调整和规制，这造成了法律上的滞后性和不确定性。

---

❶ Charles Clark. The Answer to the Machine is in the Machine, In the Future of Copyright in the Digital Environment（Hugenholtz, ed.）（1996）.

由于数字技术的规避性，在数字网络环境下对著作权的保护变得越来越困难。著作权权利人不得不考虑法律之外的手段对自己的权利进行保护。新技术不仅具有上述的逃避性，而且还具有对终端用户行为的规制性，即新技术在一些情形下可以替代法律实现对用户的行为的规制。关于新技术的规制性，美国著名网络法学者Lessig有深入的研究。他认为，代码就如同传统技术环境下的围墙、建筑一样可以对人的行为进行规制，通过代码建立起来的数字围墙可以起到对法律强制的补充作用以及对行为的规制作用。有的学者将这种利用数字技术对自己的权利进行保护的现象称为"技术自助"。[1]

二、技术保护措施的概念

技术保护措施，是指著作权的权利人通过使用数字技术对作品进行接触控制、复制控制等手段以实现对作品的使用进行控制的措施。《世界知识产权组织版权条约》（WCT）第11条对技术保护措施进行如下规定："各缔约方应规定适当的法律保护与有效的法律救济措施，制止对作者为行使本条约规定的权利而使用的对其作品未经作者许可或法律允许的行为进行约束而采取的技术措施进行规避的行为。"《世界知识产权组织表演和录音制品条约》（WPPT）第18条也有类似的规定："缔约各方应规定适当的法律保护和有效的法律补救办法，制止规避由表演者或录音制品制作者为行使本条约所规定的权利而使用的、对就其表演或录音制品进行未经该有关表演者或录音制品制作者许可或未由法律准许的行为加以约束的有效技术措施。"归纳上述对技术保护措施的不同定义，技术保护措施这一术语是对作品的接触和利用进行控制的技术的统称。

与技术保护措施相关的另一个概念是数字权利管理（Digital Rights Management）。数字权利管理是比技术保护措施更为宽泛的概念，它不仅仅是指技术保护措施，而是对数字作品的著作权内容进行描述、识别，并贯彻著作权法律规则或者权利人针对作品的接触和使用而设计的规则。数字权利管理需要技

---

[1] See Tom W. Bell, Escape from Copyright: Market Success vs. Statutory Failure in the Protection of Expressive Works, 69 U. Cin. L. Rev. 741 (2001) regime); Kenneth W. Dam, Self-Help in the Digital Jungle, 28 J. Legal Stud. 393 (1999).

术保护措施和权利管理信息❶结合起来才能实现。

目前著作权人的技术保护措施包括但不限于以下几种：❷

1. 作品进入技术保护措施：该种技术保护措施用数字化的手段对作品进行价目，要求使用者进行登记、输入密码、使用机顶盒，此种技术保护措施还可装载作品内容、作者的身份信息以及与作品使用等相关信息。

2. 防复制系统：该系统可以阻止用户进行如复制等特定行为。防复制系统中最具代表性的是"SCMS"系统（Serial Copy Management Systems），该系统不仅可控制作品的首次复制，还可控制作品的后续复制。

3. 著作权追踪系统：以技术保证数字作品始终处于著作权人的控制之下，只有在著作权人授权的情况下使用人才可使用作品。

4. 电子名片管理系统：即 ECMS（Electronic Card Management System），该技术不仅可识别作者身份，还可以对作品进行加密，同时又可以通过电子合同对使用者进行授权，收取授权费用。

5. 电子水印技术：该技术通过在作品中植入数字标识以识别作品及著作权人的基本信息，从而确定作品的真伪。

6. 标准系统：该技术措施是通过在不同的地区设定不同的技术标准从而避免对作品的侵权行为。

三、技术保护措施的性质

关于著作权技术保护措施的性质问题，自从各国立法中出现著作权技术保护措施的规定后，学术界出现了关于著作权技术保护措施性质的讨论。关于技术保护措施的性质，我国学术界目前主要存在两种观点：第一种观点认为，技术保护措施本质上属于一种民事权利。有的学者还明确提出"著作权技术保护措施权"的说法，认为著作权技术保护措施是用有形财产来保护无形财产，是一种特别的权利保护。❸另一种观点认为，著作权法上的技术保护措施，是指权利人为防止作品被复制和使用而在作品上采用的保护措施，法律所禁止的

---

❶ WCT 对权利管理信息的定义为："识别作品本身、作品的作者、对作品拥有任何权利的权利人的信息，或者关于作品使用条款的信息，以及表示此种信息的数字代码。"WCT 第 12 条。我国《信息网络传播权保护条例》关于权利管理信息的定义为："指说明作品及其作者、表演及其表演者、录音录像制品及其制作者的信息，作品、表演、录音录像制品权利人的信息和使用条件的信息，以及表示上述信息的数字或者代码。"

❷ 闫桂珍. 互联网上的版权技术保护措施 [J]. 中国版权, 2001 (3).

❸ 李扬. 试论技术措施权 [J]. 河南省政法管理干部学院学报, 2003 (3): 106.

仅是破坏著作权技术保护措施的行为，并非对著作权技术保护措施本身的保护。因此，著作权技术保护措施只是一种禁止权，该权利不是著作权的内容之一，除非技术措施本身符合作品的要件。❶

目前，关于技术保护措施的性质仍然存在较大争议。从目前世界各国对技术保护措施的态度看，美国、欧盟及相关国际条约并未对其进行明确定性，而是从实用角度规定技术保护措施是受到法律保护的，但同时对技术保护措施的限度进行了规定。本书认为，除非技术保护措施本身构成作品，否则技术保护措施不构成一种独立的权利，技术保护措施只是权利人为保护著作权而采取的自我保护手段。技术保护措施只有在满足了法律规定的特定条件时，才能受到法律保护。

第二节 对技术保护措施的立法保护

世界上不存在绝对安全的技术，即使再先进的技术保护措施也有被破解的可能。因此，技术保护措施需要法律上的保护，否则就可能发生加密和破解之间的"猫捉老鼠"游戏的不断上演，大大增加社会成本。早在1988年，英国就在《著作权、外观设计和专利法》第296条中对"防止复制系统"进行保护。❷ 但是对技术保护措施的保护成为世界各国立法潮流始于1996的《世界知识产权组织版权条约》（World Intellectual Property Organization Copyright Treaty，WCT）和《世界知识产权组织表演和录音制品条约》。

一、国际条约关于技术保护措施的规定

从1886年通过的《伯尔尼公约》算起，对知识产权的国际条约保护已经有一百年以上的历史。此后，针对新技术和商业实践的不断发展对知识产权保护带来的挑战，国际社会又不断对该条约进行相应的修改和完善，并订立了新的相关条约。《伯尔尼公约》于1971年最后一次修订后不再采用之前的修订

---

❶ 郭禾．规避技术措施行为的法律属性辨析［M］//沈仁干．数字技术与著作权．北京：法律出版社，2004：45-60.
❷ 该法案第296条规定："对于以电子形式存在的作品，著作权人有权对那些制造、进口、出售、出租、推销专门用于避开防止复制系统的人，以及公布信息、使他人得以避开防止复制系统的人提起诉讼，并可以没收其工具和设备。" See UK Copyright, Design and Patents Act 1988. 转引自王迁．知识产权法教程［M］．3版．北京：中国人民大学出版社，2011：242.

模式，而是采取"指导性发展"（Guided Development）的办法。❶世界知识产权组织通过制定相关立法建议、示范条款以及指导原则促进知识产权国际保护制度的发展。虽然著作权的技术保护措施一直是世界知识产权组织《著作权领域立法示范条款》和《保护录音制品制作者示范法》磋商进程中的重要议题。但是，国际社会逐渐发现，随着社会的快速发展，这种"指导性发展"模式无法应对新技术带来的挑战。因此，国际社会开始就缔结新的条约进行一系列的磋商和谈判。WIPO于1989年组织了"《伯尔尼公约》可能性议定专家委员会"，对《伯尔尼公约》中存在的问题进行阐明和分析，并试图缔结新的国际条约。

《与贸易有关的知识产权协议》（TRIPS协议）于1994年获得通过，该协议在《关税贸易总协定》的框架下对各缔约国必须遵循的有关知识产权保护的最低立法和司法标准进行了规定。该协议虽然也涉及了一些由数字技术引发的问题，但却未对技术保护措施问题进行规定。

1996年12月2日至20日，世界知识产权组织关于著作权和邻接权若干问题的外交会议于瑞士日内瓦召开。《世界知识产权组织版权条约》（WCT）和《世界知识产权组织表演和录音制品条约》（WPPT）两个条约在这次会议上通过。其中WCT主要是对书籍、计算机程序、音乐、电影及美术作品等文学艺术作品的作者进行保护，WPPT则主要是对表演者和录音制品作者的权利进行保护。WCT的第11条、第12条以及WPPT的第18条、第19条对技术保护措施进行了开创性的规定。❷

根据WCT第11条的规定，对技术保护措施的法律保护需要满足三个要

---

❶ See the meeting report of WIPO, WIPO Seminar for Asia and the Pacific Region on The Internet and the Protection of Intellectual Property Rights, wipo/int/sin/98/4.

❷ WCT第11条"关于技术措施的义务"规定如下：缔约各方应规定适当的法律保护和有效的法律补救办法，制止规避由作者为行使本条约所规定的权利而使用的、对就其作品进行未经该有关作者许可或未由法律准许的行为加以约束的有效技术措施。WCT第12条"关于权利管理信息的义务"规定如下：(1) 缔约各方应规定适当和有效的法律补救办法，制止任何人明知或就民事补救而言有合理根据知道其行为会诱使、促进、便利或包庇对本条约或《伯尔尼公约》所涵盖的任何权利的侵犯而故意从事以下行为：

（Ⅰ）未经许可去除或改变任何权利管理的电子信息；

（Ⅱ）未经许可发行、为发行目的进口、广播或向公众传播明知已被未经许可去除或改变权利管理电子信息的作品或作品的复制品。

(2) 本条中的用语"权利管理信息"系指识别作品、作品的作者、对作品拥有任何权利的所有人的信息，或有关作品使用的条款和条件的信息，和代表此种信息的任何数字或代码，各该项信息均附于作品的每件复制品上或在作品向公众进行传播时出现。WPPT关于技术保护措施的规定也极为类似。

件；技术保护措施的使用必须是以行使《伯尔尼公约》中所赋予的权利为目的；技术保护措施的约束对象必须是未经作者授权或者未经法律允许的行为；技术保护措施必须是"有效"的。

由于在条约形成过程中各方的利益并不一致，规则的制定必须进行一定的妥协，再加上条约的制定未能充分引进技术专家的意见，条约关于技术保护措施的规定具有相当大的模糊性。❶ 这种模糊性主要体现在三个方面：第一，条约未明确是否保护接触控制的技术保护措施，这为各国保护接触控制技术保护措施预留了立法空间。❷ 第二，条约未对技术保护措施的"有效"进行明确界定，这导致了各国立法中对技术保护措施"有效"标准的不同。第三，条约仅仅规定成员方应采取"适当的法律保护和有效的法律补救办法"，而未对各成员国应对技术保护措施保护到何种程度进行规定。这使成员国在国内立法上有很大的弹性空间，数字著作权产业发达的国家则对技术保护措施采取了较高程度的保护，数字著作权产业欠发达的国家则进行较低程度的保护。❸

然而，并不能因为以上两个条约关于技术保护措施的规定的模糊性而否定条约的开创性意义。从某种意义上讲，这种模糊性是一种必要的妥协。上述两个条约对技术保护措施的规定成为国际社会国家立法所遵循的基本原则，各国纷纷立法对技术保护措施进行法律保护。❹

二、美国对技术保护措施的保护

美国关于著作权技术保护措施制度最初源于1983年的Universal Studios, Inc公司诉Sony公司案（以下简称"索尼案"）。❺ 美国最高法院通过该案确立了关于技术保护措施的基本原则，其主要内容为：著作权人不能以保护著作权为借口而阻碍新技术的发展和进步。此后，美国又陆续通过其他几个案件，

---

❶ 章忠信．"著作权法制中的'科技保护措施'与'权利管理资讯'之探讨"[J]．万国法律，2000（10）．

❷ 王迁："对技术措施立法保护的比较研究"[J]．知识产权，2003（2）．

❸ 林静君．"论科技保护措施对著作权法公共领域之冲击"[D]．台湾逢甲大学财经法律研究所硕士学位论文，2008．

❹ 1998年，美国国会通过《千年数字版权法案》；1999年日本著作权法中增加了关于技术保护措施的规定，同年澳大利亚修改其1968年的著作权法，通过了《著作权修正与数字议程法案》，对技术保护措施进行法律保护；2001年，欧盟通过《协调信息社会版权和相关权利特定领域的指令》，对技术保护措施的保护提供了支持。费思易．论网络环境下的版权技术保护措施与权利限制[J]．知识经济，2012（24）．

❺ Sony Corp. of America v. Universal City Studios, 464 U. S. 417, 442 (1984).

创立了其他几项判例原则，其中包括"被认定为创作非侵权产品而对作品进行复制并加以研究，属于合理使用范畴"，即反向工程的适用除外规则。

  1998年10月12日，在总结以往司法实践经验以及广泛吸收各界建议的基础上，美国国会通过了"世界知识产权组织版权条约实施法案"，以实施《世界知识产权组织版权条约》的规定，该法案又被称为"数字千年版权法"（Digital Millennium Copyright Act，DMCA）。《数字千年版权法》专设"著作权保护系统和著作权管理信息"一章，对技术措施的法律保护作出了详尽规定。❶该法案是从两个基本方面来规定对于技术措施的保护的。一是从他人访问作品的角度来规定，即不得对著作权人所实施的有效控制他人访问自己作品的技术措施进行破解或破坏。二是从著作权人行使自己权利的角度来规定的，即他人不得对著作权人所实施的有效保护自己权利的技术措施进行破解或破坏。所谓"有效控制他人访问作品"的技术措施，是指在其日常的操作中，要求使用经著作权人授权的信息、程序和方式才能访问作品的措施。而所谓"有效保护著作权所有人权利"的技术措施，是指在其日常操作中，防止、限制或限定他人行使著作权人权利的技术措施。《千禧年数字版权法》将著作权技术保护措施分为两类：第一类是对作品进行有效接触控制的著作权技术保护措施，简称为"基础控制著作权技术保护措施"，目的在于保障权利人控制他人对其受保护作品的"访问"；第二类是保护著作权人权利的著作权技术保护措施，简称"权利控制技术保护措施"，即防止对作品进行非法复制、发行等的著作权技术保护措施。对禁止两类技术保护措施的规避行为方面，《千禧年数字版权法》采取了不同的模式，其中对规避第一类技术保护措施也就是"接触控制著作权技术保护措施"，采取全面禁止的方式。《千禧年数字版权法》1201（a）（1）（A）规定任何人不得避开对本法所保护的作品的接触进行有效控制的技术措施。第1201（a）（2）还规定任何人不得制造制造进口或向公众提供、供应或者以其他方式贩卖用于避开接触技术保护措施的技术、产品、服务、装置、零件。对于第二类技术保护措施，《千禧年数字版权法》1201（b）只是规定禁止为规避著作权技术保护措施的产生的技术、产品、服务、装置等的生产和流通，并没有禁止规避行为本身。美国立法之所以只禁止破解"接触控制技术保护措施"，而不禁止破解"权利控制技术保护措施"，按照美国国会司法委员会的解释，其原因是：1201（a）（1）中的禁止规避是必要的，因为在本法之前该规避行为从未被宣布违法；1201（a）（2）限制交易规

---

❶ 美国著作权法 [M]. 杜颖，张启晨，译. 北京：知识产权出版社，2013：204.

避装置是在执行对上述规避行为的禁止；之所以没有禁止规避1201（b）中的技术措施（权利保护技术措施），是因为版权法早就禁止版权侵权，因此没有必要增加新的禁止性规定。❶ 也有学者认为其原因是：《著作权法》对专有著作权专有权利已经规定了"合理使用"的例外，对保护专有权利的技术措施的破解可能是出于合理使用的需要，因此法律不应对此种破解行为全面禁止；而禁止他人未经权利人许可获取作品是保护著作权的前提，并不存在合理使用的问题。❷

仔细对比DMCA关于"接触控制技术保护措施"和"权利控制技术保护措施"的保护，还有一个重要的不同就是：在接触控制条款中，不仅禁止规避工具的非法交易行为，还禁止直接的规避行为；而在1021（b）权利控制条款中，只有禁止规避工具的非法交易条款，而没有禁止对技术保护措施的直接规避行为。根据DMCA的立法资料，这种区别主要是因为：对于接触控制技术保护措施而言，在DMCA前尚无法律对规避行为本身的违法性进行规定，故有必要对其予以规定；著作权法中本来就禁止侵权著作权的行为，故不需要新的禁止规定，而禁止规避设备的规定只是对禁止侵犯著作权规定的强化而已。❸

另外，DMCA第1201条还对上述两个国际条约中未明确规定的技术保护措施的"有效性"进行了规定。对接触控制技术保护措施的有效性的规定为：在技术措施正常运行时要获得作品需要使用经著作权人授权的信息、程序或方法。对权利控制技术保护措施有效性的规定为：在技术措施正常运行时能够阻止、制止或限制本法赋予著作权人的权利的实行。❹

三、欧盟对技术保护措施的保护

在WCT和WPPT两个国际条约缔结之前，欧盟就已经开始对技术保护措施的规避行为进行立法规制。欧洲自1991年制定《计算机程序法律保护指令》开始，至今已形成了关于技术保护措施的规范体系。❺ 该体系由《计算机

---

❶ S. Rep. No. 105-190, at 11（1998），转引自崔国斌. 著作权法：原理与案例 [M]. 北京：北京大学出版社，2014：853.
❷ 王迁. 知识产权法教程 [M]. 5版. 北京：中国人民大学出版社，2016：254.
❸ David Nimmer, Copyright and Sacred Text, Technology, and the DMCA, Hague: Kluwer Law International. 2003：399. 转引自吴伟光. 数字技术环境下的版权法危机与对策 [M]. 北京：知识产权出版社，2008：165-166.
❹ 美国版权法 [M]. 杜颖，张启晨，译. 北京：知识产权出版社，2013：206-207.
❺ Council Directive 91/250/EC on the legal protection of computer programs.

程序法律保护指令》《信息社会中著作权及其邻接权的绿皮书》《版权建议指令》以及《附条件取得信息服务的保护指令》等构成。❶

1991年制定的《计算机程序法律保护指令》中第7条第1项c款规定成员国应当提供法律救济以对抗任何基于商业目的持有或者促进流通的行为、旨在帮助未经授权的移除或者规避用以保护计算机程序的技术设备的方法。❷ 该指令对技术保护措施的保护有如下几个特点：首先，该条款的保护对象仅限于计算机程序；其次，该规定只禁止基于商业目的的持有行为或促进流通的行为，对基于个人目的的持有则不禁止；再次，该规定主要针对的用于帮助未经授权地移除或规避保护计算机程序的技术设备的方法。换言之，该规定主要针对的是对技术保护措施进行规避的准备行为。

为了落实WCT和WPPT的规定，欧盟委员会于1997年12月提出了《协调信息社会有关版权和相关权利的指令草案》。根据该草案第6条规定，成员国应当提供充分的法律救济以禁止制造或销售除规避功能之外只具有有限商业重要性用途或者目的的装置或服务。1999年5月欧盟委员会对该草案进行了修正，将上述第6条中对技术保护措施的保护范围进行了扩展，由仅仅禁止准备行为扩张至既禁止规避的准备行为，也禁止规避行为本身。❸

欧盟于2001年5月22日通过了《关于信息社会中版权和相关权某些方面的协调的指令》，并于2001年6月22日生效。❹ 指令第6条对技术保护措施进行了规定，将技术保护措施定义为：在其正常的运行过程中，任何被设计用来组织或限制未经著作权或者相关权的权利人后者Directive 96/9/EC指令中规定的特殊权利人许可的行为的技术、设备或者组件。该指令中的技术保护措施的有效性是指：作品或其他保护对象的使用能够受到权利人的控制，该控制是通过应用能够实现保护目标的接触控制或者保护过程实现的，诸如加密、干扰、对作品的转换，或者复制控制机制。值得注意的是，根据该指令第1条的规

---

❶ 闫桂珍. 互联网上的版权技术保护措施[J]. 中国版权，2001 (3).

❷ (c) any act of putting into circulation, or the possession for commercial purposes of, any means the sole intended purpose of which is to facilitate the unauthorized removal or circumvention of any technical device which may have been applied to protect a computer program.

❸ 章忠信. 著作权法制中的"科技保护措施"与"权利管理资讯"之探讨[J]. 万国法律，2000 (10).

❹ 该指令具体内容可 EC Directive 2001/29/EC on the Harmonization of Certain Aspects of Copyright and Related Rights in the Information Society -Consultation Paper on Implementation of the Directive in the United Kingdom, Department of Trade and Industry UK. Available at：http：//www.ipo.gov.uk/200121ec.pdf. (Feb 29, 2014).

定，第 6 条中关于技术保护措施的规定并适用于计算机程序，计算机程序的技术保护仍然适用于 1991 年的指令（Directive 91/250/EEC）中的第 7 条。

四、我国的技术保护措施立法及建议

我国 2001 年的《著作权法》第 47 条就已经有了关于禁止故意避开或者破坏技术保护措施的规定，但是该条规定只规定权利控制的技术保护措施，而未涉及接触控制的技术保护措施。此时的规定在逻辑上并不完善，因为 2001 年《著作权法》并未就技术保护措施以及权利管理信息的定义和相关义务进行明确规定。❶

2006 年 7 月开始实施的《信息网络传播权保护条例》（国务院令第 634 号）第 26 条对技术保护措施进行了比较详细的规定。该条使用的术语为技术措施，并规定："技术措施，是指用于防止、限制未经权利人许可浏览、欣赏作品、表演、录音录像制品的或者通过信息网络向公众提供作品、表演、录音录像制品的有效技术、装置或者部件。"该条例还对权利管理电子信息进行了规定："权利管理电子信息，是指说明作品及其作者、表演及其表演者、录音录像制品及其制作者的信息，作品、表演、录音录像制品权利人的信息和使用条件的信息，以及表示上述信息的数字或者代码。"《信息网络传播权保护条例》中的规定表明，我国立法已经开始接受接触控制的技术保护措施。因为"浏览、欣赏作品、表演、录音录像制品"都需要接触控制技术保护措施才能实现。❷ 然而值得注意的是，该条例对技术保护措施的规定虽然较 2001 年著作权法规定更为详细、具体，但该条例对于非网络环境下的技术保护措施并无规定。因此，我国于 2007 年 6 月 9 日加入上述 WCT 以及 WPPT 两个互联网条约时，我国当时的规定实际上与国际条约是存在一定差距的。

目前，我国正在进行《著作权法》第三次大规模修订，其中技术保护措施是修订的重要内容之一。修订草案第三稿基于对各国立法经验的总结，并为了与国际条约保持一致，对技术保护措施的相关规定进行了调整。首先，将《信息网络传播权保护条例》中"技术措施"的术语修改为"技术保护措施"，将"权利管理电子信息"修改为"权利管理信息"，以实现与国际条约的同步。该草案第 68 条规定："本法所称的技术保护措施，是指权利人为防止、限制作品、表演、录音制品或者广播电视节目被复制、浏览、欣赏、运行、改变

---

❶ 李明德，管育鹰，唐广良.《著作权法》专家建议稿说明 [M]. 北京：法律出版社，2012：419.
❷ 吴伟光. 数字技术环境下的版权法 [M]. 北京：知识产权出版社，2008：171.

或者通过网络传播而采取的有效技术、装置或者部件。"同时对权利管理信息进行了规定,"本法所称的权利管理信息,是指说明作品及其作者、表演及其表演者、录音制品及其制作者的信息、广播电视节目及其广播电台电视台,作品、表演、录音制品以及广播电视节目权利人的信息和使用条件的信息,以及表示上述信息的数字或者代码。"其次,由于技术保护措施严格来说并不是著作权或者相关权,❶但又与著作权和相关权密切联系,故专门设置一章对其单独规定。

以上立法虽各有差异,但其核心含义却是基本一致的,即:技术保护措施是指著作权人为防止他人非经授权利用作品、录音录像制品或广播电视节目等信息产品,以保护权利人利益而采取的技术上有效方法、程序或装置。技术保护措施的实质是权利人采取的以保护著作权为目的的自助行为。我们还可以注意到,到目前为止,我国的立法并未像美国一样将权利控制技术保护措施与接触控制技术保护措施区别开来分别给予不同的保护,而是采取统一保护的立法模式。

第三节 对技术保护措施的限制

技术保护措施表面是著作权或相关权权利人对自我权利的保护手段,但在更深层次上是不同利益集团之间在法律制度上进行博弈的结果。美国制定DMCA的初衷是对著作权制度进行修改,使著作权法律制度更加符合文化产业的利益需求,促进著作权产业新型商业模式的发展。欧盟制定著作权指令也同样是为了促进数字网络时代著作权交易授权和付费新型商业模式的发展,从而从根本上保护数字著作权产业的商业利益。可以说,技术保护措施的制度从产生以来就对著作权人利益和社会利益之间的利益平衡产生了冲击,利益的天平偏向了著作权权利人一方。❷因此,从技术保护措施的相关制度产生以来,关于该制度的争议从来就未停止。这些争议的核心问题是技术保护措施是否具有正当性?对技术保护措施进行保护的限度为何?如何平衡权利人和使用者之间

---

❶ 正是由于技术保护措施的这种特点,有国外学者将其称之为 Para-copyright,意为 alongside copyright。See Lydia Pallas Loren, Joseph Scott Miller, Intellectual Property Law: Cases & Materials, Ver. 3.0, 2012, p.511.

❷ 王喜军. 论版权技术保护措施的扩张及其限制[J]. 出版发行研究, 2012 (9).

的利益平衡?

一、技术保护措施的正当性之辨

从著作权法产生以来,其保护对象一直是作品或表演、音像制品等与作品有关的其他法定客体。著作权法通过设定一系列的权利对保护对象进行保护,从而实现著作权法上的利益平衡。如上所述,直到数字网络技术出现以后,将技术保护措施作为著作权法上的保护对象才逐渐成为立法潮流。这样,技术保护措施的正当性就成为技术保护措施制度的一个前提性问题。

如上所述,技术保护措施可分为权利控制技术措施和接触控制技术措施。著作权法通过明确赋予权利人一系列的专有权利来保护权利人的利益,而权利控制保护措施只是法律对权利人自我权利保护手段的法律确认而已,因此权利控制技术保护措施的正当性没有问题。技术保护措施的正当性问题主要集中在接触控制技术保护措施上,这是因为接触控制措施并非直接用于保护著作权。根据著作权法的基本原理,判断一项行为是否构成著作权侵权,主要的依据是行为是否受到著作权法规定的专有权利的控制。依此判断,接触(如阅读、欣赏等行为)作品的行为本身并不侵犯任何著作权专有权利,即使该作品是盗版作品。既然接触行为本身并不侵犯著作权专有权利,那么接触控制技术保护措施的正当性问题就凸显出来。

在技术保护措施立法成为世界潮流的背景下,各国学者从不同角度出发解释接触控制技术保护措施的正当性。关于接触控制技术保护措施的正当性理论,主要有以下几种:❶

(一)复制权保护说

在数字网络背景下,对作品的欣赏、浏览等接触行为离不开计算机系统的加载和读取。在计算机对作品进行加载和读取的过程中,必然会产生对作品的临时复制。复制权保护说就是基于这一事实而认为接触控制技术保护措施通过控制对作品的接触而实现对复制权的保护。

值得注意的是,该学说的一个潜在的逻辑前提是临时复制属于著作权法意义上的复制行为,即受到复制权的保护。如果临时复制不属于著作权法意义上的复制行为,则对作品的接触行为就不会对复制权产生侵害,那么复制权保护说也就失去了合理性基础。而事实上,虽然美国、欧盟等都将临时复制定性为

---

❶ 王迁. 版权法技术保护措施的正当性 [J]. 法学研究, 2011 (4).

著作权法意义上的复制，但仍有一些国家并未明确将临时复制界定为复制行为，我国就是其中之一。本书作者认为，是否将临时复制界定为著作权法上的复制行为主要不是一个技术问题或者事实问题，而是一个价值判断和利益平衡的问题。因此通过复制权保护说来证成接触控制技术保护措施的正当性存在明显的缺陷。

（二）接触权保护说

该学说认为，接触控制技术保护措施保护的并非复制权，而是一种独立存在的权利——接触权。美国著名著作权法学者 Ginsburg 就认为，在数字技术背景下，使用者对作品的使用从过去的"获取作品有形的复制件"过渡到了"直接欣赏作品内容"。她认为，DMCA 中的"接触控制接触保护措施"条款实际上是为著作权人创设了一项新的权利——"接触权"（Access Right）。❶ 我国也有学者支持这种观点。❷ 虽然学者们在法律进行解释时认为存在一种单独的接触权，但到目前为止尚无任何国家的法律明确将接触权确认为一种单独的法律权利。因此，该学说不是以明确的法律规定为基础，而是以单纯的理论解释和推断为基础来证成接触控制技术保护措施的正当性，这样有失严谨。

（三）著作权间接保护说

该观点认为接触控制技术保护措施的正当性在于其本身是通过禁止未经权利人授权的接触作品行为而实现对著作权间接保护的手段。❸ 在该学说下，控制对作品接触的技术措施只有在能够间接保护著作权专有权不受侵犯的情况下才能构成著作权法所保护的接触控制技术保护措施。

（四）正当利益保护说

我国著作权法学者王迁认为，接触控制技术保护措施的正当性源于其所保护利益的正当性。他认为，既然著作权法的目的是通过专有权利使权利人获取收益，那么权利人当然有权设置技术措施防止他人未经其许可而接触其作品，从而保护自己基于著作权的正当利益。

本书比较倾向于著作权间接保护的观点。王迁教授在对著作权间接保护说进行批判的基础上提出正当利益保护说。在他看来，著作权间接保护理论无法

---

❶ See Ginsburg, Jane C. "Essay: From Having Copies to Experiencing Works: The Development of an Access Right in US Copyright Law" J. Copyright Soc'y USA 50 (2002-2003): 113.

❷ 熊琦. 论"接触权"——著作财产权类型化的不足与克服 [J]. 法律科学，2008（5）.

❸ See Australian Federation Against Copyright Theft, Submission to House of Representative Standing Committee on Legal and Constitutional Affairs, No. 39, p. 6.

解释大量的并不具有间接保护著作权作用的接触控制技术保护措施。例如游戏控制码、软件序列号等仅仅用来防止用户未付费即对作品进行浏览、欣赏或使用的接触保护措施。王迁教授据此认为，著作权法对这类接触控制技术保护措施进行保护的正当性，无法从著作权间接保护说得到合理解释。本书作者认为，王迁教授的这一论证尚有商榷余地。众所周知，民事权利的权能可以分为积极权能和消极权能。积极权能是指权利人为实现权利、享有利益而行使的对客体的各种支配行为。消极权能是指权利人享有的禁止他人对其权利的干涉或侵害行为。著作权也同样如此，著作权的权能不仅包括防御著作权受到侵害、干涉的权能，也包括为实现著作权利益而进行的各种积极支配行为。王迁教授显然是将著作权的积极权能排除在著作权的内容之外了。在明确了著作权的内容既包括消极权能，也包括积极权能之后，没有必要提出"正当利益保护说"来涵盖权利人通过利用作品而获取利益的行为。著作权间接保护说完全可以解释接触控制技术保护措施的正当性。而且著作权间接保护理论除为接触控制技术保护措施提供正当性基础外，同样可以为防止权利人滥用接触控制技术保护措施提供理论基础。如果接触控制技术保护措施的使用超出了保护著作权的限度，就不应当受到法律保护。

二、技术保护措施与合理使用的冲突与解决

（一）技术保护措施与著作权例外制度的冲突

技术保护措施是权利人保护自己著作权的自助手段，为了实现自己利益的最大化，权利人不仅会在其受著作权保护的作品上使用技术保护措施，也会在其不受著作权保护的作品上使用技术保护措施。如上所述技术保护措施的正当性在于其对著作权专有权利的保护，如果技术保护措施保护的不是著作权专有权利，就失去了正当性，法律就应当对其进行限制。如果作品已经进入公共领域，或者对作品的使用属于合理使用的范畴，那么技术保护措施就会与著作权法的例外制度相冲突。DMCA 是当今技术保护措施立法的典范，因此本书首先以 DMCA 为样本对技术保护措施与著作权例外的冲突进行分析。尽管著作权法上有完善的著作权例外制度，但 DMCA 却允许内容提供者利用技术保护措施涉足著作权公共领域以及合理使用。

首先，技术保护措施可能与著作权公共领域相冲突。尽管 DMCA 并不禁止对公共领域内的作品之上的技术保护措施进行破解，但是如果公共领域作品与受著作权保护的作品混合在一起，那么对技术保护措施的破解就违反了

DMCA 的规定。最典型的例子就是数据库。通常数据库中既包含受著作权保护的作品，也包含已经进入公共领域内的作品。而法律禁止对数据库技术保护措施的破解，即使这种破解只是为了使用处于公共领域内的作品。因此，内容提供商可以利用这一法律空隙，仅仅在内容中加入部分受著作权保护的作品就可以取得法律的保护，即使其提供的内容中绝大部分已经进入公共领域。❶ 在这种情形下，技术保护措施就与公共领域制度产生了直接的冲突。

其次，对于以合理使用为目的或者出于其他非侵权目的而对技术保护措施采取的破解行为，DMCA 也没有设定豁免。这样，技术保护措施就与合理使用发生了冲突。尽管 DMCA 中明确表明其不影响现有的权利、救济、著作权限制、合理使用等著作权侵权免责事由，❷ 这些事项仍然由著作权法案规制。虽然有数个法案尝试使对以合理使用或使用公共领域作品为目的的破解合法化，但这些法案最终均未实行。❸ DMCA 的这种规定对司法实践产生了重要影响。在 Universal City Studios, Inc., v. Reimerdes❹ 一案中，原告 Universal City Studios 是一家电影公司，被告 Reimerdes 是一家网站运营者。原告在其 DVD 上使用了一种名为 CSS 的技术保护措施。而被告在其网站上传了名为 DeCSS 的软件，该软件可破解 CSS 从而使受到技术保护措施保护的 DVD 可以在未安装经过授权的破解技术的设备上播放原告的作品。于是原告起诉被告。法院判决认为，被告在其网站上传 DeCSS 的行为违反了 DMCA 禁止非法交易破解接触控制技术保护措施的技术的相关规定。被告抗辩称 DeCSS 可以使用户基于合理使用的非侵权目的接触被告的作品，因此并不违反 DMCA 的规定。法院并未采纳被告这一抗辩，认为既然国会立法时已经认真考虑了合理使用问题，而最终仍然选择保护权利人的技术保护措施，即使这种技术保护措施妨碍了合理使用，那么法院应尊重国会的立法。法院还根据相似的理由驳回了被告提出的索尼案❺中确立的"实质非侵权"规则免责抗辩。法院认为，索尼案中的规则并不

---

❶ See Mazzone, Jason "Copyfraud and other abuses of intellectual property law" (2011), p. 87–88.

❷ 17 U.S.C. § 1201 (c) (1).

❸ 这些法案包括《2002 年数字媒体消费者权利法案》（the Digital Media Consumers' Rights Act of 2002）、《2003 年限制预付和净消费者期望作者利益法案》（the Benefit Authors Without Limiting Advancement or Net Consumer Expectations Act of 2003）以及《2007 年自由和创新复兴创业精神法案》（the Freedom and Innovation Revitalizing U.S. Entrepreneurship Act of 2007）。

❹ Universal City Studios, Inc., v. Reimerdes, 111 F. Supp. 2d 294 (S.D.N.Y. 2000), aff'd, Universal City Studios, Inc., v. Carley, 273 F.3d 429 (2d Cir. 2001).

❺ Sony Corp. of America v. Universal City Studios, Inc., 464 U.S. 417 (1984).

能简单地适用于 DMCA 规制之下的案件。❶

这样，DMCA 就允许权利人自己决定作品使用者是否可以对其作品进行合理使用，这完全背离了著作权法案中的合理使用规则。这就使权利人对技术保护措施的使用超出了保护著作权法赋予的专有权的范围。这给使用者对作品进行合理使用造成了巨大障碍，尤其是对教育机构合理使用作品造成了很大的问题。例如，教师为了教学目的经常需要在课堂上播放某电影作品中的一小段。但是很多电影公司在发行 DVD 时使用了技术保护措施，禁止使用者从作品中截取特定的部分。如果教师使用破解技术对 DVD 进行破解，就违反了 DMCA 关于技术保护措施的规定。DMCA 的规定同时可能影响其他的在著作权法案下构成合理使用的行为，如出于评论或批评目的而使用部分作品、再混合（Remix）❷ 等。

（二）对技术保护措施进行限制的域外立法分析

为了在保护技术保护措施的同时保证使用者使用作品的权利，美国 DMCA 规定了若干例外以保证使用者的权利。

第一，法案对权利控制技术保护措施和接触控制技术保护措施区别对待。对权利控制保护措施的破解是被允许的，而对后者的破解则是被禁止的。❸ 第二，DMCA 法案中有专门条款规定该法案不影响包括合理使用在内的著作权侵权的例外。❹ 第三，法案还规定了若干禁止破解技术保护措施的例外。这些例外主要分为两类：第一类例外是法律执行和政府活动的例外；第二类例外是仅仅针对接触保护技术保护措施的例外，包括非营利性机构例外、反向工程例外、机密研究例外、保护未成年人例外、个人隐私例外以及安全测试例外。❺ 第四，法案还确立了一种新的规则制定机制，国会图书馆有权就特定种类的作

---

❶ Reimerdes, 111 F. Supp. 2d at 323. 法院在判决中认为，DCMA 禁止提供破解技术，这从根本上改变了现有的规则。虽然具有实质性非侵权用途的设备或技术可以根据著作权法案免责，但其在 DMCA §1201 下仍然能是被禁止的。

❷ See Wikipedia, Remix. Available at: http://en.wikipedia.org/wiki/Remix.

❸ 对于接触控制技术保护措施而言，破解行为以及破解技术的交易都是被禁止的；对于权利控制技术保护措施而言，破解行为未被禁止，但破解技术的交易则是被禁止的。See U. S. Copyright Office, The Digital Millennium Copyright Act of 1998: U. S. Copyright Office Summary 3-6 (Dec. 1998), available at http://www.copyright.gov/legislation/dmca.pdf.

❹ 17 U. S. C. § 1201 (c) (1).

❺ See DMCA, § 1201 (d) - (j).

品指定为期三年的禁止破解接触控制技术保护措施的例外。❶ 这一程序作为一种安全阀机制，可以对应当豁免而未被豁免的破解行为进行识别，目的在于防止技术保护措施对合法使用造成的潜在影响。❷ 其他很多国家也采取了类似的安全阀机制。在欧盟，《版权法指令》要求成员国采取适当的措施保证权利人向使用者提供某些特定的例外。❸ 英国则建立一种使用者申诉程序。按照这一程序，作品的使用者可以向国务大臣（the Secretary of State）申诉，国务大臣随后会开展调查，确定是否存在自愿性的协议以保证使用者可以在相关豁免下对作品进行使用，如果不存在自愿性协议，则要求作品权利人向使用者提供这种豁免。❹ 第五，为了使诸如个人电脑等多目的设备（Multipurpose Device）免于承担责任，DCMA规定，对破解行为的禁止仅适用于如下设备：（1）设计或生产该设备的主要目的是破解技术保护措施；（2）除了破解功能之外，对该种设备的使用仅具有有限的经济重要性；（3）该设备被当作破解工具出售。❺ DMCA还规定了一项非强制性条款（No Mandate Provision），即技术开发者在开发产品时没有义务事先将产品设计成与特定的技术保护措施相兼容。❻

欧盟关于技术保护措施的限制有两方面值得关注。首先，《信息社会指

---

❶ See 17 U.S.C. § 1201（a）（1）（C）. 另外，国会图书馆对新的例外的制定需要经过征集公众意见、版权登记处（Register of Copyright）的建议、与电信和信息管理局（NTIA）会商等过程。

❷ 目前美国在此规则制定机制下增加的破解技术保护措施的例外情形共五种：（1）某些出于批评、评论或者教育目的而对DVD上或者通过网络服务传输的电影之上的技术保护措施进行破解的行为；（2）出于研究、开发字幕或者为了残障人士而开发描述性音频技术的目的DVD上或者通过网络服务传输的电影之上的技术保护措施进行破解的行为；（3）智能手机的越狱行为；（4）智能手机解锁行为；（5）为方便盲人、视力受损者、失聪者、听力困难者而允许使用辅助技术的以电子书格式传播的文学作品。See Copyright Office, Exemption to Prohibition on Circumvention of Copyright Protection Systems for Access Control Technologies, 65 Fed. Reg. 64556, 64574（Oct. 27, 2000）; Copyright Office, Exemption to Prohibition on Circumvention of Copyright Protection Systems for Access Control Technologies, 68 Fed. Reg. 62011, 62013-14（Oct. 31, 2003）; Copyright Office, Exemption to Prohibition on Circumvention of Copyright Protection Systems for Access Control Technologies, 71 Fed. Reg. 68472, 68473-68477（Nov. 27, 2006）; Copyright Office, Exemption to Prohibition on Circumvention of Copyright Protection Systems for Access Control Technologies, 75 Fed. Reg. 43825, 43827-43834（July 27, 2010）; Copyright Office, Exemption to Prohibition on Circumvention of Copyright Protection Systems for Access Control Technologies, 77 Fed. Reg. 65260, 65262-65271（Oct. 26, 2012）. 不过值得注意的是，美国于近未对智能手机解锁行为的豁免进行延续，这在美国引起了不小的争议。See Jon Healey, Proponents of cellphone unlocking ask the White House for help, LOS ANGELES TIMES（Feb. 18, 2013）, available at：http://www.latimes.com/business/technology/la-fi-tn-cellphone-unlocking-petition-20130218, 0, 6053343.story.

❸ See EU Copyright Directive at art. 6（4）.

❹ See U.K. Copyright Designs and Patent Act（CDPA）at § 296ZE.

❺ 17 U.S.C. § 1201（a）（2），（b）（1）.

❻ 17 U.S.C. § 1201（c）（3）.

第四章　权利保护之二：权利人技术保护措施的保护与限制

令》第6条要求行为主体在对技术保护措施进行破解时主观状态为明知或者应知。无意识的规避行为则不受指令调整。其次，欧盟规定权利人有义务向合法取得作品的访问权的使用者提供必要的手段以保证使用人受益。当使用人根据例外的情形需要对技术保护措施进行规避时，有权要求权利人提供密匙等必要手段。❶ 另外，德国还在其著作权法中要求内容提供商向消费者披露其所使用的技术保护措施的范围与特性，这有助于保护消费者的知情权。❷

然而，上述域外立法对技术保护措施的限制虽然可谓详尽，但也并非尽善尽美。例如，DMCA对于以合理使用为目的或者出于其他非侵权目的而对技术保护措施采取的破解行为并没有提供豁免，这就使著作权权利人可以通过技术保护措施僭越著作权法规定的合理使用制度。正因为此，有学者认为DMCA中的反破解规定与合理使用制度发生了冲突，其不应适用于出于合理使用目的使用著作权作品或者接触已经进入公共领域作品两种情形，并呼吁美国国会尽快修改DMCA，并明确规定，只要破解行为并未对著作权造成侵权，法律就应当允许这种破解。❸

(三) 我国相关立法的分析与建议

相比国外立法对技术保护措施的限制，我国关于技术保护措施限制的规定相对简单。

1.《信息网络传播权保护条例》对技术保护措施的限制

尽管我国2001年著作权法对技术保护措施进行了规定，但却没有对技术保护措施的限制。现有立法中对技术保护措施的限制主要是《信息网络传播权保护条例》第12条。该条规定了可以对技术保护措施进行规避的四种例外情形：课堂教学或科学研究例外、非营利目的向盲人提供作品的例外、国家机关依法执行公务例外、安全性能测试例外，但使用者不得向他人提供规避技术保护措施的技术、装置或者部件。

与其他国家相比，上述规定对技术保护措施的限制是非常有限的。首先，上述规定仅仅局限于与信息网络传播权有关的技术保护措施，而对于其他的技术保护措施的限制则没有明确法律规定。其次，该条对技术保护措施的破解仅仅规定了四种例外情形，相比之下，我国《著作权法》第22条中规定了12种

---

❶ 王迁.［荷兰］Lucie Guibault. 中欧网络版权保护比较研究［M］. 北京：法律出版社，2008：129-130.

❷ 同上，131页。

❸ See Mazzone, Jason "Copyfraud and other abuses of intellectual property law" (2011), chapter 4.

合理使用的情形,《信息网络传播权保护条例》也规定了9种针对信息网络传播权的合理使用的情形。因此,作品使用者对技术保护措施进行破解的例外情形仅仅局限在非常有限的范围内。这意味着使用者如果基于以上四种例外情形的合理使用目的而对技术保护措施进行规避可能要承担侵权责任。再次,虽然使用者可以基于以上四种例外情形对技术保护措施进行规避,但使用者不得向他人提供规避技术保护措施的技术、装置或者部件。这就意味着如果使用者需要对技术保护措施进行规避或破解,其必须自己掌握规避或破解技术,而无法向第三方寻求支持。因为第三方如果向其提供相关技术或设备,则应承担侵权责任。而事实上,绝大部分作品的使用者并非技术专家,很难自己掌握规避或破解技术,因此,上述规定实际上是架空了使用者基于合理使用目的对技术保护措施进行破解的权利。

2. 我国第三次著作权法修订草案中相关规定的分析

我国目前正在进行的著作权法第三次修改也对技术保护措施问题进行了充分的考虑。以修订草案第三稿(送审稿)❶ 为例,对技术保护措施的限制主要有两个条款。

草案第69条延续了《信息网络传播权保护条例》第5条的规定,在规定"未经许可,任何组织或者个人不得故意避开或者破坏技术保护措施,不得故意制造、进口或者向公众提供主要用于避开或者破坏技术保护措施的装置或者部件,不得故意为他人避开或者破坏技术保护措施提供技术或者服务"的同时,还规定"但是法律、行政法规另有规定的除外。"这一规定就为立法机关根据需要对技术保护措施单独立法进行限制预留了空间。草案第71条规定了可以对技术保护措施进行规避的情形。该规定与《信息网络传播权保护条例》第12条基本相同,但是增加了一项例外情形:加密研究或者计算机程序反向工程研究。值得注意的是,虽然第71条规定了可以对技术保护措施进行规避的情形,但也是有限制的,即不得向他人提供避开技术保护措施的技术或者装置。另外,根据第71条,只有在根据正常途径无法获得作品的情形下,才允许对技术保护措施进行规避,这也是对技术保护措施进行限制的反限制。

3. 对我国立法关于对技术保护措施进行限制的建议

从上述对我国相关立法的分析可见,与国外对技术保护措施的限制相对而

---

❶ 目前,国家版权局官方网站尚未见著作权法修订草案送审稿,但可见于苏州市政府网站。[EB/OL]. [2014-02-20]. http://fzhb.changshu.gov.cn/changshu_fzb/InfoDetail/? InfoID=2d32cd4c-b853-4b22-8c28-a5dcc9a2e46b&CategoryNum=004.

第四章　权利保护之二：权利人技术保护措施的保护与限制

言,我国对技术保护措施限制的相关制度非常不足。首先,我国未对权利控制技术保护措施和接触控制技术保护措施区别对待,而是给予相同的保护。这样相对国外而言,利益的天平就更加向内容提供者倾斜。其次,我国未对技术保护措施的有效性进行界定。这会导致一些太过容易或者已经过时的技术保护措施同样受到法律的保护,大大不利于作品的使用者。最后,我国目前对技术保护措施的合理使用限制范围大大小于著作权法中合理使用的范围。

鉴于我国对技术保护措施限制的相关立法的上述问题,为完善技术保护措施的限制制度,在借鉴域外立法经验的基础上,本书作者认为,我国将来的立法至少应就技术保护措施的限制进行如下完善和改进:

第一,应在立法中将权利控制技术保护措施与接触控制技术保护措施区别对待。美国DMCA将两种技术保护措施区别对待是因为著作权法中本来就有对著作权专有权利的保护和限制,著作权专有权应由著作权法中对专有权的保护和限制的有关规定规制,因此DMCA并未规定禁止对权利控制技术保护措施进行规避。而对作品的接触并不属于传统的著作权专有权利范畴,之前的法律也没有关于接触作品的相关规定,故DMCA规定禁止对接触控制技术保护措施进行规避。可见DMCA对接触技术保护措施的保护的力度大于对权利控制技术保护措施的保护。而我国对两种技术保护措施相同对待,对权利控制技术保护措施给予与解除控制技术保护措施以相同的保护,这使已经倾斜的天平更加倾向于内容提供者一方。

第二,在对两种技术保护措施进行区分的基础上,扩展对接触技术保护措施的限制。在DMCA语境下,著作权法中对著作权保护的例外与DMCA中对技术保护措施保护的例外是相互平行的,两者互不影响。换句话说,对作品的合理使用并不能作为对接触技术保护措施进行规避的抗辩理由。美国法院在一些案例中也明确作出解释:DMCA中对技术保护措施的保护例外比著作权法中的合理使用范围要小。[1] 美国法院还认为,国会有意反对为了出于合理使用或公共利益目的而对技术保护措施进行规避或者提供规避工具,如果权利人已经在其作品之上使用了技术保护措施,DMCA第1201(c)便不会再以公共利益为由为规避和提供规避工具的行为提供庇护。有学者因此认为,DMCA以及相

---

[1] See Borg-Breen, Caryn C. "Garage Door Openers, Printer Toner Cartridges, and the New Age of the Digital Millennium Copyright Act." Nw. UL Rev. 100 (2006): 885.

应的司法案例已经将著作权法中的公共利益消除殆尽。❶ 观察我国的著作权法第三次修订草案,对技术保护措施进行限制的有关规定未出美国 DMCA 立法的窠臼,对技术保护措施的保护例外远远小于著作权合理使用的范围,更是没有考虑著作权法中的法定许可限制。

第三,应在立法中明确界定技术保护措施的"有效性"。不管是美国还是欧盟都对"有效性"进行了界定。美国的界定为"在技术措施正常运行时要获得作品需要使用经著作权人授权的信息、程序或者方法。"❷ 欧盟则将"有效性"界定为:如果权利人对受保护的作品或者其他客体通过其使用的访问控制或者保护程序,例如对作品或者其他客体进行加密、干扰或者其他的改变、复制控制机制,实现保护目标时,那么技术保护措施就是有效的。❸ 无论美国还是欧盟,其对"有效性"的界定是为了限制受到保护的技术保护措施的范围。如果技术保护措施根本无法对作品提供一定程度的保护,需要完全依赖法律责任来保证,那么就可以说这一技术保护措施不具有有效性。例如,如果一种技术保护措施的破解方法成为一种常识,无法为作品提供最低程度的保护,那么这种技术保护措施就不能说具有有效性。当然,"有效性"并不要求技术保护措施坚不可摧,其只需能够提供特定水平的保护即可。❹ 我国应当引进"有效性"这一工具,将无须保护的技术保护措施排除在外。当然,在引进这一制度工具的前提下,"有效性"的标准问题则是立法标准和司法标准的问题,需要根据利益平衡进行具体的界定。

第四,我国还可以考虑借鉴美国和欧盟的经验,就技术保护措施问题建立动态的利益平衡机制。首先可以借鉴美国的做法,建立禁止对技术保护措施进行规避例外情形的动态调整机制。按照 DMCA 第 1201 条的规定,如果非侵权使用特定类别的作品的能力受到或很有可能受到不利影响的,则禁止规避接触控制技术保护措施的规则不适用于该类别的作品。不过这种例外的建立需要一定的程序:国会图书馆馆长应根据版权局长的建议(版权局长则应与商务部电信和信息助理部长进行会商,并报告助理部长关于建议的观点以及评论),按照特定的标准对技术保护措施例外情形进行调整。根据 DMCA1201 条规定,

---

❶ 吴伟光. 著作权法研究——国际条约、中国立法与司法实践 [M]. 北京:清华大学出版社,2013:493.

❷ 美国版权法 [M]. 杜颖,张启晨,译. 北京:知识产权出版社,2013:206.

❸ 王迁. [荷兰] Lucie Guibault. 中欧网络版权保护比较研究 [M]. 北京:法律出版社,2008:172.

❹ 吴伟光. 著作权法研究——国际条约、中国立法与司法实践 [M]. 北京:清华大学出版社,2013:475.

这些标准包括：(1) 获得著作权作品使用的可能性；(2) 出于非营利的存档、保存以及教育目的获取作品使用的可能性；(3) 禁止对技术保护措施进行规避后，对批评、评论、新闻报道、教学、学术研究的影响；(4) 规避技术保护措施对著作权作品市场或价值的影响；(5) 国会图书馆馆长认为适当的其他事项。❶ 其次，可以考虑建立使用者为合理使用技术保护措施保护作品向权利人请求移除技术保护措施的机制。为了消除 DMCA 对著作权法上的利益平衡造成的破坏产生的负面作品，还有学者提出了"反通知和移除"程序，以缓解 DMCA 第 1201 条（a）与 1201 条（c）两款规定之间的冲突。在这一程序下，作品的使用者要对作品进行合理使用或其他合法使用之前，可以向权利人发出通知，要求其暂时消除其作品之上设置的技术保护措施。权利人必须在特定期间内对使用者的请求进行回应，要么允许，要么拒绝。如果权利人拒绝使用人的请求，则使用人可以向司法机关提出诉讼，要求权利人消除技术保护措施。❷ 在数字网络技术的发展日新月异的背景下，上述动态调整机制对于实现著作权法的利益平衡目标至关重要。

三、技术保护措施与反不正当竞争的冲突与协调

在 DMCA 通过后，一些企业很快就发现他们可以利用这一法案限制其他竞争对手的竞争。这样，对技术保护措施的保护与反不正当竞争之间又发生了一定的冲突。本部分主要通过 Chamberlain 案❸分析技术保护措施与反不正当竞争之间发生的冲突以及如何处理这种冲突。

原告 Chamberlain 公司开发了一种名称为 Security+的车库开门器（Garage Door Opener）。该开门器内置"滚动密码"计算机程序，该程序可以不断改变开门所需要的遥控器信号，从而增强安全性。被告 Skylink 是原告的竞争者，该公司生产并销售一种通用遥控器，该遥控器虽然没有内置"滚动密码"，但其可以与原告生产的 Security 车库开门系统匹配使用。原告希望自己能够成为市场上独家销售其生产的车库门的开门器的厂商，因此对被告提出了诉讼。原告的起诉理由是：根据 DMCA 被告生产的遥控器是一种可以进入开门器中受保护的软件的一种规避设备。法院判决认为根据 DMCA 被告不应承担责任。

---

❶ 美国版权法 [M]. 杜颖, 张启晨, 译. 北京：知识产权出版社, 2013：204-205.

❷ See Reichman, Jerome H., Graeme B. Dinwoodie, and Pamela Samuelson, "Reverse Notice and Takedown Regime to Enable Pubic Interest Uses of Technically Protected Copyrighted Works", Berkeley Tech. LJ 22 (2007).

❸ Chamberlain Group, Inc., v. Skylink Technologies, Inc., 381 F. 3d 1178 (Fed. Cir. 2004).

法院的判决中论述到：DCMA 中的"规避"（Circumvention）是指未经著作权人的授权而进入。DMCA 并未创造任何新的知识产权，著作权人无权禁止一种著作权法上允许的接触（Access）。[1] DMCA 只禁止与著作权法案向著作权人提供的保护有关的接触。既然著作权人并不享有一种禁止接触的权利，那么被告的接触行为就根本算不上未经授权。基于本案的事实，虽然著作权法禁止未经授权对车库开门器软件的复制，但并未禁止拥有车库门的消费者接触软件。因此，销售通用开门器并未违反 DMCA。另外，美国法院还通过 Lexmark、Storage Tech 等其他相关案件的审判，在处理技术保护措施与反不正当竞争问题的关系上做出了与 Chamberlain 案相一致的判决。[2] 这样，美国法院通过 Chamberlain 等案件确立了这样的规则：法院不保护权利人利用对技术保护措施的保护来实现与著作权本身无关的排除竞争的行为。

但值得注意的是，Chamberlain 案的判决也有一定的局限性：其并未对为合理使用而规避技术保护措施的行为是否违反 DMCA 这一问题进行回答。虽然法院认为，如果禁止规避与保护著作权无关的接触控制技术保护措施，就会导致权利人利用技术保护措施废除掉著作权法上的合理使用原则，[3] 然而法院却最终未明确回答合理使用是否能对抗基于 DMCA 的技术保护措施。其实，法院对这一问题的态度在其判决中已经非常明显。法院之所以未捅破那层薄薄的窗户纸，最可能的理由是他们不想轻易对国会的立法权进行僭越。不过，这并不排除法院在将来的案件中对这一问题进行明确回答的可能。

总结美国法院对上述几个案件的审理，我们可以初步得出以下两点结论：

第一，DMCA 只对与保护著作权和相关权利有关的技术保护措施进行保护。如果权利人的技术保护措施与著作权的保护没有关系，那么权利人则无权依据 DMCA 请求禁止使用人对技术保护措施的规避。因此，权利人利用技术保护措施实现与著作权本身无关的排除竞争的行为不受 DMCA 的保护。

第二，对于技术保护措施的例外和著作权合理使用的例外，美国立法机关虽然采取的是两条平行线的做法（即技术保护措施的例外不影响著作权的例

---

[1] Chamberlain Group, Inc., 381 F. 3d at 1202.

[2] See Lexmark International, Inc. v. Static Control Components, Inc, 387 F. 3d 522, 549（6th Cir. 2004）；Storage Technology Corp. v. Custom Hardware Eng'g & Consulting, Inc., 421 F. 3d 1307（Fed. Cir. 2005）. 在这两个案件中，法院驳回了两个案件原告（一个为可交互操作的打印机墨盒生产商，一个为自动磁带盒图书馆的生产商）的诉讼请求。关于这两个案件的具体介绍和分析，见吴伟光. 著作权法研究——国际条约、中国立法与司法实践 [M]. 清华大学出版社，2013：495-500.

[3] Chamberlain Group, Inc., 381 F. 3d, p. 1202.

第四章 权利保护之二：权利人技术保护措施的保护与限制

外，著作权的例外也不影响技术保护措施的例外）。但事实上这两条线是不可能不相互影响的，❶ 而法院在司法实践中也已经认识到了这种立法上的问题。尽管到目前为止法院并未明确指出立法是错误的，但对 DMCA 对技术保护措施的过分保护进行司法纠正似乎是一种趋势。

我国关于技术保护措施的立法与司法也体现了对技术保护措施的反不正当竞争限制。我国《著作权法》（2001）第 47 条第（6）项规定"未经著作权人或者与著作权有关的权利人许可，故意避开或者破坏权利人为其作品、录音录像制品等采取的保护著作权或者与著作权有关的权利的技术措施的"，该项规定对技术措施进行了限定，即"保护著作权或者与著作权有关的权利的技术措施"。因此，如果权利人采取技术保护措施的目的不是保护著作权或者与著作权有关的权利，则无法受到该规定的保护。另外，《信息网络传播权条例》第 4 条也对采取技术措施的目的进行了限制，即"为了保护信息网络传播权"。

与上述立法一致，我国法院在司法实践中也区分了以保护著作权为目的的技术保护措施和非以保护著作权为目的的技术保护措施。在最高人民法院指导案例 48 号北京精雕科技有限公司与上海奈凯电子科技有限公司侵害计算机软件著作权纠纷一案中，❷ 计算机软件著作权人为实现软件与机器的捆绑销售，将软件运行的输出数据设定为特定文件格式，以限制其他竞争者的机器读取以该特定文件格式保存的数据，从而将其在软件上的竞争优势扩展到机器。上海市高级人民法院认为上诉人采取的技术措施不属于《计算机软件保护条例》所规定的著作权人为保护其软件著作权而采取的技术措施，并认为上诉人精雕公司对 JDPaint 输出文件采用 Eng 格式，旨在限定 JDPaint 软件只能在"精雕 CNC 雕刻系统"中使用，其根本目的和真实意图在于建立和巩固上诉人 JDPaint 软件与其雕刻机床之间的捆绑关系。这种行为不属于为保护软件著作权而采取的技术保护措施。如果将对软件著作权的保护扩展到与软件捆绑在一起的产品上，必然超出我国著作权法对计算机软件著作权的保护范围。对恶意规避技术措施的法律限制旨在保护软件著作权，而不能作为滥用该权利者垄断市场和损害社会公共利益的工具。因此，法院最终认定该技术措施不属于著作权法所规定的著作权人为保护其软件著作权而采取的技术保护措施，被上诉人研发软件读取其设定的特定文件格式，不构成侵害计算机软件著作权。

---

❶ 吴伟光. 数字技术环境下的版权法——危机与对策 [M]. 北京：知识产权出版社，2008：209.
❷ （2006）沪高民三（知）终字第 110 号.

北京市高级人民法院在总结司法实践经验的基础上也对技术保护措施进行了相应规定，其在《北京市高级人民法院审理涉及网络环境下著作权纠纷案件若干问题的指导意见（一）（试行）》[1]中第32条规定：

"《信息网络传播权保护条例》第26条规定的技术措施是指为保护权利人在著作权法上的正当利益而采取的控制浏览、欣赏或者控制使用作品、表演、录音录像制品的技术措施。

下列情形中的技术措施不应认定为应受著作权法保护的技术措施。

（1）用于实现作品、表演、录音录像制品与产品或者服务的捆绑销售的；

（2）用于实现作品、表演、录音录像制品价格区域划分的；

（3）用于破坏未经许可使用作品、表演、录音录像制品的用户的计算机系统的；

（4）其他妨害公共利益保护、与权利人在著作权法上的正当利益无关的技术措施。"

对技术保护措施的保护和限制问题是著作权法如何适应数字网络技术的一个重要议题。新技术的发展使得对作品的大规模网上侵权成为可能，这使对权利人的技术保护措施进行保护成为必要。同时，权利人在使用技术保护措施时为了自己利益的最大化往往突破合理使用等著作权例外的边界，影响了使用人合法使用作品的正当利益，或者利用技术保护措施进行不正当竞争。因此又必须对技术保护措施进行限制。在对技术保护措施进行立法规制时必须遵循利益平衡的基本原则，平衡权利人、使用者以及其他利益相关者的利益。我国的技术保护措施立法与国外相比还显得相对不发达，我国有必要借鉴美国、欧盟的先进经验，同时避免其不足，构建一套既能够保护权利人的权利，又能保证使用者合理使用作品的正当利益的规则体系。

---

[1] 京高法发［2010］166号。

第五章　权利实现：数字网络环境下的著作权市场机制

　　法律并非万能，如果一个问题能在法律之外找到解决之道，那么向国家寻求法律救济通常只是次优选择，这在著作权领域尤其如此。著作权人面临的一个重要的问题就是消费者不对其提供的作品进行付费。著作权人通常会将其归结为著作权侵权和救济的法律问题。从本质上讲，与其说这是一个法律问题，不如说是一个市场问题。如果著作权人无法适应新技术引起的市场的变化，无法满足消费者的需要，那么他就无法获得市场的回报。一项关于P2P分享的研究表明，当消费者能够通过合法途径以公平合理的价格买到服务时，未经授权的复制量就会下降；反之，未经授权的复制量就会上升。[1] 因此，著作权市场未能很好地满足消费者的需求是大规模网上侵权长期得不到有效治理的重要因素之一。可以说，如果没有一个能够向消费者提供优质方便服务的有效著作权市场机制，再严厉的著作权执法、再精密的技术保护措施在大规模网上著作权侵权面前都只是杯水车薪、隔靴搔痒。

第一节　数字网络环境要求著作权授权模式转型

　　著作权授权不仅是著作权人实现其权利价值的基本途径，也是使用人获取作品的主要途径。[2] 在数字网络技术出现之前，著作权需要物化于一定载体之上，因此传统技术条件下著作权授权与一般有体物的权利变动并无本质区别。[3] 数字网络技术的出现对社会产生了结构性的变革作用，传统的著作权授权模式在新技术的冲击下开始显得力不从心。因此，如何实现著作权授权模式在数字网络环境中的转型，成为一个不可回避的课题。

一、数字网络技术改变传统著作权市场生态

　　数字网络技术的发展对著作权市场产生了深刻的影响。一方面，大规模地

---

[1] See Patry, William. How to fix copyright. Oxford University Press, 2012, p. 142.
[2] 使用人还可以利用著作权法中的著作权例外对作品进行使用。
[3] 熊琦. 著作权激励机制的法律构造 [M]. 1版. 中国人民大学出版社，2011：141-143.

对作品的非法复制和传播严重影响了创作者从市场上获取回报。另一方面,数字网络环境也使作品生产和发行的边际成本大大下降。新技术改变了传统著作权市场中的供应链和价值链,从而使新的著作权授权商业模式逐渐替代了传统模式。以下以音乐产业为例,分析数字网络技术对传统著作权市场的冲击。❶

数字网络技术之前,传统的音乐产业供应链很大程度上被大型唱片公司控制。人才发现、唱片制作、音乐推广以及发行这些环节都被这些唱片公司垄断。唱片公司之所以能够承担起发掘人才的功能是因为它们有足够的经济能力将星探们分派到全国各地的表演场所进行人才挖掘。当艺术家签约唱片公司之后,唱片公司就会在进行完著作权交割后帮助他们制作专辑,并承担包括录音棚费用、伴奏人员、后期混音设备以及唱片灌制等的全部成本。而一般艺术家根本没有支付这些高昂成本的经济能力。当音乐制作完成后,唱片公司便开始制作音乐产品。音乐产品的物质载体一般包括塑胶唱片、磁带、CD等。然后音乐产品会通过实体唱片商店、网上唱片商店等发行渠道进行发行。另外,唱片公司还会通过广播、音乐电视、音乐会、品牌搭售(Branding Tie-ins)、宣传单以及店面布局(Store Positioning)等方式对音乐产品进行宣传促销。

这样,唱片公司控制了除产品零售环节之外音乐产业的整个价值链,并获取了价值链中的大部分利益。有研究表明,一张未打折的售价18美元的CD,零售商会取得其中的7美元,而唱片公司则会得到剩余的11美元。从理论上讲,唱片的艺术家会从唱片公司获得的11美元中得到12%的收益。但在绝大多数情况下艺术家会一无所得,因为唱片公司会将其为艺术家提前支付的音乐录制费用、分摊的营销费用以及其他各种费用从这11美元中扣除。❷

数字网络技术的出现,大大改变了音乐产业的市场生态。传统唱片公司的

---

❶ 关于数字网络技术对音乐著作权产业以及电影产业、图书出版产业市场生态的影响,See Cameron, Lisa and Bazelon, Coleman. "The impact of digitization on business models in copyright-driven industries: A review of the economic issues". The Brattle Group, Inc., 2013. Available at: http://www.brattle.com/system/publications/pdfs/000/004/323/original/The_ Impact_ of_ Digitization_ on_ Business_ Models_ in_ Copyright-Driven_ Industries_ Cameron_ Bazelon_ Feb_ 26_ 2013.pdf? 1378772099. (Dec. 12 2013); See also Merrill, Stephen A., and William J. Raduchel, eds. "Copyright in the Digital Era: Building Evidence for Policy". National Academies Press, 2013, p. 21-34. Available at: http://www.nap.edu/download.php? record_ id=14686. (Jan. 11 2014). 关于数字网络环境下音乐产业价值链的分析另可见佟雪娜. 数字音乐的产业价值链研究[M]. 北京:清华大学出版社, 2012: 55-76.

❷ Slater, Derek, Meg Smith, Derek Bambauer, Urs Gasser, & John Palfrey "Content and Control: Assessing the Impact of Policy Choices on Potential Online Business Models in the Music and Film Industries," Berkman Center for Internet and Society at Harvard Law School January 7, 2005, at p. AI-4. Available at: http://cyber.law.harvard.edu/media/files/content_ control.pdf. (Feb 20 2014).

第五章 权利实现：数字网络环境下的著作权市场机制 ◎

人才发现、音乐录制以及音乐发行三大功能被日渐瓦解。首先，数字音乐制作和网上发行成本的大大降低，大大减小了新艺术家被发现的难度。唱片公司的发现人才功能很大程度上已被替代。一些专门的艺术家发现网站（如Fresh-Scouts、RecordScout）不断涌现，它们帮助音乐听众发现自己喜欢的艺术家。其次，随着数字技术的发展，高品质音乐录制和后期制作设备的成本不断降低。这一方面是因为音乐制作设备的相对成本以摩尔定律的速度不断降低，另一方面是音乐编辑软件可以轻易地对音乐进行编辑。如今普通的个人电脑制作的音乐就可以与以前专业录影棚制作的音乐的质量相媲美。随着如苹果公司的Garage Band等音乐制作软件的出现，任何个人都可以自己录制音乐并上传到YouTube、Facebook等网络空间。❶ 再次，数字网络技术对音乐产业价值链最深刻的改变在于其大大降低了音乐生产和发行的成本。唱片公司以及与其有密切联系的批发商和零售商在很大程度上失去对音乐发行的控制权。

数字网络技术一方面通过对传统人才发现机制的改变，改变了大型唱片公司垄断人才发现的局面，使艺术家具有更大的独立性和与唱片公司的谈判能力；另一方面通过对音乐产品制作和发行机制的影响改变了音乐产业的商业模式，各种新兴的商业模式应运而生。❷

为简明起见，可用下图总结数字网络技术对传统音乐产业市场生态的影响和改变：

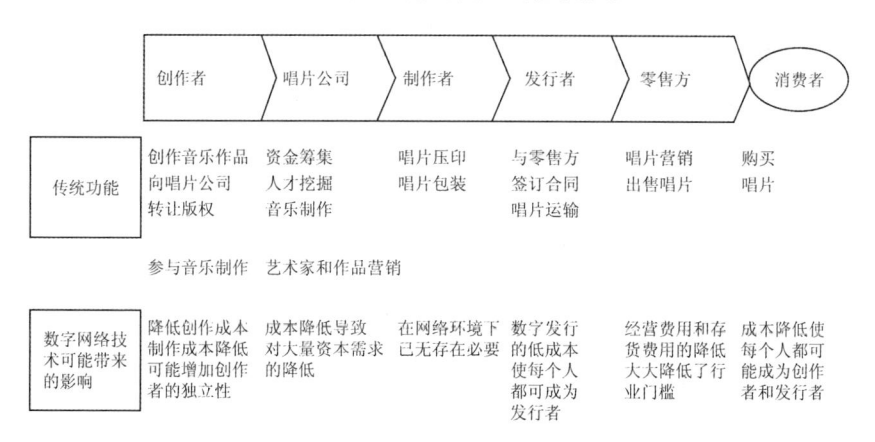

数字技术对传统音乐产业价值链的影响

	创作者	唱片公司	制作者	发行者	零售方	消费者
传统功能	创作音乐作品 向唱片公司 转让版权	资金筹集 人才挖掘 音乐制作	唱片压印 唱片包装	与零售方 签订合同 唱片运输	唱片营销 出售唱片	购买 唱片
	参与音乐制作	艺术家和作品营销				
数字网络技术可能带来的影响	降低创作成本 制作成本降低 可能增加创作者的独立性	成本降低导致对大量资本需求的降低	在网络环境下已无存在必要	数字发行的低成本使每个人都可成为发行者	经营费用和存货费用的降低大大降低了行业门槛	成本降低使每个人都可能成为创作者和发行者

---

❶ See the introduction of Garage Band at Apple Inc. website. Available at：http：//www.apple.com/ilife/garageband/.

❷ 关于数字网络环境下出现的音乐产业新兴商业模式可参见本文"使用者行为的失范与规制"一章中"开放型著作权保护机制的实践"部分的相关内容。

二、著作权权利的碎片化要求建立著作权授权信息系统

虽然在数字网络技术的影响下出现了各种新兴的商业模式，但是这些商业模式不可避免地面临的一个问题就是著作权的授权问题。这些商业模式在向网络用户提供服务之前都必须取得权利人的授权。然而，著作权本身的复杂性却给授权带来了很大的困难。著作权是由一系列权利组成的权利束❶，而每项子权利又可以被几个作者共同所有。有学者将著作权的这种特征形象地称为著作权的"碎片化"。❷ 另外权利还可能被继承，还可能被跨境、跨语种地转让，这些使著作权的授权问题变得更为复杂。著作权的碎片化意味着在很多情况下使用者需要获得多个授权才能有权对作品进行使用。

以广播电台对音乐的使用为例，如果广播电台希望将一首音乐拷贝到电脑上，然后将音乐进行播放，那么它从权利人处取得两项授权：复制权和向公众传播权。而一首歌曲中包括三个权利客体：音乐作品（The Music Work）、录音（The Sound Recording）以及表演（Performance）。因此，电台又必须就复制权与向公众传播权向三个权利客体的权利人取得授权。广播电台对作品的使用是海量的，而这些作品的权利却分散在不同权利主体手中。如果某些权利被多个权利人共同持有，电台甚至需要多达二十个授权才能实现对作品的使用。❸

上述取得授权的复杂性引发的另一个问题就是使用人如何与权利人取得联系。这样，如果没有一种更好的解决办法，使用人将需要为获取作品授权付出巨大的成本，有时授权的取得甚至根本就不可能实现。解决上述问题，使用者一方面需要能够获取作品权利的完整信息，另一方面需要能够获得一项统一授权，从而可以获得上述权利束中的多项子权利。这不仅对广播电台这种大量使

---

❶ 著作权法根据对作品使用的种类和性质的不同将著作权权利划分为很多种不同的权利。虽然不同的国家的著作权法授予权利人的具体权利有所不同，但这些权利基本上包括复制权、发行权、公开传播权以及演绎权等。该权利分类采用王迁教授的归纳。王迁．知识产权法教程［M］．3版．北京：中国人民大学出版社，2011：116-156．

❷ See Gervais, Daniel J., ed. Collective management of copyright and related rights. Kluwer Law International, 2010, p. 10. 值得提出的是，Gervais教授还分析了著作权权利碎片化的根源。他认为，这种碎片性源于著作权制度自产生起三百年来为了适应技术的发展而对著作权权利体系叠屋架床，就作品的新使用方式不断赋予权利人新权利的结果。

❸ See Gervais, Daniel J., ed. Collective management of copyright and related rights. Kluwer Law International, 2010, p. 3-4. 值得注意的是，此处关于广播电台使用作品的例子是以美国的法律规定为基础进行分析的。

用作品的使用者是必要的，对其他诸如餐厅、超市、咖啡厅等作品使用者，以及对网络音乐服务而言都是必要的。保证作品权利信息的可获得性有赖于一个完整高效的著作权信息系统的构建，而使用者以较低的成本获取大量作品的授权则需要一个运行良好的著作权集体管理体系。

三、著作权地域性与网络全球性的冲突需要建立跨境授权机制

除了上述权利的碎片化给著作权授权带来的困难之外，著作权制度的地域性与数字网络的跨国性之间的冲突是对著作权市场的又一挑战。

与其他知识产权一样，著作权是一种具有地域性的排他权，其效力范围通常只局限于一国之内。因此著作权的行使、保护通常也是以一国的法律为基础，国家的法律效力基本上止于一国的地理边界。❶ 与此相反的是，互联网是一个全球化的网络，它不受任何地域限制。这样，著作权的地域性与互联网的全球性之间就存在一种冲突。这种冲突至少表现在两个方面：第一，在网络环境中，权利人很难控制作品的网络传播。即使权利人本国著作权法仅将作品授权给国内使用者，但该国之外的使用者同样也可以通过互联网获取该作品。这样，以往通过海关控制作品跨国流通的做法在网络环境中已无法发挥作用。就著作权保护而言，一方面著作权的保护执法主要是依靠某个特定国家的法律进行的，另一方面网络中的著作权的非法复制、传播等侵权行为却是全球性的，以地理边境为基础的边境措施也将失去作用，著作权的保护就会遇到很大困难。第二，由于互联网的跨国性，著作权权利人在一国实施的著作权政策的后果会超出该国的范围而具有跨国性。例如，根据一国法律，对某种类型作品的使用属于合理使用或者法定许可的范畴，而虽然其他国家的法律可能不同，但在网络环境中其他国家的使用者也同样可以搭便车使用该作品。❷

解决著作权地域性与网络全球性之间的冲突，最明显的办法就是统一各国的著作权法或者建立一个统一的著作权体制。但是，由于著作权制度本身的复杂性以及各国利益的冲突，实现这一构想非常困难，至少在可预见的将来尚不现实。虽然从法律制度建设的角度解决著作权地域性和互联网全球性之间的冲突存在困难，但很多国家已经认识到，通过市场力量，构建一个高效的跨境网

---

❶ 尽管《伯尔尼公约》中已经规定了国民待遇原则，但这仍然无法改变著作权制度的地域性，国际公约只是在著作权制度的地域性上增添了一些国际元素而已。See J. Axhamn (Ed.), Copyright in a borderless online environment. Stockholm: Norstedts Juridik. (2012), p. 23.

❷ 吴伟光．著作权法研究——国际条约、中国立法与司法实践 [M]．北京：清华大学出版社，2013：641-642.

上授权才是上述问题的解决之道。❶ 建立一个有效的跨境网上授权机制，一方面需要一个完整的著作权信息系统，另一方面需要有完善的著作权集体管理制度。

四、数字网络时代著作权授权的线上迁移

与传统的人工谈判方式相比，网络著作权授权更加具有效率，而且不受工作时间的限制。尤其对于单笔交易金额较小的授权而言，需要较大成本的传统谈判方式根本不现实，自动网络授权就显得尤为必要。尽管目前网络授权方式尚未得到充分发展，但目前在一些领域已经有了相关实践。

以美国音乐产业为例，目前至少在以下领域内可以实现网络著作权授权：在机械权（Mechanical Right）领域，❷ 独立艺术家可以在网上通过一站式服务取得机械权授权。只要艺术家在网上提交其所使用的音乐的信息以及其使用的方式，就可以取得授权。❸ 在公开表演权领域，ASCAP 以及 BMI 等集体管理组织均可以实现在线授权，并且可以支持手机客户端。❹ 一些网站还可提供同步权在线授权（Synchronization Licensing）服务。❺ 一些唱片公司也就他们自己的唱片提供全部或部分权利的在线授权。❻

---

❶ 目前，欧盟已经在致力于通过建立统一著作权集体管理制度构建跨境网络授权机制。European Commission, Proposal for a Directive of the European Parliament and of the Council on the collective management of copyright and related rights and multi-territorial licensing of rights in musical works for online uses in the internal market, COM (2012) 372 final arts. 21-33 (July 11, 2012). Available at: http://ec.europa.eu/internal_market/copyright/docs/management/com-2012-3722_en.pdf. (Nov. 11 2013). 该指令于 2014 年 2 月 4 日被欧洲议会正式通过。See IP Watch, EU Parliament Passes Directive On Collective Rights Management, Pan-EU Licences. Avaible at: http://www.ip-watch.org/2014/02/04/eu-parliament-passes-directive-on-collective-rights-management-pan-eu-licences/. (Feb 20, 2014).

❷ See 17 U.S.C. §§106 (1) and (3). 在美国，这种权利属于强制许可的范围，任何支付法定的许可费使用者都可以取得这种许可。

❸ 这种一站式服务的典型例子有 Limelight 以及 HFA Songfile。Limelight: https://www.songclearance.com/about/；HFA Songfile: http://www.harryfox.com/public/songfile.jsp。

❹ 关于 ASCAP 网址及手机客户端授权，参见 http://www.ascap.com/licensing/types/web-mobile.aspx；关于 BMI 的在线授权服务参见 https://naxoasp01.bmi.org/licensing/nmwebsite.jsf。

❺ 同步权控制的是对视听作品音轨中歌曲的使用，即声音与运动图像的同步。同步使用必须就录音和曲作取得双重授权。提供同步权线上授权的服务包括 Sir Groovy，GreenLight Music Licensing，Rumblefish Music Licensing Store 等。关于 Sir Groovy 参见：http://www.musiclicensingstore.com/；关于 GreenLight Music Licensing 参见 http://www.greenlightmusic.com/music-licensing/education/how-it-works；关于 Rumblefish Music Licensing Store 参见 http://www.musiclicensingstore.com。

❻ 此类的服务如 Magnatune 和 Beggars Group Licensing Requests。关于 Magnatune 参见：http://magnatune.com/info/licensing；Beggars Group Licensing Requests 参见 http://licensing.beggars.com/。

第五章　权利实现：数字网络环境下的著作权市场机制

在音乐领域之外，对文字作品、图片作品的在线授权服务在国外也已广泛存在。例如，美国的著作权清算中心（Copyright Clearance Center，CCC）可以就文字作品提供复杂的授权工具。该中心不仅可以提供一揽子授权，还可以就每次使用提供单次授权；不仅可以提供在美国出版的作品的授权，还可以提供在其他很多国家出版的作品的授权。[1] 再如，可以支持用户上传图片的商业服务 Flickr 也对其图片提供在线授权服务。[2]

基于上述分析，为适应数字网络技术的发展，著作权授权模式必须实现网络化、跨地域的转型，并建设一个完善的集体管理机制。

第二节　网络著作权授权信息系统的基本框架

实现著作权授权的网络化和跨地域的转型，首先应该保证使用者能够以较低的成本获取权利人的信息和便捷的授权渠道，这一目标的实现需要完整高效的著作权信息系统来保证。

一、网络著作权信息系统的国际实践

虽然根据《伯尔尼公约》第 5 条的规定，国家立法不应为著作权的享有和行使设置任何手续，即权利人无须进行权利登记就可享有著作权。但是，著作权登记无论对于著作权交易还是著作权保护都非常重要。它不仅可以向公众提供作品著作权的基本信息，而且可向权利人提供其享有著作权的表面证据。[3] 此外，按照一些国家的规定，著作权登记是取得法定损害赔偿的前提条件。[4] 本部分着重介绍美国建立和完善著作权信息系统的经验。

美国的著作权登记不仅要登记权利的归属，还登记权利的转让情况，以及转让合同等相关信息。[5] 信息查询者不仅可以到档案馆查询权利登记的纸质版

---

[1] See http：//www.copyright.com/content/cc3/en.html；see also Copyright Clearance Center, Pay-Per-Use Services, available at：http：//www.copyright.com/content/dam/cc3/marketing/documents/pdfs/Search-Instructions-PPU.pdf.

[2] See Flickr, http：//www.gettyimages.com/creative/frontdoor/flickrphotos？isource=usa_ nav_ images_ whatsnew_ flickr.

[3] 17 U.S.C. § 410 (c).

[4] 17 U.S.C. § 408-412.

[5] 17 U.S.C. § 205；U.S. Copyright Office, Circular 12：Recordation of Transfers and Other Documents, available at http：//www.copyright.gov/circs/circ12.pdf.

· 113 ·

本，还可以通过网络查询1978年以后的登记信息。到2011年，有80%的著作权登记是通过数字形式提交，未采用数字化申请的登记信息也可以在网络上查询。[1] 而对于1978年之前的登记则以4500万张纸质卡片和缩微胶片的形式保存。这些记录既可以在著作权局查询，也可以在很多图书馆以及网络检索中心查询。著作权局还可以提供付费出具书面著作权登记报告的服务。[2] 可见，美国在著作权登记方面已经实现了一定程度的电子化和网络化。但是，就为著作权授权提供信息这一功能而言，美国的著作权登记尚存在如下问题：（1）由于1988年之后著作权登记采取自愿形式，因此目前的著作权登记信息无法覆盖全部的著作权作品；（2）部分的登记信息仍然无法通过网络查询；（3）只有著作权登记时的著作权相关信息，而无法查询后续交易等信息。

鉴于著作权信息系统的重要性以及数字网络技术给著作权登记带来的影响，美国正在致力于改进目前的著作权登记系统。首先，考虑改进在线著作权登记和信息记录系统，增加公共数据信息的准确性和易搜索性。这些考虑包括：如何为登记申请人设计一种网络操作界面、采用何种措施保证数据的安全、应当公开的信息的范围、应当提取那些元数据（Metadata）等。[3] 其次，鉴于数字网络环境下海量网页、博客中的内容的著作权登记问题，考虑如何设计一种简单可行的登记制度。目前，美国版权局正在考虑一种针对网页、博客内容著作权的集合著作权登记机制，即允许用一个单一的著作权登记覆盖一定期限内产生的所有内容的著作权。[4] 再次，将以往关于著作权转让、授权以及其他与权属有关的记录进行数字化，并致力于将所有著作权登记信息数据化、网络化。[5]

从美国著作权信息系统的建设和完善的经验来看，在数字网络背景下，将著作权登记信息进行数字化、在线化，并增强登记信息查询的用户友好性，是新技术背景下促进著作权授权的需要。另外，针对网络环境下网页、博客等网

---

[1] U. S. Copyright Office, Priorities and Special Projects of the United States Copyright Office, p. 3. Available at：http://www.copyright.gov/docs/priorities.pdf.

[2] The U. S. Department of Commerce Internet Policy Task Force Report, Copyright policy, Creativity, and Innovation in the Digital Economy (July 2013), p. 90. Available at：http://www.uspto.gov/news/publications/copyrightgreenpaper.pdf.

[3] See U. S. Copyright Office, Priorities and Special Projects of the United States Copyright Office, p. 13. Available at：http://www.copyright.gov/docs/priorities.pdf.

[4] Id, p. 11.

[5] See Mike Burke, Copyright digitization：Moving right along！(Mar 22, 2013). Available at：http://blogs.loc.gov/copyrightdigitization/2013/03/copyright-digitization-moving-right-along/.

络空间中的内容，单独设计合理、高效的著作权登记机制，也是值得考虑的现实问题。

在美国，除了上述公共著作权登记系统外还有很多私人登记系统。这些系统主要由著作权人会员组织后者其他机构运营。首先，集体管理组织掌握着大量的著作权信息。由于集体管理组织需要承担着联结权利人和使用者的作用，还要征收、分配版税，因此准确而且保持最新的权利信息就显得尤为重要。如在音乐领域，三大集体管理组织 ASCAP，BMI 以及 SESAC 所有拥有的数据库可以覆盖其所有曲库中所有作品的权利信息，而且这些信息都可以在线查询。❶ 另外，Sound Exchange，Copyright Clearance Center 等组织也都有自己相关领域的著作权信息数据库。

世界上其他国家或地区有的也已经拥有或者开始建立著作权登记系统。然而，世界知识产权组织对其成员国的调查和统计表明，从全球角度来看，著作权信息系统的建设和发展并不乐观。在被统计国家中，只有46%拥有权利信息检索系统，只有16%的国家可以提供网上检索服务。❷ 而且，各个国家对于可以登记的作品的种类以及登记信息的内容也都不尽一致。更大的问题还在于，在拥有著作权信息系统的国家中，大部分都未实现将其数据库与其他官方数据库或私有机构数据库进行互联。❸

二、著作权信息系统的跨境整合

正如上所述，现有的不同作品领域、不同国家之间的著作权信息系统之间是相互孤立的。而在数字网络环境下，一方面很多作品的创作需要使用多种类型的作品才能实现，另一方面著作权的交易很多情形下是跨国界的。因此，如果著作权信息系统之间无法进行互联、整合，根本无法满足网络环境下的在线跨领域、跨国界著作权授权的要求，其充其量只能算是一个个数据孤岛。使不同的著作权信息系统之间相互连接，实现数据和功能的整合，是建立网络著作

---

❶ ASCAP 的数据库网址：https://www.ascap.com/Home/ace-title-search/.index.aspx；BMI 数据库网址 http://repertoire.bmi.com/.startpage.asp；SESAC 的曲库网址：http://www.sesac.com/Repertory/Terms.aspx.

❷ WIPO, Summary of the Responses to the Questionnaire for Survey on Copyright Registration and Deposit Systems, Annex A. 4, p. 2-3. Available at：http://www.wipo.int/export/sites/www/copyright/en/registration/pdf/a4_charts.pdf.

❸ WIPO, Summary of the Responses to the Questionnaire for Survey on Copyright Registration and Deposit Systems. Available at：http://www.wipo.int/export/sites/www/copyright/en/registration/pdf/registration_summary_responses.pdf.

权授权信息系统的重要一环。目前，国际社会已经开始致力于著作权信息系统之间的联结和整合。

(一) 著作权信息系统跨境整合的实践

1. 全球曲目数据库 (Global Repertoire Database，以下简称 GRD)

鉴于当时世界上尚没有一个能够向曲作者、出版社、授权人以及被授权人开放的，提供关于音乐作品全球曲库的权威的、全面的、跨地域的数据库，2008 年 9 月，时任欧盟竞争委员会委员 Neelie Kroes 主持了一系列圆桌会议，邀请音乐产业的利益相关方讨论在线音乐发行面临的法律方面和操作方面的障碍。最后会议达成的一致意见认为，应当建立一个能够整合音乐产业现有权利信息数据的一般框架。为实现这一目标，GRD 工作组于 2009 年年底成立，重点是如何实现上述整合现有权利信息目标。❶ 目前，GRD 正在筹备中，预计 2015 年可初步投入运营。该数据库将直接接受来自出版商、作曲家以及集体管理组织的权利登记，而且这些登记通过在线注册端口进行，出版商可以自愿选择是否直接向 GRD 登记。出版商选择登记后，GRD 将会把登记信息转发给不同的协会。虽然目前创作者仍然会通过其所属的协会向 GRD 登记，但将来也可能是创作者直接向 GRD 登记。这样，在所有权利信息都想 GRD 登记后，GRD 就可以提供集中的、一步到位的著作权信息登记机制。❷

2. 著作权枢纽 (Copyright Hub)

著作权枢纽的构想是由 Hargreaves 与 2011 年接受英国政府委托对英国知识产权法进行重新审视而形成的报告中提出的。❸ Hargreaves 在报告中指出，为了建立一个能够提供著作权交易的统一平台，可以设立一个数字著作权交易所。该项目的一份后续报告中对设想中的数字著作权交易所进行了如下描述：由产业牵头的非营利性的著作权交易枢纽；该枢纽与其他国家的相关著作权交易机构、登记机构以及其他相关数据库相互对接，从而拥有跨作品领域和跨国界的数据；交易枢纽的建立采用选择进入 (Opt‐in)、非排他性 (Non‐exclusive) 以及促进竞争 (Procompetitive) 的原则。❹

---

❶ 关于全球曲目数据库筹备的详细背景，请参见：http：//www.globalrepertoiredatabase.com/.

❷ See Richard Hooper and Ros Lynch, Copyright works: Streamlining copyright licensing for the digital age (July 2012), p.41. Available at: http://www.ipo.gov.uk/dce-report-phase2.pdf.

❸ Ian Hargreaves, Digital Opportunity: A Review of Intellectual Property and Growth (May 2011). Available at: http://www.ipo.gov.uk/ipreview-finalreport.pdf.

❹ Richard Hooper and Ros Lynch, Copyright works: Streamlining copyright licensing for the digital age (July 2012), p.1. Available at: http://www.ipo.gov.uk/dce-report-phase2.pdf.

第五章　权利实现：数字网络环境下的著作权市场机制

值得注意的是，由于大宗著作权交易（如网络音乐网站 Spotify 与 Universal Music Group 之间的著作权交易）的授权机制目前已经形成固定流程，已经比较完善并且高效，因此该著作权枢纽主要是针对海量的，但单个金额却又较低的著作权交易提供自动交易服务。❶ 该著作权枢纽已于 2013 年 7 月进入在线测试阶段。❷

3. 国际音乐登记中心（International Music Registry，以下简称 IMR）

在国际层面，WIPO 正在致力于建设一个国际音乐登记中心——能够覆盖音乐著作权所有领域的利益相关者之间的合作机制。之所以称之为一种合作机制，是因为 IMR 的目的并不在于创建一个独立的数据库，而是促进音乐著作权数据库建设的进步，促进不同数据库之间的合作，从而促进能够向用户提供完整著作权授权信息的数据系统的形成。❸ 换句话说，IMR 是为了创建一个能够接入全球不同著作权权利信息系统的接入点。目前，WIPO 正在就 IMR 的架构等重要问题进行讨论研究。❹

（二）著作权信息系统跨境整合的数据标准问题

要实现著作权信息系统跨作品领域、跨国界整合，首先面临的问题就是著作权信息的技术标准问题。不同数据库要实现无缝连接，必须采用统一的技术标准。在著作权领域，不同类型的作品领域的权利登记采用各不相同的技术标准。目前国际上主要有以下四种技术标准：音乐作品的识别采用国际标准工作码（ISWC）；❺ 录音作品的识别采用国际标准记录码（ISRC）；❻ 电影、电视等视听作品采用国际标准视听码（ISAN）；❼ 图书作品则采用国际标准图书码（ISBN）。❽

上述不同类型的作品采用不同的识别码不利于著作权信息系统跨领域的整合，因此有必要开发一种通用技术标准，以促进著作权交易的授权的进行。

---

❶ *Ibid*, p. 2.

❷ 参见 Copyright Hub 主页：http：//www.copyrighthub.co.uk/. 根据其主页介绍，著作权枢纽在测试阶段只能与有限数量的著作权组织链接，正式运营后会提供更加全面的服务。

❸ See Nicholas Garnett, Study on the Role and Functions of the International Music Registry, p. 5-6. Available at: http://www.internationalmusicregistry.org/export/sites/imr/portal/en/pdf/imr_scoping_study.pdf.

❹ See FAQ at http：//www.internationalmusicregistry.org/portal/en/faqs.html.

❺ ISWC, http：//www.iswc.org/.

❻ IFPI, Resources-ISRC, http：//www.ifpi.org/content/section_resources/isrc.html.

❼ ISAN, http://www.isan.org/portal/page?_pageid=168,1&_dad=portal&_schema=PORTAL.

❽ ISBN, http：//www.isbn.org/standards/home/about/index.html.

WIPO正在考虑的IMR的目标之一就是促进在音乐领域形成通用的技术标准。另外，欧洲出版委员会也正在与产业界合作，通过建立一个内容联结联盟（Linked Content Coalition）促进统一技术标准的形成，从而使跨作品领域、跨国界的授权成为可能。❶

三、我国著作权信息系统存在的问题和完善建议

对于一个国家而言，合理完善的著作权登记制度是实现高效网络著作权授权的基本保证。我国目前的著作权登记制度主要体现在相关的条例、办法中，❷《著作权法》虽然在第26条对著作权出质登记进行了规定，但没有关于著作权登记的一般性规定。我国目前的著作权登记制度并不完善。不断改进我国的著作权登记制度，促进登记制度的数字化、网络化和国际化，是促进数字网络技术背景下版权交易，从而推动我国著作权产业升级的需要。

（一）我国著作权登记存在的问题

总结起来，我国的著作权登记制度目前存在登记机关不统一、登记效力不明确、登记内容不完整等问题。

首先，著作权登记机关不统一。目前，我国法律并未规定统一的著作权登记机关。《著作权法》第26条规定了以著作权出质情形下质权人与出质人向著作权行政管理部门进行登记。《计算机软件保护条例》第7条则规定，软件著作权人可向著作权行政管理部门认可的登记机构进行权利登记。实践中，中国版权保护中心是软件著作权的统一登记机构。另外，国家版权局《作品自愿登记试行办法》第3条还规定，各省、自治区和直辖市版权局负责本区域的作品的版权登记工作。从上述规定看，在我国不仅不同类型的作品的著作权登记机构不同，即使对同一类型作品而言，著作权登记机构也可分为中央一级的版权保护中心和地方版权局及其认可的登记机构。著作权登记机关的混乱不仅不利于著作权人进行权利登记，也不利于相关利益方进行著作权信息查询，著作权登记的公信力和可靠性大打折扣。

其次，著作权登记的效力不明确。我国相关法律并未明确对著作权登记的法律效力进行规定。虽然《作品自愿登记试行办法》第1条中提到该办法的目的是为解决著作权纠纷提供初步证据，但其并未明确规定登记的具体效力。

---

❶ Project Plan: Linked Content Coalition (Oct. 27, 2011). Available at: http://media.wix.com/ugd/bff7bc_ffefdfc161440b32d37e7bb227b8a4d2.pdf.

❷ 参见《计算机软件登记办法》《作品自愿登记试行办法》《著作权质权登记办法》。

而且该办法效力层级较低，即使有明确的规定也难以起到相应的作用。这种现状非常不利于著作权纠纷的解决，进而减少了权利人进行登记的动力。事实上，在著作权制度发达的国家，法律通常赋予著作权登记特定的法律效力。例如美国，著作权登记有多重法律效力。一方面，著作权登记是权利人提起侵权诉讼的前提条件，❶ 另一方面，著作权登记还有享有著作权的推定效力。❷ 另外，著作权登记也是要求侵权人进行著作权侵权法定损害赔偿并支付律师费的条件。❸ 否则，如果法律不赋予著作权登记法律效力，权利人进行权利登记的积极性就大大降低。

最后，著作权登记的内容不完整。我国目前的著作权登记的内容主要是权属登记以及质权登记，而对于权利继承、转让等权利变动情况并不要求登记。事实上，著作权发生继承、转让等权利变动情况经常发生，如果著作权登记内容不包括权利变动，则起不到权利公示的作用，反而会成为著作权授权的障碍。

(二) 完善著作权登记制度的建议

针对我国著作权登记存在的上述问题，本书对完善我国著作权登记制度提出如下建议：

第一，鉴于著作权登记在著作权授权信息系统的重要作用，著作权法应当增加对著作权登记的一般性规定，提高其法律地位。在著作权法中明确规定统一的著作权登记机关，避免当前多头登记的混乱局面。第二，借鉴国外的先进经验，在著作权法中明确规定著作权登记的法律效力。第三，明确规定著作权登记的具体内容，改变以往不登记权利转让登记的局面。为了满足著作权交易的需要，著作权登记的内容至少应当包括权利人的信息、首次登记信息、权利范围信息、权利变动信息。

值得注意的是，我国著作权法第三次修订草案送审稿已经就上述一些问题进行了新的规定。首先，为了降低著作权交易风险，避免权属争议，草案在"总则"一章第8条中对著作权登记进行了一般性的规定，将著作权登记提升到前所未有的法律地位。该条首次对著作权登记的法律效力作出了规定，即著作权登记文书是著作权权属的初步证明。可以说，该条对著作权效力的规定与美国的权利推定效力有异曲同工之妙。其次，为了解决著作权交易中的"一

---

❶ 17 U.S.C. § 411.

❷ 17 U.S.C. § 410 (c).

❸ 17 U.S.C. § 412.

女二嫁"的问题,保护著作权交易合同相对方的正当权益,保障交易的安全,在"权利的行使"一章第 59 条增加了关于专有许可合同和转让合同登记的规定。根据该条规定,使用者可以自愿向登记机构进行登记,未经登记的不具有对抗善意第三人的效力,这借鉴了物权法中的登记对抗要件主义。另外,草案第 60 条延续了以往关于著作权出质情况下的登记制度。

可以说,上述草案解决了我国著作权登记存在的一些问题,但仍未解决统一登记机关以及明确登记内容的问题。本书建议我国借第三次全面修订著作权法的机会对这些问题予以解决。

(三) 政府在网络著作权信息系统构建中的作用

鉴于在数字网络环境下统一的著作权信息系统对著作权授权、交易的重要作用,我国国家版权局已经认识到了各地著作权登记机构存在登记程序、登记证书、登记信息不统一以及无法统一公告和查询等问题。为了强化著作权登记服务功能,逐步实现著作权登记的统一管理,建立全国统一的作品著作权登记体系,于 2011 年 10 月向地方版权局下发了《关于进一步规范作品登记程序等有关工作的通知》(国版字〔2011〕14 号),通知要求地方版权局的著作权登记实行证书统一、编号统一、管理统一、公告统一、查询统一"五个统一";建立作品登记数据库,并将登记信息报送中国版权中心,进入国家登记档案。❶ 目前,致力于建设统一著作权登记信息数据库的全国作品登记信息数据库管理平台已于 2013 年上线运行,各地版权局将著作权登记信息都上传到该管理平台。❷

可以说,上述举措是一个良好的开始。政府在网络著作权信息系统的建设中还可以发挥更多的作用。除建立统一的著作权登记信息数据库之外,还应当考虑建立类似于英国目前正在考虑的著作权交易枢纽,促进著作权交易。同时,我国还应积极参与国际层面的合作,保持与国际先进经验的同步。

---

❶ 国家知识产权局. 全国作品登记信息数据库将建立. [EB/OL]. [2011-11-25]. http://www.sipo.gov.cn/mtjj/2011/201111/t20111125_ 633162.html.

❷ 全国作品登记信息数据库管理平台网址:http://111.205.32.11:8082/.

第三节　数字网络技术背景下的著作权集体管理制度

一、传统技术背景下的著作权集体管理

17世纪中期以后，第二次工业革命带来了社会经济的飞速发展。在这一时期，大量的文学艺术作品问世，并得到广泛的传播。作品的广泛传播的一个直接后果就是作品的使用量大大增加，作者对作品的使用无法一一收取使用费已经变得非常困难。尤其在机械复制技术被广泛应用之后，著作权权利人更是无法控制作品的复制、传播和使用，大量未经授权的对作品的使用影响了作者权益的实现。[1] 在这种情况下，著作权的权利人便选择联合起来，通过集体的力量管理自己的权利，著作权集体管理制度应运而生。

（一）集体管理制度历史发展

著作权集体管理制度最初起源于18世纪的法国。剧作家博马舍（Pierre-Augustin Caron de Beaumarchais）第一次提出了著作权集体管理的观念。1777年，他创造了法国戏剧总章程（General Statutes of Drama in Paris），由最初的22名剧作家对经济问题的讨论逐渐转向权利集体保护这一话题。最后，他们创建了法国剧作家协会。[2] 1838年，巴尔扎克与雨果又成立了作者协会，统一从出版商征收版税。[3] 著作权集体管理成为当时使作者获得经济回报的最实际有效的途径。这样，在当时的文化背景下，集体管理发展起来并逐渐扩散到其他国家。

随着著作权集体管理在各个国家的发展，不同集体管理组织之间产生了在国际层面进行合作和协调的需要。为了解决不同国家的集体管理组织之间的冲突，外国作者协会代表组织委员会（The Committee for the Organization of Congresses of Foreign Authors' Societies）于1925年成立。与此同时，Firmin Gémier

---

[1] 崔丹妮. 版权集体管理制度的变革——从机械到代码 [M] // 网络法律评论（第14卷）. 北京：北京大学出版社，2013：129.

[2] See Gervais, Daniel J., ed. Collective management of copyright and related rights. Kluwer Law International, 2010, p. 171.

[3] 参见法国文人协会（La Société des Gens de Lettres）网址：http://www.sgdl.org/sgdl/presentation/histoire.

创立了统一戏剧协会（Universal Theatrical Society）。这两个协会的成立促成了1926年国际作者与作曲者协会联合会（International Confederation of Societies of Authors and Composers，CISAC）的成立。CISAC旨在就版税的征收和作品的保护在各国建立统一的原则和方法，以确保文学艺术财产在世界范围内得到保护。如今，CISAC拥有来自118个国家的225个集体管理组织会员。❶ 目前，集体管理组织的全球网络已经初步形成，在国际上具有举足轻重地位的国际组织除CISAC之外，还有国际复制权组织联合会（IFRRO）及欧洲表演者组织协会（AEPO）等。

（二）集体管理制度的运作原理

WIPO对著作权集体管理的含义解释如下：集体管理是指有明显"集体特征"的那些著作权管理方式；这些集体特征涵盖授权费率、授权条款以及收费分配规则等方面；集体管理组织代表其成员的利益行使权利；集体管理通常还有权利管理之外的一些集体性质的功能。❷ 根据我国的《著作权法》第8条以及《著作权集体管理条例》第2条的规定，著作权集体管理是指集体管理组织经过著作权和相关权的权利人的授权而以自己的名义集中行使权利人的权利。这些行使权利的活动包括签订许可使用合同、向使用者收取使用费、向权利人分配使用费以及进行诉讼、仲裁等。虽然集体管理制度在不同的国家以及不同的领域会有所差异，但集体管理组织工作的基本原理是一致的。集体管理组织的工作原理基本上可以分为取得授权资格、向使用人授权、分配使用费。

1. 取得授权资格

集体管理组织取得授权资格可以分为三个层面。

首先，集体管理组织需要国家法律对其法律地位的确认。大多数情形下，在一个领域内只有一个集体管理组织。例如，根据我国《著作权集体管理条例》第6条规定，除依本条例设立的集体管理组织，任何组织和个人都不得从事集体管理业务。这样，在大多数国家，著作权集体管理在其领域内形成了事实上的垄断地位。不过也有例外情形，如在美国的音乐公开表演权领域就存在三个集体管理组织。❸

---

❶ See Gervais, Daniel J., ed. Collective management of copyright and related rights. Kluwer Law International, 2010, p. 3-5.

❷ See Ficsor, Mihály. Collective Management of Copyright and Related Rights. WIPO, 2002, p. 12.

❸ 在美国的音乐公开表演权领域，有ASCAP、BMI以及AESAC三个集体管理组织。See Gervais, Daniel J., ed. Collective management of copyright and related rights. Kluwer Law International, 2010, p. 340.

第五章　权利实现：数字网络环境下的著作权市场机制

其次，集体管理组织设立后需要从权利人处取得进行集体管理活动的权限。集体管理组织是由某一领域的著作权权利人发起成立的。其对作品使用的授权是从权利人处取得。按照集体管理组织取得授权权限的不同，这种授权可分为排他性授权和非排他性授权。我国《著作权集体管理条例》第19条规定，权利人可与集体管理组织签订著作权集体管理合同，授权集体管理组织对其著作权和相关权进行集体管理。

最后，集体管理组织还可能与其他集体管理组织签订相互代表协议，取得该集体管理组织的相关授权。如我国《著作权集体管理管理条例》第22条就规定，我国集体管理组织可以与国外集体管理组织签订相互代表协议。外国人可以通过与我国集体管理组织签订互相代表协议的国外集体管理组织，授权我国的集体管理组织管理其在中国的著作权。

2. 向使用人授权

集体管理组织在取得营业资格以及授权权限后，下一步工作就授权设定授权使用费率及相关条款。我国《著作权集体管理条例》规定使用费的费率应由集体管理组织会员大会制定，但同时又规定集体管理组织费率的确定不得与国务院著作权行政管理部门公告的收费标准冲突。❶ 其他国家也都对使用费费率的确定进行一定的监管。在美国，联邦法官有权确定合适的费率。在澳大利亚、加拿大和英国，由专门的著作权法院或委员会解决费率的争议问题。有些国家则直接由政府以法令的形式确定费率。❷ 在解决费率问题后，集体管理组织就可以向使用者进行授权，并收取使用费。

3. 使用费的分配

集体管理组织在收取使用费后，将对使用费进行分配。扣除集体管理组织的管理费用后，使用费将向权利人分配。在使用费分配过程中，相关的数据起到举足轻重的作用。这些相关数据主要包括权利归属的数据以及作品使用的数据。前者用于确定权利人的身份，后者用于确定向权利人分配的具体数额。我国《著作权集体管理条例》规定集体管理组织应当建立权利信息查询系统，同时又规定使用者在支付使用费时应当提交其对作品的使用的方式、数量和时间等相关使用信息。❸ 根据这些数据，集体管理组织就会科学合理地将收到的

---

❶ 参见《著作权集体管理条例》（国务院令第429号）第2条、第25条。

❷ See Gervais, Daniel J., ed. Collective management of copyright and related rights. Kluwer Law International, 2010, p.7.

❸ 参见《著作权集体管理条例》（国务院令第429号）第24条、第27条。

使用费分配到相关权利人。

(三) 集体管理制度在传统技术背景下的优势

著作权集体管理是在对著作权进行单独行使不可能或成本过高时，由集体管理组织代表权利人行使著作权的一种方式❶。集体管理组织通过对权利人的权利进行集体管理，解决了对作品的大规模使用的授权问题，其与权利人和使用人之间的单独授权相比有着明显的优势。

这种优势主要体现在集体管理有利于大大降低著作权交易成本。著作权价值的实现依赖于著作权交易。一般而言，任何交易都会产生搜索和信息成本、缔约谈判成本、合约执行成本❷。首先，集体管理组织作为链接权利人和使用人的媒介大大降低了著作权交易双方的搜索信息成本。其次，集体管理组织能够发挥集体优势，增强权利人在著作权交易中的谈判地位，从而降低权利人的谈判成本。集体管理组织还通过一揽子合同的形式解决了签订单个合同并进行单独谈判的问题，对于交易双方而言都大大节省了缔约成本。再次，集体管理组织通过专业集中的管理为权利人收取、分配使用费用，节省了合约的执行费用。经过权利人授权，集体管理组织还可以自己的名义提起诉讼，维护著作权人的权利。

此外，集体管理组织还有一定的社会文化功能。其可以通过各种形式促进权利人的福利，并促进社会文化的发展。例如，很多集体管理组织为成员支付医疗保险等社会保障费用，并根据使用费的收取情况向著作权人支付退休年金，参与慈善活动等。❸

二、数字网络背景下著作权集体管理制度的可能作为

在传统技术条件下，对作品的零散个人使用并不会从根本上影响著作权权利人的利益，因此权利人并不在意这些对作品的个人使用。数字网络技术出现之后，这种局面逐渐改变。网上对作品的大规模未经授权使用大大影响权利人的利益，并在一定程度上导致了传统唱片、图书等行业的萎缩。对此，无论权利人、著作权产业，都必须对传统的思维模式进行审视。传统的以减少违法使

---

❶ 参见 WIPO 对著作权集体管理的定义。See http://www.wipo.int/about-ip/zh/about_collective_mngt.html.

❷ 吴伟光．著作权法研究——国际条约、中国立法与司法实践 [M]．北京：清华大学出版社，508.

❸ 崔丹妮．版权集体管理制度的变革——从机械到代码 [M] // 网络法律评论（第 14 卷）．北京：北京大学出版社，2013：131.

第五章　权利实现：数字网络环境下的著作权市场机制 ◎

用为目的的"闭锁型"保护模式应当向以增加合法使用为目的的"开放型"保护模式转变。面对网络上的海量作品，著作权权利人和使用者都非常需要一种高效、低成本的作品使用授权途径，这就需要找到一种办法对网上大规模对作品的使用进行市场化。❶ 著作权集体管理不失为组织这一巨大新市场，将未经授权的使用转变为合法使用，并使权利人获得市场回报的理想机制。

在此，我们以本书关于开放型著作权保护模式一节中各种商业实践为例对集体管理制度在数字网络环境下的作用进行分析。如上所述，集体管理组织基本工作原理主要有三步：(1) 从权利所有人处获取授权权利源；(2) 设定授权条件和价格并向用户授权；(3) 收集授权数据并对收入进行分配。❷ 对于零售模式而言，iTune Store 虽然不是官方或者根据权利人间的私人协议成立，但事实上它是一种民间集体管理模式。❸ iTune store 首先从权利所有人（主要是唱片公司）手中取得授权，然后向消费者出售音乐，最后根据音乐的下载情况向权利所有人分配收入。对订阅服务而言，相关权利的分配虽然因为订阅服务分交互式和非交互式而稍微复杂，❹ 但无论如何，该商业模式下向音乐作品作者、出版者以及录音制品表演者和制作者分配收益都是依靠集体管理组织来进行的。❺ 对于非交互式传输的网络广播服务而言，与订阅服务中的非交互传输方式一样，也要依靠集体管理组织向相关权利人分配收益。对于自愿授权集体授权模式而言，无论是自由前线基金白皮书中建议成立的组织还是加拿大作曲家协会设计方案中新设立的公司，其本质上都是集体管理组织。在

---

❶ See Gervais, Daniel J., ed. Collective management of copyright and related rights. Kluwer Law International, 2010, p. 17.

❷ See Fuxiao Jiang and Daniel Gervais (2012), Collective Management Organizations in China: Practice, Problems and Possible Solutions. The Journal of World Intellectual Property, 15: 221-237.

❸ See Wikipedia, Copyright Collective. http://en.wikipedia.org/wiki/Copyright_collective. 另见杨浩鹏．《音乐著作权集体管理收费音乐网站或许是出路》，载中国文化报 2011 年 4 月 20 日，转引自中新网，网址：http://www.chinanews.com/cul/2011/04-20/2986785.shtml。在该报道中，北大新闻与传播学院史学军博士认为 iTune Store 实际上是一种民间集体管理。

❹ 在美国，著作权法对音乐作品作者的保护由来已久，但对录音制品的表演者和制作者的保护却是从《1995 年录音制品数字表演权法案》(Digital Performance Right in Sound Recordings Act of 1995) 开始。但对其保护也仅限于如网络广播的非交互式传输以及特定的交互式传输。对于非交互式传输，国会对其施加进一步的限制，即其授权模式采用法定许可制。其对口集体管理组织为 SoundExchange。而交互式传输则没有相应集体管理组织，因此交互式服务需要与每个权利所有者进行谈判。See Glynn Lunney (2010) "Copyright CMOs and Collecting Societies: The United States Experience", in Gervais, D. (ed.) Collective Management of Copyright and Related Rights, p.365-367.

❺ ASCAP、BMI、SESAC 三家集体管理组织负责向曲作者分配收益；SoundExchange 向表演者和唱片公司分配收益。

· 125 ·

这些商业模式中，集体管理组织通过两种方式发挥作用：在订阅模式和网络广播模式下，集体管理组织是作为授权商业模式的合作伙伴发挥分配收益的作用；在零售模式和自愿集体授权模式下，集体管理组织是作为核心角色对音乐作品的使用进行授权。

集体管理组织在网络著作权授权中具有如此的重要地位并非偶然。首先，著作权的复杂性和碎片化使作品的使用者取得授权变得非常复杂。❶ 如果没有集体管理制度，很多领域的作品授权就会变得不现实。其次，在网络技术背景下，作品的个人作者和个人使用者都爆炸式增长，从而引发网上大规模使用作品的问题，网上使用作品海量授权问题使集体管理制度的作用得以凸显。再次，网络技术使作品的网上使用和授权跨越了国界限制，而目前世界各国几乎都有自己的集体管理组织，而且集体管理组织间存在国际合作机制。这使集体管理在解决网上作品使用授权的问题上优势更加突出。这些因素使得著作权集体管理制度成为解决网络环境下大规模作品使用授权问题的枢纽，也是网络著作权授权机制的重要基础设施❷。

三、著作权集体管理制度对数字网络技术的因应之策

虽然集体管理制度能够解决著作权授权个别化授权不可能或成本过高的问题，并有望解决数字网络技术背景下对作品大规模使用的授权问题，但数字网络技术大发展也给集体管理制度带来了挑战。著作权集体管理制度只有不断完善以适应新技术的发展，才能实现其制度价值和潜在功能。

---

❶ 著作权集体管理领域权威学者 Daniel Gervais 教授对集体管理制度的作用有精辟的阐述。他以广播电台取得其所播放歌曲的授权为例进行分析。认为如果没有集体管理制度，广播电台如果想将音乐复制到自己电脑中并向公众播放，则需要就其播放的每首歌曲向曲作者、录音制作者以及艺术家取得授权，涉及的权利有复制权和公开表演权。如果这些权利再被转让给不同的权利人，则授权就更为复杂，一首歌曲可能需要多达二十个授权。这样，如果没有集体管理制度，对于作品使用者而言，取得作品的授权几乎是不现实的。See Daniel Gervais（2010a）"Collective Management of Copyright: Theory and Practice in the Digital Age", in Gervais, D. (ed.) Collective Management of Copyright and Related Rights, p. 2, 10-13.

❷ 著作权集体管理制度的作用得到了欧盟的高度重视，欧盟委员会于 2012 年 11 月提出了集体管理制度指南建议草案。该草案主要有两个目的：确保通过集体管理组织使艺术家和曲作者得到适当的报酬；使音乐服务提供商能够更加容易地从权利人处取得授权。See European Commission, "Proposal for A Directive of the European Parliament and of the Council on Collective Management of Copyright and Related Rights and Multi-territorial Licensing of Rights in Musical Works for Online Uses in the Internal Market", Nov. 7, 2012. Available at: http://ec.europa.eu/internal_ market/copyright/docs/management/com-2012-3722_en.pdf.

第五章 权利实现：数字网络环境下的著作权市场机制

（一）数字网络技术对著作权集体管理的挑战

数字网络技术的发展不仅对作品的创作、传播和使用方式产生了深刻的影响，给传统的著作权集体管理制度也带来了一定的挑战。

首先，数字网络技术条件下著作权客体的复杂性给著作权集体管理制度带来了挑战。在传统技术条件下，音乐作品、文字作品、美术作品、摄影作品等不同种类的作品几乎都是独立存在的。数字网络技术的发展产生了多媒体这种新的著作权存在形式。由于多媒体通常是由多种作品构成，因此多媒体的使用可能不仅需要从多媒体著作权人处取得授权，还需要从组成多媒体的素材的著作权人处取得授权，这大大增加了授权的复杂性。

其次，网络环境中作品和使用人的海量规模对集体管理组织的功能发挥提出了挑战。在传统技术条件下，集体管理组织通常是由职业作者或者唱片公司等商业组织组成，因此会员制的管理模式具有较高的效率。在新的技术背景下，作品创作门槛的大大降低使当今成为"人人创作"时代，这使作者和作品都达到海量规模，这对集体管理组织如何代表这些海量作者提出了挑战。

再次，数字网络技术也对传统的集体管理使用统计和收入分配模式提出了新的要求。在传统技术条件下，集体管理组织对作品使用情况的统计主要是依据使用者提交的数据进行统计，并据此进行收入分配。而在网络环境下，作品的使用方式的多样化和使用数量的海量规模给集体管理组织使用信息的获取和收益的分配也带来了困难。

因此，著作权集体管理制度是否能够对自身做出调整以适应数字网络技术的发展，是其是否能够在新的技术条件下发挥应有作用的关键。

（二）著作权集体管理对数字网络技术的因应

为了解决数字网络技术对集体管理机制带来的挑战，各国都在尝试采取不同的方式对集体管理制度进行完善，以使其适应新技术的要求。

1. 整合现有集体管理组织实现一站式授权平台

为了应对多媒体技术给著作权集体管理带来的挑战，有的国家提出了通过整合现有集体管理组织实现"一站式"授权的思路。这种思路的基本原理是：通过一个综合的信息平台将各个领域内的集体管理组织整合到一起。多媒体作者的使用者只要访问综合平台网站就可以获取所有作品的权利管理信息，并通过该平台取得授权。

其中法国的 SESAM 是这种尝试的一个典型。SESAM 作为法国境内不同集体管理组织的联盟成立于 1995 年至 1996 年。该联盟包括了视觉艺术家协会、剧作家协会、曲作家和出版商协会、多媒体作者协会、机械复制权协会等各个领域的集体管理组织。SESAM 使用其成员单位的曲库对多媒体的使用进行集体管理授权，从而避免同一个使用需取得多个授权的问题。总结起来，一站式授权平台具有如下功能：提供使用者需要使用的作品来源的信息；为使用者与相关集体管理组织之间的权利提供中介服务；代表相关集体管理组织发放使用许可证。类似的一站式服务还有德国的 CMMV 以及爱尔兰的 MCCI 等。❶

2. 集体管理系统电子化促进网络著作权集体管理

随着新技术的发展，越来越多的作品将以数字形式通过互联网进行传播和使用。为了适应新形势，许多集体管理组织开始利用新技术开发各种系统，对作品的使用情况进行监控，并实现使用费的精确分配。目前比较流行的解决方案是称作电子版权管理系统（Electronic Copyright Management System）的权利管理模式。这一系统主要由授权条件信息系统、权利人与使用人身份信息系统、使用费支付结算系统三大部分。❷ 通过这种管理模式，就可以解决网络环境中作品和使用人的海量规模引发的问题，并能实现高效准确地分配使用费。

另外，值得注意的是，欧盟于 2014 年 2 月通过了一项关于对音乐作品进行集体管理和跨境许可的指令。根据这一指令，在欧盟区内网络音乐服务提供商可以通过集体管理机构获得多个成员国的授权许可。这是集体管理制度进行网络化、跨境授权的最新进展。❸

（三）对我国著作权集体管理制度的完善建议

尽管著作权集体管理制度在我国只有二十多年的历史，❹ 我国的集体管理制度仍然取得了非常大的发展。目前我国已经有音乐著作权协会、音像著作权集体管理协会、文字著作权协会、摄影著作权协会，以及电影著作权协会。这五个集体管理组织的集体管理范围基本上覆盖了作品使用的各个领域。然而，我国集体管理制度仍然存在不少问题。这些问题归结起来主要有两个方面，一方面是集体管理制度基础架构的问题；另一方面是数字网络技术的发展带来的新的问题。

---

❶ Ficsor, Mihály. Collective management of copyright and related rights. World Intellectual Property Organization. (2002), p. 108-109.

❷ 曹世华. 论数字时代技术创新与著作权集体管理制度的互动 [J]. 法学评论, 2006 (1).

❸ IP-Watch, EU Parliament Passes Directive On Collective Rights Management, Pan-EU Licences, website: http://www.ip-watch.org/2014/02/04/eu-parliament-passes-directive-on-collective-rights-management-pan-eu-licences/.

❹ 我国第一个集体管理组织是音著协（MCSC）成立于 1992 年。

第五章 权利实现：数字网络环境下的著作权市场机制

关于我国集体管理制度基本机构存在的问题，有学者指出我国集体管理制度存在着排除市场价格机制的弊端、法定垄断下的非营利性组织形式的弊端。❶ 但本书认为，这两个问题其实可以归结为一个问题，即如何对待目前我国集体管理组织的垄断地位以及如何对集体管理组织进行监管的问题。关于集体管理组织的法律地位和监管模式，当今世界有两种模式。第一种模式是以欧洲民法法系国家为代表的垄断+监管模式。在该模式下，一个领域内只允许一个集体管理组织存在，政府对集体管理组织监管，防止其滥用垄断地位。❷ 第二种模式是以美国为代表的竞争模式。在该模式下，一个领域内可以有多个集体管理组织存在，通过反垄断法对集体管理组织进行规制。由于我国的民法法系传统，我国采用了垄断+监管的模式，即在一个领域内只允许一个集体管理组织存在，由著作权行政管理机构对其进行监管。事实证明，由于法律赋予的垄断地位以及监管不力，目前的垄断+监管模式并不成功，我国的集体管理组织在费率制定、收益分配、提取管理费等方面存在滥用垄断地位的问题。❸

我国集体管理组织垄断地位的滥用很大程度上源自其与监管部门之间的密切关系。因此在我国现实背景下，如果不采取新的措施，很难在短时间内改变集体管理组织垄断地位滥用的局面。本书认为，改变我国集体管理组织垄断地位的滥用，可以考虑如下两种方案：

第一种方案是建立一个有裁判权的专门监管机构对集体管理组织进行监管。该专门监管机构应当由独立法律专业人士以及经济财务专业人士组成，以保持其中立性。该组织对集体管理组织的设立、费率设定、收益分配，以及财务年报等事项进行监管。该模式的一个成功典范是加拿大的著作权委员会。❹ 我国于2013年11月15日公布的《中共中央关于全面深化改革若干重大问题的决定》中明确提出要探索建立专门的知识产权法院。这对我国建立新的集体管理组织监管模式是一个良好的契机，我国在建立知识产权法院时可以考虑

---

❶ 吴伟光. 著作权法研究——国际条约、中国立法与司法实践 [M]. 北京：清华大学出版社, 2013：519-539.

❷ Dietz, Adolf. "Legal regulation of collective management of copyright (Collecting Societies Law) in Western and Eastern Europe." J. Copyright Soc'y USA 49 (2001)：897.

❸ See Jiang, Fuxiao, and Daniel Gervais. "Collective Management Organizations in China: Practice, Problems and Possible Solutions." The Journal of World Intellectual Property 15, no. 3 (2012)：230.

❹ 加拿大著作权委员会是独立的专业法庭。关于其具体运作情况请参见 Mario, B. (2010) "Collective Management in Commonwealth Jurisdictions: Comparing Canada with Australia", in Gervais, D. (ed.), Collective Management of Copyright and Related Rights, Kluwer Law International BV, The Netherlands, p. 324-330.

赋予其对集体管理组织的监管职能。

第二种方案是采用竞争模式，即允许在一个领域内存在多个集体管理组织，通过市场竞争改变集体管理组织滥用垄断地位的问题。目前，这种模式只在美国取得了一定的成功。但是，由于著作权集体管理领域存在着规模效应的难题，❶ 因此采用这个方案可能影响集体管理的效率，并形成市场分割等新的问题。

此外，也可以考虑将两种方案进行结合，一方面成立一个中立的专门监管机构对现有集体管理组织进行监管，防止其滥用垄断地位；另一方面赋予该监管机构设立新的集体管理组织的权利。即使该监管机构永不行使这一权利，这把悬在现有集体管理组织头顶的达摩克利斯之剑，加上中立监管机构的监管，滥用垄断地位的难题也有望解决。

关于如何应对数字网络技术的发展带来的新的问题，我国集体管理组织已经取得了显著的进步。如各集体管理组织均设立网站，向社会提供很多信息服务。但是，在建设著作权信息系统以及信息系统的整合方面，我国的集体管理制度仍要很大的改善空间。我国集体管理组织一方面应当着力于建设一个信息完整全面的著作权信息系统；另一方面集体管理组织之间应当相互合作，整合各个领域的信息系统，实现授权的一站式服务。另外，我国的集体管理组织还应积极参与国际集体管理领域的合作，这在我国文化产业蓬勃发展并逐步走向世界的今天，无疑非常有利于维护我国著作权权利人在国外的权利。

数字网络技术在给著作权集体管理带来挑战的同时，也给其带来了完善发展自己的机遇。通过在权利管理实践中充分利用数字网络技术，集体管理组织完全可以适应新技术的发展。我国应当积极探索著作权集体管理在数字网络技术环境下的因应之策，实现集体管理机制的转型和升级。从现有的国际实践来看，著作权集体管理制度不仅可以继续发挥其传统功能，而且还会在新的技术背景下对网络著作权授权发挥更大的作用。

---

❶ 这里的规模效应难题是指：一方面一定的规模是集体管理有效运行的前提条件；另一方面当规模达到一定程度或者形成垄断地位时，集体管理组织又可能滥用这种垄断地位，从而又导致低效率。See Jiang, Fuxiao and Daniel Gervais. "Collective Management Organizations in China: Practice, Problems and Possible Solutions." The Journal of World Intellectual Property 15, no. 3 (2012): 229.

结 论

三百年前印刷机的发明促成了著作权法的诞生。其后，著作权法又随着模拟技术的进步不断扩张、不断完善，适应了摄影、自动钢琴、复印机、录音机、录像机等各种新技术的发展。历史表明，在模拟技术时代，新技术虽然给著作权制度带来一定挑战，但主要是促进了著作权制度的不断完善。可以说，新技术为著作权制度的发展不断创造新的机遇。

然而，在20世纪90年代以来，对著作权法有史以来的最大挑战——数字网络技术出现了。数字网络技术的开放性、平等性和全球性使其对著作权法产生了革命性的影响。传统的著作权规则系统在这一新的技术面前变得苍白无力：传统著作权法通过创造稀缺保护著作权人的利益，而数字网络技术则使人人创作、免费复制成为可能；传统著作权法的规制对象主要是专业的权利人和使用者，而数字网络技术则使数以亿计的网络用户成为主要的作品使用者；传统著作权法具有强烈的国家性和地域性，而数字网络技术则具有天然的无国界性。数字网络技术对著作权法的基础架构、权利保护模式、权利实现方式都提出了严峻的挑战。陷入窘境的著作权法在新的技术面前何去何从，成为一个不得不思考的问题。

经过本书的认真研究和思考，作者对这个问题有了一些初步结论。

第一，在著作权的基础架构和权利原始配置方面，数字与网络技术动摇了著作权法的基础架构，对著作权法上的复制权概念以及首次销售原则、合理使用等支柱性制度产生了严重冲击。但通过对国外立法司法经验的研究，通过对著作权法的架构进行调整，至少到目前为止还可以较好地处理新技术带来的问题。更重要的是，有些问题如首次销售原则在数字网络环境下的适用问题会随着技术的不断发展逐渐消解。

第二，在权利保护方面，数字网络技术对著作权法提出了最为严峻的考验。新技术引发大规模的网上侵权，传统的以减少侵权为主旨的"闭锁型"著作权保护模式已经无法适应数字网络技术的发展。事实证明，在数字网络环境下，著作权的保护和实现模式应转向以增加合法使用为核心的"开放型"

著作权保护模式。另外，为适应数字网络技术对著作权保护带来的挑战，著作权人采用技术保护措施对自己的权利进行保护。但人的自利性决定了技术保护措施很容易被滥用，技术保护措施在一些情况下与合理使用、市场竞争秩序存在一定的冲突。因此，在对技术保护措施进行保护的同时，应当对其进行适当的限制，以平衡不同利益主体之间的利益。

第三，在权利实现方面，传统的著作权授权模式固然可以解决传统技术条件下的一些作品使用的授权问题，但对于网上作品大规模的使用和传播根本无能为力。网络授权市场机制的建设和完善应当是未来很长一段时期内著作权价值实现的关键所在。网络著作权授权信息系统是网络环境下著作权市场机制有效运行的基础。集体管理制度在应对作品的大规模网上使用问题上有着不可替代的制度优势和潜力。在数字网络技术以前所未有的速度发展的背景之下，著作权法与技术发展同步已不可欲。在新的技术环境下，不断发展和完善著作权市场机制对实现和保持各方主体的利益平衡有着关键的作用。法律的调整和规制应着眼于市场的发展和需求，不断实现不同利益的动态平衡。在数字网络世界中，最有价值的已不再是内容本身，而是让使用者与内容的无缝链接。正如Daniel Gervais 教授所言，著作权法从来就不是水坝，它应该是河流。❶ 著作权法面对数字网络技术，采用大禹治水以疏代堵的思路可能是更加务实有效的选择。

值得说明的是：关于数字网络技术背景下著作权的困境与出路问题，有不少学者主张通过各种方式"重构著作权法"，甚至主张废除著作权制度。❷ 不能否认这些主张都不乏真知灼见。但作者认为，这些主张忽略了一个最重要的问题：在著作权法领域，世界上大部分国家都被各种国际条约联系到一起。除非条约之内的全部国家采取集体行动，否则单个国家对本国著作权制度进行颠覆性修改几乎是不现实的。基于这一考虑，作者对"重构著作权法"的主张持保留态度。

作为结语，作者在这里引用欧洲议会的议员、著作权法学者 Rapporteur

---

❶ Daniel J. Gervais, Use of Copyright Content on the Internet: Considerations on Excludability and Collective Licensing. In the Public Interest: The Future of Canadian Copyright Law, Michael Geist ed., Chapter 18, p. 526, Irwin Law, 2005.

❷ 易建雄. 技术发展与版权扩张 [M]. 北京：法律出版社，2009：198-209.

Marielle Gallo 的一句话:"事实证明,著作权并不是数字时代的敌人。"❶ 其实对于本书来说,这句话反过来更为合适:数字时代并不是著作权法的敌人。著作权法会与过去一样,在与新技术的互动中不断实现自我发展和完善。

---

❶ See IP Watch, EU Parliament Passes Directive On Collective Rights Management, Pan-EU Licences. Avaible at: http://www.ip-watch.org/2014/02/04/eu-parliament-passes-directive-on-collective-rights-management-pan-eu-licences/. (Feb 20, 2014).

参考文献

一、中文著作

[1] 王利明. 侵权责任法研究 [M]. 北京：中国人民大学出版社，2010.

[2] 杨立新. 侵权法论 [M]. 5 版. 北京：人民法院出版社，2013.

[3] 吴汉东. 知识产权基本问题研究 [M]. 2 版. 北京：中国人民大学出版社，2009.

[4] 郑成思. 知识产权法：新世纪初的若干研究重点 [M]. 北京：法律出版社，2004.

[5] 王迁. 知识产权法教程 [M]. 3 版. 北京：中国人民大学出版社，2011.

[6] 易建雄. 技术发展与版权扩张 [M]. 北京：法律出版社，2009.

[7] 吕炳斌. 网络时代版权制度的变革与创新 [M]. 北京：中国民主法制出版社，2012.

[8] 吴伟光. 数字技术环境下的版权法——危机与对策 [M]. 北京：知识产权出版社，2008.

[9] 熊琦. 著作权激励机制的法律构造 [M]. 北京：中国人民大学出版社，2011.

[10] 张今. 版权法中私人复制问题研究 [M]. 北京：中国政法大学出版社，2009.

[11] 冯晓青，胡梦云. 动态平衡中的著作权法 [M]. 北京：中国政法大学出版社，2011.

[12] 于玉. 著作权合理使用制度研究——应对数字网络环境挑战 [M]. 北京：知识产权出版社，2012.

[13] 丛立先. 国际著作权制度发展趋向与我国著作权法的修改 [M]. 北京：知识产权出版社，2012.

[14] 黄海峰. 知识产权的话语与现实——版权、专利与商标史论 [M]. 武汉：华中科技大学出版社，2011.

[15] 薛虹. 十字路口的国际知识产权法 [M]. 北京：法律出版社，2012.

[16] 知识产权组织. 知识产权指南——政策、法律及应用 [M]. 北京：知识产权出版社，2012.

[17] 王迁. 网络环境中的著作权保护研究 [M]. 北京：法律出版社，2011.

[18] 王迁，[荷兰] Lucie Guibault. 中欧网络版权保护比较研究 [M]. 北京：法律出版社，2008.

[19] 曹伟. 计算机软件版权保护的反思与超越 [M]. 北京：法律出版社，2010.

[20] 陈明涛. 网络服务提供商版权责任研究 [M]. 北京：知识产权出版社，2011.

[21] 尹锋林.平行进口知识产权法律规则研究［M］.北京：知识产权出版社，2012.
[22] 马乐.国际知识产权贸易中平行进口法律规制研究［M］.北京：法律出版社，2011.
[23] 罗向京.著作权集体管理组织的发展与变异［M］.北京：知识产权出版社，2011.
[24] 黄虚锋.美国版权法与音乐产业［M］.北京：法律出版社，2012.
[25] 佟雪娜.数字音乐的产业价值链研究［M］.北京：清华大学出版社，2012.
[26] 宋海燕.中国版权新问题：网络侵权责任、Google 图书馆案、比赛转播权［M］.北京：商务印书馆，2011.
[27] 李明德，管育鹰，唐广良.《著作权法》专家建议稿说明［M］.北京：法律出版社，2012.
[28] 吴伟光.著作权法研究——国际条约、中国立法与司法实践［M］.北京：清华大学出版社，2013.

二、中文译著

[1] ［美］劳伦斯·M. 弗里德曼.美国法律史［M］.苏彦新，等，译.北京：中国社会科学出版社，2007.
[2] ［美］丹尼尔·李·克莱曼.科学技术在社会中——从生物技术到互联网［M］.北京：商务印书馆，2009.
[3] ［美］威廉·W. 费舍尔.说话算数——技术、法律以及娱乐的未来［M］.李旭，译.北京：上海三联出版社，2008.
[4] ［美］劳伦斯·莱斯格.代码 2.0：网络空间中的法律［M］.李旭，沈伟伟，译.北京：清华大学出版社，2009.
[5] ［美］劳伦斯·莱斯格.免费文化［M］.王师，译.北京：中信出版社，2009.
[6] ［美］劳伦斯·莱斯格.思想的未来［M］.李旭，译.北京：中信出版社，2004.
[7] ［加］迈克尔·盖斯特.为了公共利益——加拿大版权法的未来［M］.李静，译.北京：知识产权出版社，2008.
[8] ［日］北川善太郎.著作权交易市场——信息社会的法律基础［M］.郭慧琴，译.武汉：华中科技大学出版社，2011.
[9] ［美］约翰·冈次，杰克·罗彻斯特.数字时代盗版无罪［M］.周晓琪，译.北京：法律出版社，2008.
[10] ［美］保罗·戈斯汀.著作权之道：从古登堡到数字点播机［M］.金海军，译.北京：北京大学出版社，2008.
[11] ［美］迈克尔·A. 埃因霍恩.媒体、技术和版权：经济与法律的融合［M］.赵启杉，译.北京：北京大学出版社，2012.
[12] ［美］乔纳森·奇特林.互联网的未来［M］.康国平，刘乃清，译.北京：东方

出版社，2011．

[13] [美] 吴修铭．总开关：信息帝国的兴衰变迁［M］．顾佳，译．北京：中信出版社，2011．

[14] 维克托·迈尔-舍恩伯格，肯尼思·库克耶．大数据时代：生活、工作与思维的大变革［M］．盛杨燕，周涛，译．北京：浙江人民出版社，2012．

[15] 丹尼斯·劳埃德著，M.D.A.弗里曼修订．法理学［M］．许章润，译．北京：法律出版社，2007．

三、中文论文

[1] 万勇．美国版权法改革方案述评［J］．知识产权，2014（1）．

[2] 胡波．信息自由与版权法的变革［J］．现在法学，2016（6）．

[3] 吴汉东．网络版权的技术革命、产业变革与制度创新［J］．中国版权，2016（6）．

[4] 陈少玲．"三振出局"版权保护机制设计研究［J］．中国版权，2014（4）．

[5] 熊琦．Web.2.0时代的著作权法：问题、争议与应对［J］．政法论坛，2014（4）．

[6] 管育鹰．版权领域发行权用尽原则探讨［J］．法学杂志，2014（10）．

[7] 李杨．互联网环境下的版权理论续造与治理构想［J］．大连理工大学学报（社会科学版），2014（3）．

[8] 董慧娟．对技术措施直接规避行为构成独立的版权侵权的质疑［J］．知识产权，2015（7）．

[9] 林秀芹，黄钱欣．我国著作权集体管理组织的模式选择［J］．知识产权，2016（9）．

[10] 高富平．寻求数字时代的版权法生存法则［J］．知识产权，2011（2）．

[11] 宋廷徽，郭禾．对版权保护扩张趋势的反思［J］．法学家，2010（6）．

[12] 熊文聪．技术、商业模式与版权法的未来［N］．中国社会科学报，2010-07-29（4）．

[13] 熊文聪．数字技术与版权制度的未来［J］．东方法学，2011（1）．

[14] 王晶．数字环境下版权技术保护的法律问题［J］．中国出版，2010（22）．

[15] 梅术文．我国著作权法上的传播权整合［J］．法学，2010（9）．

[16] 梁志文．版权法上的"选择退出"制度及其合法性问题［J］．法学，2010（6）．

[17] 刘铁光．著作权正当性的危机与出路［J］．法制与社会发展，2010（2）．

[18] 李扬．知识产权法定义及其适用［J］．法学研究，2006（2）．

[19] 张今．数字环境下的版权补偿金制度［J］．政法论坛，2010（1）．

[20] 李凤莲．试析数字技术给中国版权制度带来的挑战［J］．中国出版，2010（20）．

[21] 乔生．网络版权保护的趋势与发展——兼论合理使用的抗争［J］．法学杂志，2009（2）．

[22] 叶姗．著作权保护的现代发展：从侵权限止到交易励进［J］．河北法学，2009（4）．

[23] 王迁．网络环境中版权制度的发展［J］．网络法律评论，2008（1）．

[24] 李雨峰．著作权制度的反思与改组［J］．法学论坛，2008（2）．
[25] 李雨峰．版权、市民社会与国家［J］．知识产权，2006（3）．
[26] 李雨峰．版权制度的困境［J］．比较法研究，2006（3）．
[27] 冯晓青．著作权扩张及其缘由透视［J］．政法论坛，2006（6）．
[28] 李雨峰．版权扩张：一种合法性的反思［J］．现代法学，2001（5）．
[29] 唐艳．数字化作品与首次销售原则——以著作权法修改为背景［J］．知识产权，2012（1）．
[30] 陈青．权利用尽原则的国际适用与发展［J］．河北法学，2012（1）．
[31] 张敏．论版权平行进口中"首次销售原则"的适用——美国联邦最高法院好市多诉欧米茄案谈起［J］．电子知识产权，2011（11）．
[32] 王迁．论网络环境中的"首次销售原则"［J］．法学杂志，2006（3）．
[33] 詹爱岚．美国版权耗尽与平行进口立法及其司法实践解析［J］．科技进步与对策，2005（3）．
[34] 宫士友．我国著作权法律制度面临的困惑——写在著作权法修订之际［J］．知识产权，2012（2）．
[35] 吴汉东．著作权法第三次修改草案的立法方案和内容安排［J］．知识产权，2012（5）．
[36] 刘春田．《著作权法》三次修改是国情巨变的要求［J］．知识产权，2012（5）．
[37] 阎晓宏．《著作权法》第三次修改的几个问题［J］．知识产权，2012（5）．
[38] 李明德．我国《著作权法》的第三次修改与建议［J］．知识产权，2012（5）．
[39] 吴汉东．《著作权法》第三次修改的背景、体例和重点［J］．法商研究，2012（4）．
[40] 王迁．著作权法借鉴国际条约与国外立法：问题与对策［J］．中国法学，2012（3）．
[41] 焦和平．三网融合下广播权与信息网络传播权的重构——兼析《著作权法（修改草案）》前两稿的相关规定［J］．法律科学（西北政法大学学报），2013（1）．
[42] 熊琦．著作权法定许可的误读与解读兼评《著作权法》第三次修改草案第46条［J］．电子知识产权，2012（4）．
[43] 王兰萍．中国法制近代化过程中的三部著作权法［J］．比较法研究，2005（3）．
[44] 高卢麟．中国著作权法修改初析［J］．知识产权，2002（3）．
[45] 熊琦．论著作权集体管理中的私人自治——兼评我国集体管理制度立法的谬误［J］．法律科学（西北政法大学学报），2013（1）．
[46] 熊琦．著作权许可的私人创制与法定安排［J］．政法论坛，2012（6）．
[47] 熊琦．音乐著作权许可的制度失灵与法律再造［J］．当代法学，2012（5）．
[48] 熊琦．论"接触权"——著作财产权类型化的不足与克服［J］．法律科学，2008（5）．
[49] 王吉法，李阁霞．集体管理组织与著作权保护困境［J］．烟台大学学报（哲学社会科学版），2011（3）．

[50] 卢海君,洪毓吟.著作权延伸性集体管理制度的质疑[J].知识产权,2013(2).
[51] 张平.数字图书馆版权纠纷及授权模式探讨[J].法律适用,2010(1).
[52] 王艺.网络传播与著作权集体管理[J].知识产权,2000(2).
[53] 张耕,黄细江.略论云计算环境下的著作权保护[J].法学杂志,2013(1).
[54] 李雨峰,张惠彬.云计算环境下的著作权司法保护[J].人民司法,2012(17).
[55] 何天翔.音视频分享网站的版权在先许可研究——以美国YouTube的新版权商业模式为例[J].知识产权,2012(10).
[56] 姚洪军.中美处理网络服务提供者著作权问题的比较[J].比较法研究,2011(5).
[57] 梁志文.云计算、技术中立与版权责任[J].法学,2011(3).
[58] 吴伟光.版权制度与新媒体技术之间的裂痕与弥补[J].现代法学,2011(3).
[59] 刘家瑞.版权法上的转承责任研究[J].知识产权,2011(3).
[60] 王迁.版权法保护技术措施的正当性[J].法学研究,2011(4).
[61] 姚鹤徽,王太平.著作权技术保护措施之批判、反思与正确定位[J].知识产权,2009(6).
[62] 吴汉东.论网络服务提供者的著作权侵权责任[J].中国法学,2011(2).
[63] 王迁.新型P2P技术对传统版权间接侵权责任理论的挑战——Grokster案评述[J].电子知识产权,2011(10).
[64] 翁鸣江,武雷.Napster诉讼案及其对美国版权法的影响[J].法制与社会发展,2002(2).
[65] 李瑞登.网络版权制度功效缺失的文化因素解析[J].知识产权,2010(5).
[66] 张岚.美国版权产业法律变化管窥——以新技术为背景[J].人民论坛,2010(26).
[67] 王迁.发达国家网络版权司法保护的现状与趋势[J].法律适用,2009(12).
[68] 陈锦川.网络环境下的著作权法律调整及其研究[J].人民司法,2006(3).
[69] 翟中鞠."网络时代的著作权保护"国际研讨会综述[J].法商研究,2004(4).
[70] 李明德.网络环境中的版权保护[J].环球法律评论,2001(1).
[71] 熊琦.著作权间接责任制度的扩张与限制——美国判例的启示[J].知识产权,2009(6).
[72] 沈伟伟.P2P技术下网络版权许可模式初探[J].网络法律评论,2009(1).
[73] 张耕,施鹏鹏.法国著作权法的最新重大改革及评论[J].比较法研究,2008(2).
[74] 张今.版权法上"技术中立"的反思与评析[J].知识产权,2008(1).
[75] 张平.网络环境下著作权许可模式的变革[J].华东政法大学学报,2007(4).
[76] 曹世华.论数字时代的版权补偿金制度及其导入[J].法律科学(西北政法学院学报),2006(6).
[77] 曹世华.论数字时代技术创新与著作权集体管理制度的互动[J].法学评论,

2006（1）.

[78] 刘润涛. 数字时代著作权授权方式研究 [J]. 知识产权, 2005（5）.

[79] 王迁. P2P 软件最终用户版权侵权问题研究 [J]. 知识产权, 2004（5）.

四、英文著作

[1] Litman, Jessica. Digital copyright. (2006).

[2] Patry, William. How to fix copyright. Oxford University Press, USA. (2011).

[3] Mazzone, Jason. Copyfraud and other abuses of intellectual property law. (2011).

[4] Patterson, Lyman Ray. Copyright in historical perspective. Vanderbilt University Press. (1968).

[5] Robert A. Gorman, Jane C. Ginsburg, and R. Anthony Reese, Copyright: cases and materials. Foundation Press. (2011).

[6] Ficsor, Mihály. Collective management of copyright and related rights. World Intellectual Property Organization. (2002).

[7] Gervais, Daniel J. Collective management of copyright and related rights. Kluwer Law International. (2010).

[8] Hetcher, Steven Anthony. Norms in a wired world. Cambridge: Cambridge University Press. (2004).

[9] Torremans, Paul. Global Copyright: Three Hundred Years since the Statute of Anne, from 1709 to Cyberspace. Edward Elgar Publishing. (2010).

[10] Strowel, Alain. Peer-to-peer File Sharing and Secondary Liability in Copyright Law. Edward Elgar Pub. (2009).

[11] Giblin, Rebecca. Code Wars: 10 Years of P2P Software Litigation. Edward Elgar Publishing. (2011).

[12] Moser, David J., and Cheryl L. Slay. Music Copyright Law. (2012).

[13] Rosen, Ronald S. Music and Copyright. Oxford University Press, USA. (2008).

[14] Dahl, Kurt. The Future of Copyright and Artist Rights in the Music Industry, Verlag Dr. Müller. (2009).

[15] Irini A. Stamatoudi, ed. Copyright Enforcement and the Internet. Vol. 21. Kluwer Law International. (2010).

[16] J. Axhamn (Ed.), Copyright in a Borderless Online Environment. Stockholm: Norstedts Juridik. (2012).

[17] Lessig, Lawrence. Remix: Making Art and Commerce Thrive in the Hybrid Economy. Penguin Pr, 2008.

[18] Pitt, Ivan L., Economic Analysis of Music Copyright: Income, Media and Performances.

Springer New York. (2010).

［19］ Grimmelmann, James, Internet Law: Cases and Problems. Semaphore Press. (2012).

［20］ Ficsor, Mihály. Collective Management of Copyright and Related Rights. WIPO. (2002).

［21］ Sinacore-Guinn, David. Collective Administration of Copyrights and Neighboring Rights: International Practices, Procedures, and Organizations. Boston, MA: Little, Brown, 1993.

［22］ The Evolution and Equilibrium of Copyright in the Digital Age, edited by Susy Frankel and Daniel Gervais, Cambridge Univ. Press, 2014.

［23］ Daniel Gervais , Restructuring Copyright: A Comprehensive Path to International Copyright Reform, Edward Elgar, 2017.

五、英文论文

［1］ Nimmer, David. "Appreciating Legislative History: The Sweet and Sour Spots of the DMCA's Commentary." Cardozo L. Rev. 23 (2001): 909.

［2］ Nimmer, David. "Back from the Future: A Proleptic Review of the Digital Millennium Copyright Act." Berk. Tech. LJ 16 (2001).

［3］ Nimmer, David. "Codifying Copyright Comprehensibly." UCLA L. Rev. 51 (2003): 1233.

［4］ Nimmer, David. "Puzzles of the Digital Millennium Copyright Act." J. Copyright Soc'y USA 46 (1998): 401.

［5］ Ginsburg, Jane C. "Copyright legislation for the digital millennium." Colum. -Vla JL & Arts 23 (1999): 137.

［6］ Marke, Julius J. "United States copyright revision and its legislative history." Law Libr. J. 70 (1977): 121.

［7］ Friedman, Matthew. "Nine Years and Still Waiting: While Congress Continues to Hold off on Amending Copyright Law for the Digital Age, Commercial Industry Has Largely Moved On." Vill. Sports & Ent. LJ 17 (2010): 637.

［8］ Davis, Randall. "The digital dilemma." Communications of the ACM 44, no. 2 (2001): 77-83.

［9］ Samuelson, Pamela, and Randall Davis. "The digital dilemma: A perspective on intellectual property in the information age." In 28th Annual Telecommunications Policy Research Conference, Arlington, VA. 2000.

［10］ Gervais, Daniel J. "The Regulation of Inchoate Technologies." Houston Law Review 47, no. 3 (2010): 665-705.

［11］ Ginsburg, Jane C. "Copyright and control over new technologies of dissemination." Columbia Law Review (2001): 1613-1647.

［12］ Wu, Tim. "When Code Isn't Law." Virginia Law Review (2003): 679-751.

[13] Depoorter, Ben. "Technology and Uncertainty: The Shaping Effect on Copyright Law." University of Pennsylvania Law Review (2009): 1831-1868.

[14] Dusollier, Severine. "DRM at the intersection of copyright law and technology: a case study for regulation." (2012): 297-317.

[15] Dizon, Michael Anthony C. "Does Technology Trump Intellectual Property?: Re-Framing the Debate About Regulating New Technologies." Re-Framing the Debate About Regulating New Technologies (August 17, 2011). SCRIPTed 8 (2011): 124.

[16] Hutchison, Cameron J., "Interpreting Copyright Law & Internet Facts". Canadian Journal of Law and Technology, Vol. 43, 2010.

[17] Rub, Guy. "The Economics of Kirtsaeng v. John Wiley & Sons: The Efficiency of a Balanced Approach to the First Sale Doctrine." (2013).

[18] McIntyre, Stephen J. "Game Over For First Sale." (2013).

[19] Reese, R. Anthony. "The First Sale Doctrine in the Era of Digital Networks." BCL Rev. 44 (2002): 577.

[20] Gervais, Daniel J. "The Price of Social Norms: Towards a Liability Regime for File-Sharing." J. of Intell. Prop. Law 12, no. 1 (2003): 39-74.

[21] Yu, Peter. "P2P and the Future of Private Copying." University of Colorado Law Review 76 (2005).

[22] Yu, Peter. "Digital Copyright and Confuzzling Rhetoric." Vanderbilt Journal of Entertainment and Technology Law 13 (2011): 881-939.

[23] Bridy, Annemarie. "Why pirates (still) won't behave: Regulating P2P in the decade after Napster." (2009).

[24] Litman, Jessica. "Revising copyright law for the information age." Or. L. Rev. 75 (1996): 19.

[25] Litman, Jessica. "Real copyright reform." Iowa Law Review 96, no. 1 (2010): 1-55.

[26] Wood, Jessica. "The Darknet: A Digital Copyright Revolution". XVI Rich. J. L. & Tech. 14 (2010).

[27] Samuelson, Pamela. "Is Copyright Reform Possible?" Harv. L. Rev. 126 (2013): 740-868.

[28] Samuelson, Pamela. "The Copyright Principles Project: Directions for Reform." Berkeley Technology Law Journal 25 (2010).

[29] Samuelson, Pamela. "Preliminary thoughts on copyright reform." Utah L. Rev. (2007): 551.

[30] Pallante, Maria A., "The Next Great Copyright Act." Twenty-sixth Horace S. Manage Lecture. (2013).

[31] Tehranian, John, "Infringement Nation: Copyright Reform and the Law/Norm Gap (2007)". Utah Law Review, Vol. 2007, p. 537, 2007.

[32] Gard, Elizabeth Townsend, "Conversations with Renowned Professors on the Future of Copyright". 12 Tul. J. Tech. & Intell. Prop. 35. (2009).

[33] Boyle, James, "The Second Enclosure Movement and the Construction of the Public Domain." Law and Contemporary Problems, Vol. 66, p. 33-74, Winter-Spring 2003.

[34] Merges, Robert P. "To Waive and Waive Not: Property and Flexibility in the Digital Era" (April 2, 2011). Available at SSRN: http://ssrn.com/abstract=1854731 or http://dx.doi.org/10.2139/ssrn.1854731.

[35] Kaufman, Justin M. "The Creative Rights Act of 2020: Rethinking Copyright for the Future" (April 17, 2012). Available at SSRN: http://ssrn.com/abstract=2135862 or http://dx.doi.org/10.2139/ssrn.2135862.

[36] Daniel J. Gervais. "The Role of Copyright Collectives in Web 2.0 Music Markets" WIPO/Vanderbilt Law School Conference of Collective Management. Nashville. Oct. 2007.

[37] Strowel, Alain. "The European Extended Collective Licensing Model" Colum. JL & Arts 34 (2010): 665.

[38] Riis, Thomas, and Jens Schovsbo. "Extended Collective Licenses and the Nordic Experience: It's a Hybrid but is it a Volvo or a Lemon." Colum. JL & Arts 33 (2009): 471.

[39] Gyertyanfy, Peter. "Why is a European Directive on Collective Management Necessary-A Perspective from a New Member State of the EU." J. Copyright Soc'y USA 53 (2005): 71.

[40] Karnell, Gunnar. "Extended Collective License Clauses and Agreements in Nordic Copyright Law." Colum.-VLA JL & Arts 10 (1985): 73.

[41] Gervais, Daniel J. "Application of an extended collective licensing regime in Canada: principles and issues related to implementation." (2003).

[42] Gervais, Daniel J. "The Landscape of collective management schemes." Columbia Journal of Law & the arts 34, no. 4 (2011): 423-449.

[43] Reichman, Jerome H., Graeme B. Dinwoodie, and Pamela Samuelson. "Reverse Notice and Takedown Regime to Enable Pubic Interest Uses of Technically Protected Copyrighted Works", Berkeley Tech. LJ 22 (2007).

附录 1

17 U. S. Code § 512 – Limitations on liability relating to material online

(a) **Transitory Digital Network Communications.** —A service provider shall not be liable for monetary relief, or, except as provided in subsection (j), for injunctive or other equitable relief, for infringement of copyright by reason of the provider's transmitting, routing, or providing connections for, material through a system or network controlled or operated by or for the service provider, or by reason of the intermediate and transient storage of that material in the course of such transmitting, routing, or providing connections, if—

(1) the transmission of the material was initiated by or at the direction of a person other than the service provider;

(2) the transmission, routing, provision of connections, or storage is carried out through an automatic technical process without selection of the material by the service provider;

(3) the service provider does not select the recipients of the material except as an automatic response to the request of another person;

(4) no copy of the material made by the service provider in the course of such intermediate or transient storage is maintained on the system or network in a manner ordinarily accessible to anyone other than anticipated recipients, and no such copy is maintained on the system or network in a manner ordinarily accessible to such anticipated recipients for a longer period than is reasonably necessary for the transmission, routing, or provision of connections; and

(5) the material is transmitted through the system or network without modification of its content.

(b) System Caching. —

(1) **Limitation on liability.** —A service provider shall not be liable for monetary relief, or, except as provided in subsection (j), for injunctive or other equitable relief, for infringement of copyright by reason of the intermediate and

temporary storage of material on a system or network controlled or operated by or for the service provider in a case in which—

(A) the material is made available online by a person other than the service provider;

(B) the material is transmitted from the person described in subparagraph (A) through the system or network to a person other than the person described in subparagraph (A) at the direction of that other person; and

(C) the storage is carried out through an automatic technical process for the purpose of making the material available to users of the system or network who, after the material is transmitted as described in subparagraph (B), request access to the material from the person described in subparagraph (A),

if the conditions set forth in paragraph (2) are met.

(2) Conditions. —The conditions referred to in paragraph (1) are that—

(A) the material described in paragraph (1) is transmitted to the subsequent users described in paragraph (1)(C) without modification to its content from the manner in which the material was transmitted from the person described in paragraph (1)(A);

(B) the service provider described in paragraph (1) complies with rules concerning the refreshing, reloading, or other updating of the material when specified by the person making the material available online in accordance with a generally accepted industry standard data communications protocol for the system or network through which that person makes the material available, except that this subparagraph applies only if those rules are not used by the person described in paragraph (1)(A) to prevent or unreasonably impair the intermediate storage to which this subsection applies;

(C) the service provider does not interfere with the ability of technology associated with the material to return to the person described in paragraph (1)(A) the information that would have been available to that person if the material had been obtained by the subsequent users described in paragraph (1)(C) directly from that person, except that this subparagraph applies only if that technology—

(i) does not significantly interfere with the performance of the provider's system or network or with the intermediate storage of the material;

(ii) is consistent with generally accepted industry standard communications protocols; and

(iii) does not extract information from the provider's system or network other than the information that would have been available to the person described in paragraph (1)(A) if the subsequent users had gained access to the material directly from that person;

(D) if the person described in paragraph (1)(A) has in effect a condition that a person must meet prior to having access to the material, such as a condition based on payment of a fee or provision of a password or other information, the service provider permits access to the stored material in significant part only to users of its system or network that have met those conditions and only in accordance with those conditions; and

(E) if the person described in paragraph (1)(A) makes that material available online without the authorization of the copyright owner of the material, the service provider responds expeditiously to remove, or disable access to, the material that is claimed to be infringing upon notification of claimed infringement as described in subsection (c)(3), except that this subparagraph applies only if—

(i) the material has previously been removed from the originating site or access to it has been disabled, or a court has ordered that the material be removed from the originating site or that access to the material on the originating site be disabled; and

(ii) the party giving the notification includes in the notification a statement confirming that the material has been removed from the originating site or access to it has been disabled or that a court has ordered that the material be removed from the originating site or that access to the material on the originating site be disabled.

(c) Information Residing on Systems or Networks At Direction of Users. —

(1) In general. —A service provider shall not be liable for monetary relief, or, except as provided in subsection (j), for injunctive or other equitable relief, for infringement of copyright by reason of the storage at the direction of a user of material that resides on a system or network controlled or operated by or for the service provider, if the service provider—

(A)

(i) does not have actual knowledge that the material or an activity using the material on the system or network is infringing;

(ii) in the absence of such actual knowledge, is not aware of facts or circumstances from which infringing activity is apparent; or

(iii) upon obtaining such knowledge or awareness, acts expeditiously to remove, or disable access to, the material;

(B) does not receive a financial benefit directly attributable to the infringing activity, in a case in which the service provider has the right and ability to control such activity; and

(C) upon notification of claimed infringement as described in paragraph (3), responds expeditiously to remove, or disable access to, the material that is claimed to be infringing or to be the subject of infringing activity.

(2) **Designated agent.** —The limitations on liability established in this subsection apply to a service provider only if the service provider has designated an agent to receive notifications of claimed infringement described in paragraph (3), by making available through its service, including on its website in a location accessible to the public, and by providing to the Copyright Office, substantially the following information:

(A) the name, address, phone number, and electronic mail address of the agent.

(B) other contact information which the Register of Copyrights may deem appropriate.

The Register of Copyrights shall maintain a current directory of agents available to the public for inspection, including through the Internet, and may require payment of a fee by service providers to cover the costs of maintaining the directory.

(3) **Elements of notification.** —

(A) To be effective under this subsection, a notification of claimed infringement must be a written communication provided to the designated agent of a service provider that includes substantially the following:

(i) A physical or electronic signature of a person authorized to act on behalf of the owner of an exclusive right that is allegedly infringed.

(ii) Identification of the copyrighted work claimed to have been infringed, or, if multiple copyrighted works at a single online site are covered by a single notification, a representative list of such works at that site.

(iii) Identification of the material that is claimed to be infringing or to be the subject of infringing activity and that is to be removed or access to which is to be disabled, and information reasonably sufficient to permit the service provider to locate the material.

(iv) Information reasonably sufficient to permit the service provider to contact the complaining party, such as an address, telephone number, and if available, an electronic mail address at which the complaining party may be contacted.

(v) A statement that the complaining party has a good faith belief that use of the material in the manner complained of is not authorized by the copyright owner, its agent, or the law.

(vi) A statement that the information in the notification is accurate, and under penalty of perjury, that the complaining party is authorized to act on behalf of the owner of an exclusive right that is allegedly infringed.

(B)

(i) Subject to clause (ii), a notification from a copyright owner or from a person authorized to act on behalf of the copyright owner that fails to comply substantially with the provisions of subparagraph (A) shall not be considered under paragraph (1)(A) in determining whether a service provider has actual knowledge or is aware of facts or circumstances from which infringing activity is apparent.

(ii) In a case in which the notification that is provided to the service provider's designated agent fails to comply substantially with all the provisions of subparagraph (A) but substantially complies with clauses (ii), (iii), and (iv) of subparagraph (A), clause (i) of this subparagraph applies only if the service provider promptly attempts to contact the person making the notification or takes other reasonable steps to assist in the receipt of notification that substantially complies with all the provisions of subparagraph (A).

(d) **Information Location Tools.** —A service provider shall not be liable for monetary relief, or, except as provided in subsection (j), for injunctive or other equitable relief, for infringement of copyright by reason of the provider referring or linking users to an online location containing infringing material or infringing activity, by using information location tools, including a directory, index, reference, pointer, or hypertext link, if the service provider—

(1)

(A) does not have actual knowledge that the material or activity is infringing;

(B) in the absence of such actual knowledge, is not aware of facts or circumstances from which infringing activity is apparent; or

(C) upon obtaining such knowledge or awareness, acts expeditiously to remove, or disable access to, the material;

(2) does not receive a financial benefit directly attributable to the infringing activity, in a case in which the service provider has the right and ability to control such activity; and

(3) upon notification of claimed infringement as described in subsection (c)(3), responds expeditiously to remove, or disable access to, the material that is claimed to be infringing or to be the subject of infringing activity, except that, for purposes of this paragraph, the information described in subsection (c)(3)(A)(iii) shall be identification of the reference or link, to material or activity claimed to be infringing, that is to be removed or access to which is to be disabled, and information reasonably sufficient to permit the service provider to locate that reference or link.

(e) Limitation on Liability of Nonprofit Educational Institutions. —

(1) When a public or other nonprofit institution of higher education is a service provider, and when a faculty member or graduate student who is an employee of such institution is performing a teaching or research function, for the purposes of subsections (a) and (b) such faculty member or graduate student shall be considered to be a person other than the institution, and for the purposes of subsections (c) and (d) such faculty member's or graduate student's knowledge or awareness of his or her infringing activities shall not be attributed to the institution, if—

(A) such faculty member's or graduate student's infringing activities do not involve the provision of online access to instructional materials that are or were required or recommended, within the preceding 3-year period, for a course taught at the institution by such faculty member or graduate student;

(B) the institution has not, within the preceding 3-year period, received more than two notifications described in subsection (c)(3) of claimed infringement by such faculty member or graduate student, and such notifications of claimed infringement were not actionable under subsection (f); and

(C) the institution provides to all users of its system or network informational materials that accurately describe, and promote compliance with, the laws of the United States relating to copyright.

(2) For the purposes of this subsection, the limitations on injunctive relief contained in subsections (j)(2) and (j)(3), but not those in (j)(1), shall apply.

(f) **Misrepresentations.** —Any person who knowingly materially misrepresents under this section—

(1) that material or activity is infringing, or

(2) that material or activity was removed or disabled by mistake or misidentification,

shall be liable for any damages, including costs and attorneys' fees, incurred by the alleged infringer, by any copyright owner or copyright owner's authorized licensee, or by a service provider, who is injured by such misrepresentation, as the result of the service provider relying upon such misrepresentation in removing or disabling access to the material or activity claimed to be infringing, or in replacing the removed material or ceasing to disable access to it.

(g) **Replacement of Removed or Disabled Material and Limitation on Other Liability.** —

(1) No liability for taking down generally. —

Subject to paragraph (2), a service provider shall not be liable to any person for any claim based on the service provider's good faith disabling of access to, or removal of, material or activity claimed to be infringing or based on facts or circumstances from which infringing activity is apparent, regardless of whether the material or activity is ultimately determined to be infringing.

(2) Exception. —Paragraph (1) shall not apply with respect to material residing at the direction of a subscriber of the service provider on a system or network controlled or operated by or for the service provider that is removed, or to which access is disabled by the service provider, pursuant to a notice provided under subsection (c)(1)(C), unless the service provider—

(A) takes reasonable steps promptly to notify the subscriber that it has removed or disabled access to the material;

(B) upon receipt of a counter notification described in paragraph (3), promptly provides the person who provided the notification under subsection (c)(1)(C) with a copy of the counter notification, and informs that person that it will replace the removed material or cease disabling access to it in 10 business days; and

(C) replaces the removed material and ceases disabling access to it not less than 10, nor more than 14, business days following receipt of the counter notice, unless its designated agent first receives notice from the person who submitted the notification under subsection (c)(1)(C) that such person has filed an action seeking a court order to restrain the subscriber from engaging in infringing activity relating to the material on the service provider's system or network.

(3) **Contents of counter notification.** —To be effective under this subsection, a counter notification must be a written communication provided to the service provider's designated agent that includes substantially the following:

(A) A physical or electronic signature of the subscriber.

(B) Identification of the material that has been removed or to which access has been disabled and the location at which the material appeared before it was removed or access to it was disabled.

(C) A statement under penalty of perjury that the subscriber has a good faith belief that the material was removed or disabled as a result of mistake or misidentification of the material to be removed or disabled.

(D) The subscriber's name, address, and telephone number, and a statement that the subscriber consents to the jurisdiction of Federal District Court for the judicial district in which the address is located, or if the subscriber's address is outside of the United States, for any judicial district in which the service provider may be found, and that the subscriber will accept service of process from the person who provided notification under subsection (c)(1)(C) or an agent of such person.

(4) **Limitation on other liability.** —

A service provider's compliance with paragraph (2) shall not subject the service provider to liability for copyright infringement with respect to the material identified in the notice provided under subsection (c)(1)(C).

(h) Subpoena To Identify Infringer. —

(1) Request. —

A copyright owner or a person authorized to act on the owner's behalf may request the clerk of any United States district court to issue a subpoena to a service provider for identification of an alleged infringer in accordance with this subsection.

(2) **Contents of request.** —The request may be made by filing with the clerk—

(A) a copy of a notification described in subsection (c)(3)(A);

(B) a proposed subpoena; and

(C) a sworn declaration to the effect that the purpose for which the subpoena is sought is to obtain the identity of an alleged infringer and that such information will only be used for the purpose of protecting rights under this title.

(3) **Contents of subpoena.** —

The subpoena shall authorize and order the service provider receiving the notification and the subpoena to expeditiously disclose to the copyright owner or person authorized by the copyright owner information sufficient to identify the alleged infringer of the material described in the notification to the extent such information is available to the service provider.

(4) **Basis for granting subpoena.** —

If the notification filed satisfies the provisions of subsection (c)(3)(A), the proposed subpoena is in proper form, and the accompanying declaration is properly executed, the clerk shall expeditiously issue and sign the proposed subpoena and return it to the requester for delivery to the service provider.

(5) **Actions of service provider receiving subpoena.** —

Upon receipt of the issued subpoena, either accompanying or subsequent to the receipt of a notification described in subsection (c)(3)(A), the service provider shall expeditiously disclose to the copyright owner or person authorized by the copyright owner the information required by the subpoena, notwithstanding any other provision of law and regardless of whether the service provider responds to the notification.

(6) **Rules applicable to subpoena.** —

Unless otherwise provided by this section or by applicable rules of the court, the procedure for issuance and delivery of the subpoena, and the remedies for noncompliance with the subpoena, shall be governed to the greatest extent practicable by those provisions of the Federal Rules of Civil Procedure governing the issuance, service, and enforcement of a subpoena duces tecum.

(i) **Conditions for Eligibility.** —

(1) **Accommodation of technology.** —The limitations on liability established by this section shall apply to a service provider only if the service provider—

(A) has adopted and reasonably implemented, and informs subscribers and account holders of the service provider's system or network of, a policy that provides for the termination in appropriate circumstances of subscribers and account holders of the service provider's system or network who are repeat infringers; and

(B) accommodates and does not interfere with standard technical measures.

(2) **Definition.** —As used in this subsection, the term "standard technical measures" means technical measures that are used by copyright owners to identify or protect copyrighted works and—

(A) have been developed pursuant to a broad consensus of copyright owners and service providers in an open, fair, voluntary, multi-industry standards process; and

(B) are available to any person on reasonable and nondiscriminatory terms; and

(C) do not impose substantial costs on service providers or substantial burdens on their systems or networks.

(j) **Injunctions.** —The following rules shall apply in the case of any application for an injunction under section 502 against a service provider that is not subject to monetary remedies under this section:

(1) **Scope of relief.** —

(A) With respect to conduct other than that which qualifies for the limitation on remedies set forth in subsection (a), the court may grant injunctive relief with respect to a service provider only in one or more of the following forms:

(i) An order restraining the service provider from providing access to infringing material or activity residing at a particular online site on the provider's system or network.

(ii) An order restraining the service provider from providing access to a subscriber or account holder of the service provider's system or network who is engaging in infringing activity and is identified in the order, by terminating the accounts of the subscriber or account holder that are specified in the order.

(iii) Such other injunctive relief as the court may consider necessary to prevent or restrain infringement of copyrighted material specified in the order of the court at a particular online location, if such relief is the least burdensome to the service provider among the forms of relief comparably effective for that purpose.

(B) If the service provider qualifies for the limitation on remedies described in subsection (a), the court may only grant injunctive relief in one or both of the following forms:

(i) An order restraining the service provider from providing access to a subscriber or account holder of the service provider's system or network who is using the provider's service to engage in infringing activity and is identified in the order, by terminating the accounts of the subscriber or account holder that are specified in the order.

(ii) An order restraining the service provider from providing access, by taking reasonable steps specified in the order to block access, to a specific, identified, online location outside the United States.

(2) **Considerations.** —The court, in considering the relevant criteria for injunctive relief under applicable law, shall consider—

(A) whether such an injunction, either alone or in combination with other such injunctions issued against the same service provider under this subsection, would significantly burden either the provider or the operation of the provider's system or network;

(B) the magnitude of the harm likely to be suffered by the copyright owner in the digital network environment if steps are not taken to prevent or restrain the infringement;

(C) whether implementation of such an injunction would be technically feasible and effective, and would not interfere with access to noninfringing material at other online locations; and

(D) whether other less burdensome and comparably effective means of preventing or restraining access to the infringing material are available.

(3) Notice and ex parte orders. —

Injunctive relief under this subsection shall be available only after notice to the service provider and an opportunity for the service provider to appear are provided, except for orders ensuring the preservation of evidence or other orders having no material adverse effect on the operation of the service provider's communications network.

(k) Definitions. —

(1) Service provider. —

(A) As used in subsection (a), the term "service provider" means an entity offering the transmission, routing, or providing of connections for digital online communications, between or among points specified by a user, of material of the user's choosing, without modification to the content of the material as sent or received.

(B) As used in this section, other than subsection (a), the term "service provider" means a provider of online services or network access, or the operator of facilities therefor, and includes an entity described in subparagraph (A).

(2) Monetary relief. —

As used in this section, the term "monetary relief" means damages, costs, attorneys' fees, and any other form of monetary payment.

(l) Other Defenses Not Affected. —

The failure of a service provider's conduct to qualify for limitation of liability under this section shall not bear adversely upon the consideration of a defense by the service provider that the service provider's conduct is not infringing under this title or any other defense.

(m) Protection of Privacy. —Nothing in this section shall be construed to condition the applicability of subsections (a) through (d) on—

(1) a service provider monitoring its service or affirmatively seeking facts indicating infringing activity, except to the extent consistent with a standard technical measure complying with the provisions of subsection (i); or

(2) a service provider gaining access to, removing, or disabling access to material in cases in which such conduct is prohibited by law.

(n) Construction. —

Subsections (a), (b), (c), and (d) describe separate and distinct functions for purposes of applying this section. Whether a service provider qualifies for the limitation on liability in any one of those subsections shall be based solely on the criteria in that subsection, and shall not affect a determination of whether that service provider qualifies for the limitations on liability under any other such subsection.

(Added Pub. L. 105-304, title Ⅱ, § 202(a), Oct. 28, 1998, 112 Stat. 2877; amended Pub. L. 106-44, § 1(d), Aug. 5, 1999, 113 Stat. 222; Pub. L. 111-295, § 3(a), Dec. 9, 2010, 124 Stat. 3180.)

注：基于DMCA实施将近二十年互联网产业的发展，美国版权局目前正在实施一项旨在评估《美国法典》第17题第512条中安全港条款影响和有效性的研究。为此，美国版权局发布了征求公众意见的公告。至第一轮公开意见截止日2016年4月1日，版权局收到超过9200份书面意见。版权局又于5月2日、3日在纽约，5月12日、13日在旧金山召开公开圆桌会议以征求关于第512条进一步的意见。目前，纽约和旧金山圆桌会议的会议记录已经可以在线查看和下载。进一步书面公众意见的提交于2017年2月21日截止，书面的经验研究提交于2017年3月22日截止。上述美国版权局征求意见公告、会议记录、书面的公众意见以及经验研究可参见美国国家版权局网站，网址：https://www.copyright.gov/policy/section512/。

附录 2

Directive 2001/29/EC of the European Parliament and of the Council of 22 May 2001 on the harmonisation of certain aspects of copyright and related rights in the information society

THE EUROPEAN PARLIAMENT AND THE COUNCIL OF THE EUROPEAN UNION,

Having regard to the Treaty establishing the European Community, and in particular Articles 47(2), 55 and 95 thereof,

Having regard to the proposal from the Commission(1),

Having regard to the opinion of the Economic and Social Committee(2),

Acting in accordance with the procedure laid down in Article 251 of the Treaty (3),

Whereas:

(1) The Treaty provides for the establishment of an internal market and the institution of a system ensuring that competition in the internal market is not distorted. Harmonisation of the laws of the Member States on copyright and related rights contributes to the achievement of these objectives.

(2) The European Council, meeting at Corfu on 24 and 25 June 1994, stressed the need to create a general and flexible legal framework at Community level in order to foster the development of the information society in Europe. This requires, inter alia, the existence of an internal market for new products and services. Important Community legislation to ensure such a regulatory framework is already in place or its adoption is well under way. Copyright and related rights play an important role in this context as they protect and stimulate the development and marketing of new products and services and the creation and exploitation of their creative content.

(3) The proposed harmonisation will help to implement the four freedoms of the

internal market and relates to compliance with the fundamental principles of law and especially of property, including intellectual property, and freedom of expression and the public interest.

(4) A harmonised legal framework on copyright and related rights, through increased legal certainty and while providing for a high level of protection of intellectual property, will foster substantial investment in creativity and innovation, including network infrastructure, and lead in turn to growth and increased competitiveness of European industry, both in the area of content provision and information technology and more generally across a wide range of industrial and cultural sectors. This will safeguard employment and encourage new job creation.

(5) Technological development has multiplied and diversified the vectors for creation, production and exploitation. While no new concepts for the protection of intellectual property are needed, the current law on copyright and related rights should be adapted and supplemented to respond adequately to economic realities such as new forms of exploitation.

(6) Without harmonisation at Community level, legislative activities at national level which have already been initiated in a number of Member States in order to respond to the technological challenges might result in significant differences in protection and thereby in restrictions on the free movement of services and products incorporating, or based on, intellectual property, leading to a refragmentation of the internal market and legislative inconsistency. The impact of such legislative differences and uncertainties will become more significant with the further development of the information society, which has already greatly increased transborder exploitation of intellectual property. This development will and should further increase. Significant legal differences and uncertainties in protection may hinder economies of scale for new products and services containing copyright and related rights.

(7) The Community legal framework for the protection of copyright and related rights must, therefore, also be adapted and supplemented as far as is necessary for the smooth functioning of the internal market. To that end, those national provisions on copyright and related rights which vary considerably from one Member State to another or which cause legal uncertainties hindering the smooth functioning of the internal market and the proper development of the information society in Europe should be adjusted, and inconsistent national responses to the technological developments should be avoided, whilst differences not adversely affecting the functioning of the internal market need not be removed or prevented.

(8) The various social, societal and cultural implications of the information soci-

ety require that account be taken of the specific features of the content of products and services.

(9) Any harmonisation of copyright and related rights must take as a basis a high level of protection, since such rights are crucial to intellectual creation. Their protection helps to ensure the maintenance and development of creativity in the interests of authors, performers, producers, consumers, culture, industry and the public at large. Intellectual property has therefore been recognised as an integral part of property.

(10) If authors or performers are to continue their creative and artistic work, they have to receive an appropriate reward for the use of their work, as must producers in order to be able to finance this work. The investment required to produce products such as phonograms, films or multimedia products, and services such as "on-demand" services, is considerable. Adequate legal protection of intellectual property rights is necessary in order to guarantee the availability of such a reward and provide the opportunity for satisfactory returns on this investment.

(11) A rigorous, effective system for the protection of copyright and related rights is one of the main ways of ensuring that European cultural creativity and production receive the necessary resources and of safeguarding the independence and dignity of artistic creators and performers.

(12) Adequate protection of copyright works and subject-matter of related rights is also of great importance from a cultural standpoint. Article 151 of the Treaty requires the Community to take cultural aspects into account in its action.

(13) A common search for, and consistent application at European level of, technical measures to protect works and other subject-matter and to provide the necessary information on rights are essential insofar as the ultimate aim of these measures is to give effect to the principles and guarantees laid down in law.

(14) This Directive should seek to promote learning and culture by protecting works and other subject-matter while permitting exceptions or limitations in the public interest for the purpose of education and teaching.

(15) The Diplomatic Conference held under the auspices of the World Intellectual Property Organisation (WIPO) in December 1996 led to the adoption of two new Treaties, the "WIPO Copyright Treaty" and the "WIPO Performances and Phonograms Treaty", dealing respectively with the protection of authors and the protection of performers and phonogram producers. Those Treaties update the international protection for copyright and related rights significantly, not least with regard to the so-called "digital agenda", and improve the means to fight piracy world-wide. The Community and a majority of Member States have already signed the Treaties and the

process of making arrangements for the ratification of the Treaties by the Community and the Member States is under way. This Directive also serves to implement a number of the new international obligations.

(16) Liability for activities in the network environment concerns not only copyright and related rights but also other areas, such as defamation, misleading advertising, or infringement of trademarks, and is addressed horizontally in Directive 2000/31/EC of the European Parliament and of the Council of 8 June 2000 on certain legal aspects of information society services, in particular electronic commerce, in the internal market ("Directive on electronic commerce") (4), which clarifies and harmonises various legal issues relating to information society services including electronic commerce. This Directive should be implemented within a timescale similar to that for the implementation of the Directive on electronic commerce, since that Directive provides a harmonised framework of principles and provisions relevant inter alia to important parts of this Directive. This Directive is without prejudice to provisions relating to liability in that Directive.

(17) It is necessary, especially in the light of the requirements arising out of the digital environment, to ensure that collecting societies achieve a higher level of rationalisation and transparency with regard to compliance with competition rules.

(18) This Directive is without prejudice to the arrangements in the Member States concerning the management of rights such as extended collective licences.

(19) The moral rights of rightholders should be exercised according to the legislation of the Member States and the provisions of the Berne Convention for the Protection of Literary and Artistic Works, of the WIPO Copyright Treaty and of the WIPO Performances and Phonograms Treaty. Such moral rights remain outside the scope of this Directive.

(20) This Directive is based on principles and rules already laid down in the Directives currently in force in this area, in particular Directives 91/250/EEC(5), 92/100/EEC(6), 93/83/EEC(7), 93/98/EEC(8) and 96/9/EC(9), and it develops those principles and rules and places them in the context of the information society. The provisions of this Directive should be without prejudice to the provisions of those Directives, unless otherwise provided in this Directive.

(21) This Directive should define the scope of the acts covered by the reproduction right with regard to the different beneficiaries. This should be done in conformity with the acquis communautaire. A broad definition of these acts is needed to ensure legal certainty within the internal market.

(22) The objective of proper support for the dissemination of culture must not be

achieved by sacrificing strict protection of rights or by tolerating illegal forms of distribution of counterfeited or pirated works.

(23) This Directive should harmonise further the author's right of communication to the public. This right should be understood in a broad sense covering all communication to the public not present at the place where the communication originates. This right should cover any such transmission or retransmission of a work to the public by wire or wireless means, including broadcasting. This right should not cover any other acts.

(24) The right to make available to the public subject-matter referred to in Article 3(2) should be understood as covering all acts of making available such subject-matter to members of the public not present at the place where the act of making available originates, and as not covering any other acts.

(25) The legal uncertainty regarding the nature and the level of protection of acts of on-demand transmission of copyright works and subject-matter protected by related rights over networks should be overcome by providing for harmonised protection at Community level. It should be made clear that all rightholders recognised by this Directive should have an exclusive right to make available to the public copyright works or any other subject-matter by way of interactive on-demand transmissions. Such interactive on-demand transmissions are characterised by the fact that members of the public may access them from a place and at a time individually chosen by them.

(26) With regard to the making available in on-demand services by broadcasters of their radio or television productions incorporating music from commercial phonograms as an integral part thereof, collective licensing arrangements are to be encouraged in order to facilitate the clearance of the rights concerned.

(27) The mere provision of physical facilities for enabling or making a communication does not in itself amount to communication within the meaning of this Directive.

(28) Copyright protection under this Directive includes the exclusive right to control distribution of the work incorporated in a tangible article. The first sale in the Community of the original of a work or copies thereof by the rightholder or with his consent exhausts the right to control resale of that object in the Community. This right should not be exhausted in respect of the original or of copies thereof sold by the rightholder or with his consent outside the Community. Rental and lending rights for authors have been established in Directive 92/100/EEC. The distribution right provided for in this Directive is without prejudice to the provisions relating to the rental and lending rights contained in Chapter I of that Directive.

(29) The question of exhaustion does not arise in the case of services and on-

line services in particular. This also applies with regard to a material copy of a work or other subject-matter made by a user of such a service with the consent of the rightholder. Therefore, the same applies to rental and lending of the original and copies of works or other subject-matter which are services by nature. Unlike CD-ROM or CD-I, where the intellectual property is incorporated in a material medium, namely an item of goods, every on-line service is in fact an act which should be subject to authorisation where the copyright or related right so provides.

(30) The rights referred to in this Directive may be transferred, assigned or subject to the granting of contractual licences, without prejudice to the relevant national legislation on copyright and related rights.

(31) A fair balance of rights and interests between the different categories of rightholders, as well as between the different categories of rightholders and users of protected subject-matter must be safeguarded. The existing exceptions and limitations to the rights as set out by the Member States have to be reassessed in the light of the new electronic environment. Existing differences in the exceptions and limitations to certain restricted acts have direct negative effects on the functioning of the internal market of copyright and related rights. Such differences could well become more pronounced in view of the further development of transborder exploitation of works and cross-border activities. In order to ensure the proper functioning of the internal market, such exceptions and limitations should be defined more harmoniously. The degree of their harmonisation should be based on their impact on the smooth functioning of the internal market.

(32) This Directive provides for an exhaustive enumeration of exceptions and limitations to the reproduction right and the right of communication to the public. Some exceptions or limitations only apply to the reproduction right, where appropriate. This list takes due account of the different legal traditions in Member States, while, at the same time, aiming to ensure a functioning internal market. Member States should arrive at a coherent application of these exceptions and limitations, which will be assessed when reviewing implementing legislation in the future.

(33) The exclusive right of reproduction should be subject to an exception to allow certain acts of temporary reproduction, which are transient or incidental reproductions, forming an integral and essential part of a technological process and carried out for the sole purpose of enabling either efficient transmission in a network between third parties by an intermediary, or a lawful use of a work or other subject-matter to be made. The acts of reproduction concerned should have no separate economic value on their own. To the extent that they meet these conditions, this exception should in-

clude acts which enable browsing as well as acts of caching to take place, including those which enable transmission systems to function efficiently, provided that the intermediary does not modify the information and does not interfere with the lawful use of technology, widely recognised and used by industry, to obtain data on the use of the information. A use should be considered lawful where it is authorised by the rightholder or not restricted by law.

(34) Member States should be given the option of providing for certain exceptions or limitations for cases such as educational and scientific purposes, for the benefit of public institutions such as libraries and archives, for purposes of news reporting, for quotations, for use by people with disabilities, for public security uses and for uses in administrative and judicial proceedings.

(35) In certain cases of exceptions or limitations, rightholders should receive fair compensation to compensate them adequately for the use made of their protected works or other subject-matter. When determining the form, detailed arrangements and possible level of such fair compensation, account should be taken of the particular circumstances of each case. When evaluating these circumstances, a valuable criterion would be the possible harm to the rightholders resulting from the act in question. In cases where rightholders have already received payment in some other form, for instance as part of a licence fee, no specific or separate payment may be due. The level of fair compensation should take full account of the degree of use of technological protection measures referred to in this Directive. In certain situations where the prejudice to the rightholder would be minimal, no obligation for payment may arise.

(36) The Member States may provide for fair compensation for rightholders also when applying the optional provisions on exceptions or limitations which do not require such compensation.

(37) Existing national schemes on reprography, where they exist, do not create major barriers to the internal market. Member States should be allowed to provide for an exception or limitation in respect of reprography.

(38) Member States should be allowed to provide for an exception or limitation to the reproduction right for certain types of reproduction of audio, visual and audio-visual material for private use, accompanied by fair compensation. This may include the introduction or continuation of remuneration schemes to compensate for the prejudice to rightholders. Although differences between those remuneration schemes affect the functioning of the internal market, those differences, with respect to analogue private reproduction, should not have a significant impact on the development of the information society. Digital private copying is likely to be more widespread and have a

greater economic impact. Due account should therefore be taken of the differences between digital and analogue private copying and a distinction should be made in certain respects between them.

(39) When applying the exception or limitation on private copying, Member States should take due account of technological and economic developments, in particular with respect to digital private copying and remuneration schemes, when effective technological protection measures are available. Such exceptions or limitations should not inhibit the use of technological measures or their enforcement against circumvention.

(40) Member States may provide for an exception or limitation for the benefit of certain non-profit making establishments, such as publicly accessible libraries and equivalent institutions, as well as archives. However, this should be limited to certain special cases covered by the reproduction right. Such an exception or limitation should not cover uses made in the context of on-line delivery of protected works or other subject-matter. This Directive should be without prejudice to the Member States' option to derogate from the exclusive public lending right in accordance with Article 5 of Directive 92/100/EEC. Therefore, specific contracts or licences should be promoted which, without creating imbalances, favour such establishments and the disseminative purposes they serve.

(41) When applying the exception or limitation in respect of ephemeral recordings made by broadcasting organisations it is understood that a broadcaster's own facilities include those of a person acting on behalf of and under the responsibility of the broadcasting organisation.

(42) When applying the exception or limitation for non-commercial educational and scientific research purposes, including distance learning, the non-commercial nature of the activity in question should be determined by that activity as such. The organisational structure and the means of funding of the establishment concerned are not the decisive factors in this respect.

(43) It is in any case important for the Member States to adopt all necessary measures to facilitate access to works by persons suffering from a disability which constitutes an obstacle to the use of the works themselves, and to pay particular attention to accessible formats.

(44) When applying the exceptions and limitations provided for in this Directive, they should be exercised in accordance with international obligations. Such exceptions and limitations may not be applied in a way which prejudices the legitimate interests of the rightholder or which conflicts with the normal exploitation of his work

or other subject-matter. The provision of such exceptions or limitations by Member States should, in particular, duly reflect the increased economic impact that such exceptions or limitations may have in the context of the new electronic environment. Therefore, the scope of certain exceptions or limitations may have to be even more limited when it comes to certain new uses of copyright works and other subject-matter.

(45) The exceptions and limitations referred to in Article 5(2), (3) and (4) should not, however, prevent the definition of contractual relations designed to ensure fair compensation for the rightholders insofar as permitted by national law.

(46) Recourse to mediation could help users and rightholders to settle disputes. The Commission, in cooperation with the Member States within the Contact Committee, should undertake a study to consider new legal ways of settling disputes concerning copyright and related rights.

(47) Technological development will allow rightholders to make use of technological measures designed to prevent or restrict acts not authorised by the rightholders of any copyright, rights related to copyright or the sui generis right in databases. The danger, however, exists that illegal activities might be carried out in order to enable or facilitate the circumvention of the technical protection provided by these measures. In order to avoid fragmented legal approaches that could potentially hinder the functioning of the internal market, there is a need to provide for harmonised legal protection against circumvention of effective technological measures and against provision of devices and products or services to this effect.

(48) Such legal protection should be provided in respect of technological measures that effectively restrict acts not authorised by the rightholders of any copyright, rights related to copyright or the sui generis right in databases without, however, preventing the normal operation of electronic equipment and its technological development. Such legal protection implies no obligation to design devices, products, components or services to correspond to technological measures, so long as such device, product, component or service does not otherwise fall under the prohibition of Article 6. Such legal protection should respect proportionality and should not prohibit those devices or activities which have a commercially significant purpose or use other than to circumvent the technical protection. In particular, this protection should not hinder research into cryptography.

(49) The legal protection of technological measures is without prejudice to the application of any national provisions which may prohibit the private possession of devices, products or components for the circumvention of technological measures.

(50) Such a harmonised legal protection does not affect the specific provisions

on protection provided for by Directive 91/250/EEC. In particular, it should not apply to the protection of technological measures used in connection with computer programs, which is exclusively addressed in that Directive. It should neither inhibit nor prevent the development or use of any means of circumventing a technological measure that is necessary to enable acts to be undertaken in accordance with the terms of Article 5(3) or Article 6 of Directive 91/250/EEC. Articles 5 and 6 of that Directive exclusively determine exceptions to the exclusive rights applicable to computer programs.

(51) The legal protection of technological measures applies without prejudice to public policy, as reflected in Article 5, or public security. Member States should promote voluntary measures taken by rightholders, including the conclusion and implementation of agreements between rightholders and other parties concerned, to accommodate achieving the objectives of certain exceptions or limitations provided for in national law in accordance with this Directive. In the absence of such voluntary measures or agreements within a reasonable period of time, Member States should take appropriate measures to ensure that rightholders provide beneficiaries of such exceptions or limitations with appropriate means of benefiting from them, by modifying an implemented technological measure or by other means. However, in order to prevent abuse of such measures taken by rightholders, including within the framework of agreements, or taken by a Member State, any technological measures applied in implementation of such measures should enjoy legal protection.

(52) When implementing an exception or limitation for private copying in accordance with Article 5(2)(b), Member States should likewise promote the use of voluntary measures to accommodate achieving the objectives of such exception or limitation. If, within a reasonable period of time, no such voluntary measures to make reproduction for private use possible have been taken, Member States may take measures to enable beneficiaries of the exception or limitation concerned to benefit from it. Voluntary measures taken by rightholders, including agreements between rightholders and other parties concerned, as well as measures taken by Member States, do not prevent rightholders from using technological measures which are consistent with the exceptions or limitations on private copying in national law in accordance with Article 5(2)(b), taking account of the condition of fair compensation under that provision and the possible differentiation between various conditions of use in accordance with Article 5(5), such as controlling the number of reproductions. In order to prevent abuse of such measures, any technological measures applied in their implementation should enjoy legal protection.

(53) The protection of technological measures should ensure a secure environment for the provision of interactive on-demand services, in such a way that members of the public may access works or other subject-matter from a place and at a time individually chosen by them. Where such services are governed by contractual arrangements, the first and second subparagraphs of Article 6(4) should not apply. Non-interactive forms of online use should remain subject to those provisions.

(54) Important progress has been made in the international standardisation of technical systems of identification of works and protected subject-matter in digital format. In an increasingly networked environment, differences between technological measures could lead to an incompatibility of systems within the Community. Compatibility and interoperability of the different systems should be encouraged. It would be highly desirable to encourage the development of global systems.

(55) Technological development will facilitate the distribution of works, notably on networks, and this will entail the need for rightholders to identify better the work or other subject-matter, the author or any other rightholders, and to provide information about the terms and conditions of use of the work or other subject-matter in order to render easier the management of rights attached to them. Rightholders should be encouraged to use markings indicating, in addition to the information referred to above, inter alia their authorisation when putting works or other subject-matter on networks.

(56) There is, however, the danger that illegal activities might be carried out in order to remove or alter the electronic copyright-management information attached to it, or otherwise to distribute, import for distribution, broadcast, communicate to the public or make available to the public works or other protected subject-matter from which such information has been removed without authority. In order to avoid fragmented legal approaches that could potentially hinder the functioning of the internal market, there is a need to provide for harmonised legal protection against any of these activities.

(57) Any such rights-management information systems referred to above may, depending on their design, at the same time process personal data about the consumption patterns of protected subject-matter by individuals and allow for tracing of on-line behaviour. These technical means, in their technical functions, should incorporate privacy safeguards in accordance with Directive 95/46/EC of the European Parliament and of the Council of 24 October 1995 on the protection of individuals with regard to the processing of personal data and the free movement of such data(10).

(58) Member States should provide for effective sanctions and remedies for in-

fringements of rights and obligations as set out in this Directive. They should take all the measures necessary to ensure that those sanctions and remedies are applied. The sanctions thus provided for should be effective, proportionate and dissuasive and should include the possibility of seeking damages and/or injunctive relief and, where appropriate, of applying for seizure of infringing material.

(59) In the digital environment, in particular, the services of intermediaries may increasingly be used by third parties for infringing activities. In many cases such intermediaries are best placed to bring such infringing activities to an end. Therefore, without prejudice to any other sanctions and remedies available, rightholders should have the possibility of applying for an injunction against an intermediary who carries a third party's infringement of a protected work or other subject–matter in a network. This possibility should be available even where the acts carried out by the intermediary are exempted under Article 5. The conditions and modalities relating to such injunctions should be left to the national law of the Member States.

(60) The protection provided under this Directive should be without prejudice to national or Community legal provisions in other areas, such as industrial property, data protection, conditional access, access to public documents, and the rule of media exploitation chronology, which may affect the protection of copyright or related rights.

(61) In order to comply with the WIPO Performances and Phonograms Treaty, Directives 92/100/EEC and 93/98/EEC should be amended,

HAVE ADOPTED THIS DIRECTIVE:

CHAPTER I

OBJECTIVE AND SCOPE

Article 1

Scope

1. This Directive concerns the legal protection of copyright and related rights in the framework of the internal market, with particular emphasis on the information society.

2. Except in the cases referred to in Article 11, this Directive shall leave intact and shall in no way affect existing Community provisions relating to:

(a) the legal protection of computer programs;

(b) rental right, lending right and certain rights related to copyright in the field of intellectual property;

(c) copyright and related rights applicable to broadcasting of programmes by satellite and cable retransmission;

(d) the term of protection of copyright and certain related rights;

(e) the legal protection of databases.

CHAPTER II
RIGHTS AND EXCEPTIONS

Article 2
Reproduction right

Member States shall provide for the exclusive right to authorise or prohibit direct or indirect, temporary or permanent reproduction by any means and in any form, in whole or in part:

(a) for authors, of their works;

(b) for performers, of fixations of their performances;

(c) for phonogram producers, of their phonograms;

(d) for the producers of the first fixations of films, in respect of the original and copies of their films;

(e) for broadcasting organisations, of fixations of their broadcasts, whether those broadcasts are transmitted by wire or over the air, including by cable or satellite.

Article 3
Right of communication to the public of works and right of making available to the public other subject-matter

1. Member States shall provide authors with the exclusive right to authorise or prohibit any communication to the public of their works, by wire or wireless means, including the making available to the public of their works in such a way that members of the public may access them from a place and at a time individually chosen by them.

2. Member States shall provide for the exclusive right to authorise or prohibit the making available to the public, by wire or wireless means, in such a way that members of the public may access them from a place and at a time individually chosen by them:

(a) for performers, of fixations of their performances;

(b) for phonogram producers, of their phonograms;

(c) for the producers of the first fixations of films, of the original and copies of their films;

(d) for broadcasting organisations, of fixations of their broadcasts, whether these broadcasts are transmitted by wire or over the air, including by cable or satellite.

3. The rights referred to in paragraphs 1 and 2 shall not be exhausted by any act of communication to the public or making available to the public as set out in this Article.

Article 4
Distribution right

1. Member States shall provide for authors, in respect of the original of their works or of copies thereof, the exclusive right to authorise or prohibit any form of distribution to the public by sale or otherwise.

2. The distribution right shall not be exhausted within the Community in respect of the

original or copies of the work, except where the first sale or other transfer of ownership in the Community of that object is made by the rightholder or with his consent.

Article 5

Exceptions and limitations

1. Temporary acts of reproduction referred to in Article 2, which are transient or incidental [and] an integral and essential part of a technological process and whose sole purpose is to enable:

(a) a transmission in a network between third parties by an intermediary, or

(b) a lawful use

of a work or other subject-matter to be made, and which have no independent economic significance, shall be exempted from the reproduction right provided for in Article 2.

2. Member States may provide for exceptions or limitations to the reproduction right provided for in Article 2 in the following cases:

(a) in respect of reproductions on paper or any similar medium, effected by the use of any kind of photographic technique or by some other process having similar effects, with the exception of sheet music, provided that the rightholders receive fair compensation;

(b) in respect of reproductions on any medium made by a natural person for private use and for ends that are neither directly nor indirectly commercial, on condition that the rightholders receive fair compensation which takes account of the application or non-application of technological measures referred to in Article 6 to the work or subject-matter concerned;

(c) in respect of specific acts of reproduction made by publicly accessible libraries, educational establishments or museums, or by archives, which are not for direct or indirect economic or commercial advantage;

(d) in respect of ephemeral recordings of works made by broadcasting organisations by means of their own facilities and for their own broadcasts; the preservation of these recordings in official archives may, on the grounds of their exceptional documentary character, be permitted;

(e) in respect of reproductions of broadcasts made by social institutions pursuing non-commercial purposes, such as hospitals or prisons, on condition that the rightholders receive fair compensation.

3. Member States may provide for exceptions or limitations to the rights provided for in Articles 2 and 3 in the following cases:

(a) use for the sole purpose of illustration for teaching or scientific research, as long as the source, including the author's name, is indicated, unless this turns out to be impossible and to the extent justified by the non-commercial purpose to be achieved;

(b) uses, for the benefit of people with a disability, which are directly related to the disability and of a non-commercial nature, to the extent required by the specific disability;

(c) reproduction by the press, communication to the public or making available of published articles on current economic, political or religious topics or of broadcast works or other subject-matter of the same character, in cases where such use is not expressly reserved, and as long as the source, including the author's name, is indicated, or use of works or other subject-matter in connection with the reporting of current events, to the extent justified by the informatory purpose and as long as the source, including the author's name, is indicated, unless this turns out to be impossible;

(d) quotations for purposes such as criticism or review, provided that they relate to a work or other subject-matter which has already been lawfully made available to the public, that, unless this turns out to be impossible, the source, including the author's name, is indicated, and that their use is in accordance with fair practice, and to the extent required by the specific purpose;

(e) use for the purposes of public security or to ensure the proper performance or reporting of administrative, parliamentary or judicial proceedings;

(f) use of political speeches as well as extracts of public lectures or similar works or subject-matter to the extent justified by the informatory purpose and provided that the source, including the author's name, is indicated, except where this turns out to be impossible;

(g) use during religious celebrations or official celebrations organised by a public authority;

(h) use of works, such as works of architecture or sculpture, made to be located permanently in public places;

(i) incidental inclusion of a work or other subject-matter in other material;

(j) use for the purpose of advertising the public exhibition or sale of artistic works, to the extent necessary to promote the event, excluding any other commercial use;

(k) use for the purpose of caricature, parody or pastiche;

(l) use in connection with the demonstration or repair of equipment;

(m) use of an artistic work in the form of a building or a drawing or plan of a building for the purposes of reconstructing the building;

(n) use by communication or making available, for the purpose of research or private study, to individual members of the public by dedicated terminals on the premises of establishments referred to in paragraph 2(c) of works and other subject-matter not subject to purchase or licensing terms which are contained in their collections;

(o) use in certain other cases of minor importance where exceptions or limitations already exist under national law, provided that they only concern analogue uses and do not affect the free circulation of goods and services within the Community, without prejudice to the other exceptions and limitations contained in this Article.

4. Where the Member States may provide for an exception or limitation to the right of reproduction pursuant to paragraphs 2 and 3, they may provide similarly for an exception or limitation to the right of distribution as referred to in Article 4 to the extent justified by the

purpose of the authorised act of reproduction.

5. The exceptions and limitations provided for in paragraphs 1, 2, 3 and 4 shall only be applied in certain special cases which do not conflict with a normal exploitation of the work or other subject-matter and do not unreasonably prejudice the legitimate interests of the rightholder.

CHAPTER III
PROTECTION OF TECHNOLOGICAL MEASURES AND RIGHTS-MANAGEMENT INFORMATION

Article 6
Obligations as to technological measures

1. Member States shall provide adequate legal protection against the circumvention of any effective technological measures, which the person concerned carries out in the knowledge, or with reasonable grounds to know, that he or she is pursuing that objective.

2. Member States shall provide adequate legal protection against the manufacture, import, distribution, sale, rental, advertisement for sale or rental, or possession for commercial purposes of devices, products or components or the provision of services which:

(a) are promoted, advertised or marketed for the purpose of circumvention of, or

(b) have only a limited commercially significant purpose or use other than to circumvent, or

(c) are primarily designed, produced, adapted or performed for the purpose of enabling or facilitating the circumvention of,

any effective technological measures.

3. For the purposes of this Directive, the expression "technological measures" means any technology, device or component that, in the normal course of its operation, is designed to prevent or restrict acts, in respect of works or other subject-matter, which are not authorised by the rightholder of any copyright or any right related to copyright as provided for by law or the sui generis right provided for in Chapter III of Directive 96/9/EC. Technological measures shall be deemed "effective" where the use of a protected work or other subject-matter is controlled by the rightholders through application of an access control or protection process, such as encryption, scrambling or other transformation of the work or other subject-matter or a copy control mechanism, which achieves the protection objective.

4. Notwithstanding the legal protection provided for in paragraph 1, in the absence of voluntary measures taken by rightholders, including agreements between rightholders and other parties concerned, Member States shall take appropriate measures to ensure that rightholders make available to the beneficiary of an exception or limitation provided for in national law in accordance with Article 5(2)(a), (2)(c), (2)(d), (2)(e), (3)(a), (3)(b) or (3)(e) the means of benefiting from that exception or limitation, to the extent necessary to benefit from that exception or limitation and where that beneficiary has legal access to the

protected work or subject-matter concerned.

A Member State may also take such measures in respect of a beneficiary of an exception or limitation provided for in accordance with Article 5(2)(b), unless reproduction for private use has already been made possible by rightholders to the extent necessary to benefit from the exception or limitation concerned and in accordance with the provisions of Article 5(2)(b) and (5), without preventing rightholders from adopting adequate measures regarding the number of reproductions in accordance with these provisions.

The technological measures applied voluntarily by rightholders, including those applied in implementation of voluntary agreements, and technological measures applied in implementation of the measures taken by Member States, shall enjoy the legal protection provided for in paragraph 1.

The provisions of the first and second subparagraphs shall not apply to works or other subject-matter made available to the public on agreed contractual terms in such a way that members of the public may access them from a place and at a time individually chosen by them.

When this Article is applied in the context of Directives 92/100/EEC and 96/9/EC, this paragraph shall apply mutatis mutandis.

Article 7

Obligations concerning rights-management information

1. Member States shall provide for adequate legal protection against any person knowingly performing without authority any of the following acts:

(a) the removal or alteration of any electronic rights-management information;

(b) the distribution, importation for distribution, broadcasting, communication or making available to the public of works or other subject-matter protected under this Directive or under Chapter III of Directive 96/9/EC from which electronic rights-management information has been removed or altered without authority,

if such person knows, or has reasonable grounds to know, that by so doing he is inducing, enabling, facilitating or concealing an infringement of any copyright or any rights related to copyright as provided by law, or of the sui generis right provided for in Chapter III of Directive 96/9/EC.

2. For the purposes of this Directive, the expression "rights-management information" means any information provided by rightholders which identifies the work or other subject-matter referred to in this Directive or covered by the sui generis right provided for in Chapter III of Directive 96/9/EC, the author or any other rightholder, or information about the terms and conditions of use of the work or other subject-matter, and any numbers or codes that represent such information.

The first subparagraph shall apply when any of these items of information is associated with a copy of, or appears in connection with the communication to the public of, a work or other subjectmatter referred to in this Directive or covered by the sui generis right provided for in Chapter III of Directive 96/9/EC.

CHAPTER IV
COMMON PROVISIONS

Article 8
Sanctions and remedies

1. Member States shall provide appropriate sanctions and remedies in respect of infringements of the rights and obligations set out in this Directive and shall take all the measures necessary to ensure that those sanctions and remedies are applied. The sanctions thus provided for shall be effective, proportionate and dissuasive.

2. Each Member State shall take the measures necessary to ensure that rightholders whose interests are affected by an infringing activity carried out on its territory can bring an action for damages and/or apply for an injunction and, where appropriate, for the seizure of infringing material as well as of devices, products or components referred to in Article 6(2).

3. Member States shall ensure that rightholders are in a position to apply for an injunction against intermediaries whose services are used by a third party to infringe a copyright or related right.

Article 9
Continued application of other legal provisions

This Directive shall be without prejudice to provisions concerning in particular patent rights, trade marks, design rights, utility models, topographies of semi-conductor products, type faces, conditional access, access to cable of broadcasting services, protection of national treasures, legal deposit requirements, laws on restrictive practices and unfair competition, trade secrets, security, confidentiality, data protection and privacy, access to public documents, the law of contract.

Article 10
Application over time

1. The provisions of this Directive shall apply in respect of all works and other subject-matter referred to in this Directive which are, on 22 December 2002, protected by the Member States' legislation in the field of copyright and related rights, or which meet the criteria for protection under the provisions of this Directive or the provisions referred to in Article 1(2).

2. This Directive shall apply without prejudice to any acts concluded and rights acquired before 22 December 2002.

Article 11
Technical adaptations

1. Directive 92/100/EEC is hereby amended as follows:
(a) Article 7 shall be deleted;

(b) Article 10(3) shall be replaced by the following: "3. The limitations shall only be applied in certain special cases which do not conflict with a normal exploitation of the subject-matter and do not unreasonably prejudice the legitimate interests of the rightholder."

2. Article 3(2) of Directive 93/98/EEC shall be replaced by the following: "2. The rights of producers of phonograms shall expire 50 years after the fixation is made. However, if the phonogram has been lawfully published within this period, the said rights shall expire 50 years from the date of the first lawful publication. If no lawful publication has taken place within the period mentioned in the first sentence, and if the phonogram has been lawfully communicated to the public within this period, the said rights shall expire 50 years from the date of the first lawful communication to the public.

However, where through the expiry of the term of protection granted pursuant to this paragraph in its version before amendment by Directive 2001/29/EC of the European Parliament and of the Council of 22 May 2001 on the harmonisation of certain aspects of copyright and related rights in the information society(11) the rights of producers of phonograms are no longer protected on 22 December 2002, this paragraph shall not have the effect of protecting those rights anew."

Article 12

Final provisions

1. Not later than 22 December 2004 and every three years thereafter, the Commission shall submit to the European Parliament, the Council and the Economic and Social Committee a report on the application of this Directive, in which, inter alia, on the basis of specific information supplied by the Member States, it shall examine in particular the application of Articles 5, 6 and 8 in the light of the development of the digital market. In the case of Article 6, it shall examine in particular whether that Article confers a sufficient level of protection and whether acts which are permitted by law are being adversely affected by the use of effective technological measures. Where necessary, in particular to ensure the functioning of the internal market pursuant to Article 14 of the Treaty, it shall submit proposals for amendments to this Directive.

2. Protection of rights related to copyright under this Directive shall leave intact and shall in no way affect the protection of copyright.

3. A contact committee is hereby established. It shall be composed of representatives of the competent authorities of the Member States. It shall be chaired by a representative of the Commission and shall meet either on the initiative of the chairman or at the request of the delegation of a Member State.

4. The tasks of the committee shall be as follows:

(a) to examine the impact of this Directive on the functioning of the internal market, and to highlight any difficulties;

(b) to organise consultations on all questions deriving from the application of this Directive;

(c) to facilitate the exchange of information on relevant developments in legislation and case-law, as well as relevant economic, social, cultural and technological developments;

(d) to act as a forum for the assessment of the digital market in works and other items, including private copying and the use of technological measures.

Article 13

Implementation

1. Member States shall bring into force the laws, regulations and administrative provisions necessary to comply with this Directive before 22 December 2002. They shall forthwith inform the Commission thereof.

When Member States adopt these measures, they shall contain a reference to this Directive or shall be accompanied by such reference on the occasion of their official publication. The methods of making such reference shall be laid down by Member States.

2. Member States shall communicate to the Commission the text of the provisions of domestic law which they adopt in the field governed by this Directive.

Article 14

Entry into force

This Directive shall enter into force on the day of its publication in the Official Journal of the European Communities.

Article 15

Addressees

This Directive is addressed to the Member States.

Done at Brussels, 22 May 2001.

For the European Parliament
The President
N. Fontaine

For the Council
The President
M. Winberg

(1) OJ C 108, 7.4.1998, p. 6 and
OJ C 180, 25.6.1999, p. 6.

(2) OJ C 407, 28.12.1998, p. 30.

(3) Opinion of the European Parliament of 10 February 1999 (OJ C 150, 28.5.1999, p. 171), Council Common Position of 28 September 2000 (OJ C 344, 1.12.2000, p. 1) and

Decision of the European Parliament of 14 February 2001 (not yet published in the Official Journal). Council Decision of 9 April 2001.

(4) OJ L 178, 17. 7. 2000, p. 1.

(5) Council Directive 91/250/EEC of 14 May 1991 on the legal protection of computer programs (OJ L 122, 17. 5. 1991, p. 42). Directive as amended by Directive 93/98/EEC.

(6) Council Directive 92/100/EEC of 19 November 1992 on rental right and lending right and on certain rights related to copyright in the field of intellectual property (OJ L 346, 27. 11. 1992, p. 61). Directive as amended by Directive 93/98/EEC.

(7) Council Directive 93/83/EEC of 27 September 1993 on the coordination of certain rules concerning copyright and rights related to copyright applicable to satellite broadcasting and cable retransmission (OJ L 248, 6. 10. 1993, p. 15).

(8) Council Directive 93/98/EEC of 29 October 1993 harmonising the term of protection of copyright and certain related rights (OJ L 290, 24. 11. 1993, p. 9).

(9) Directive 96/9/EC of the European Parliament and of the Council of 11 March 1996 on the legal protection of databases (OJ L 77, 27. 3. 1996, p. 20).

(10) OJ L 281, 23. 11. 1995, p. 31.

(11) OJ L 167, 22. 6. 2001, p. 10.

附录 3

EUROPEAN COMMISSION

Brussels, 14.9.2016
COM(2016) 593 final

2016/0280 (COD)

Proposal for a

DIRECTIVE OF THE EUROPEAN PARLIAMENT AND OF THE COUNCIL

on copyright in the Digital Single Market

(Text with EEA relevance)

{SWD(2016) 301 final}
{SWD(2016) 302 final}

EXPLANATORY MEMORANDUM

1. CONTEXT OF THE PROPOSAL
• Reasons for and objectives of the proposal

The evolution of digital technologies has changed the way works and other protected subject-matter are created, produced, distributed and exploited. New uses have emerged as well as new actors and new business models. In the digital environment, cross-border uses have also intensified and new opportunities for consumers to access copyright-protected content have materialised. Even though the objectives and principles laid down by the EU copyright framework remain sound, there is a need to adapt it to these new realities. Intervention at EU level is also needed to avoid fragmentation in the internal market. Against this background, the Digital Single Market Strategy[1] adopted in May 2015 identified the need "to reduce the differences between national copyright regimes and allow for wider online access to works by users across the EU". This Communication highlighted the importance to enhance cross-border access to copyright-protected content services, facilitate new uses in the fields of research and education, and clarify the role of online services in the distribution of works and other subject-matter. In December 2015, the Commission issued a Communication "Towards a modern, more European copyright framework"[2]. This Communication outlined targeted actions and a long-term vision to modernise EU copyright rules. This proposal is one of the measures aiming at addressing specific issues identified in that Communication.

Exceptions and limitations to copyright and neighbouring rights are harmonised at EU level. Some of these exceptions aim at achieving public policy objectives, such as research or education. However, as new types of uses have recently emerged, it remains uncertain whether these exceptions are still adapted to achieve a fair balance

---

[1] COM(2015) 192 final.
[2] COM(2015) 626 final.

between the rights and interests of authors and other rightholders on the one hand, and of users on the other. In addition, these exceptions remain national and legal certainty around cross-border uses is not guaranteed. In this context, the Commission has identified three areas of intervention: digital and cross-border uses in the field of education, text and data mining in the field of scientific research, and preservation of cultural heritage. The objective is to guarantee the legality of certain types of uses in these fields, including across borders. As a result of a modernised framework of exceptions and limitations, researchers will benefit from a clearer legal space to use innovative text and data mining research tools, teachers and students will be able to take full advantage of digital technologies at all levels of education and cultural heritage institutions (i. e. publicly accessible libraries or museums, archives or film or audio heritage institutions) will be supported in their efforts to preserve the cultural heritage, to the ultimate advantage of EU citizens.

Despite the fact that digital technologies should facilitate cross-border access to works and other subject-matter, obstacles remain, in particular for uses and works where clearance of rights is complex. This is the case for cultural heritage institutions wanting to provide online access, including across borders, to out-of-commerce works contained in their catalogues. As a consequence of these obstacles European citizens miss opportunities to access cultural heritage. The proposal addresses these problems by introducing a specific mechanism to facilitate the conclusion of licences for the dissemination of out-of-commerce works by cultural heritage institutions. As regards audiovisual works, despite the growing importance of video-on-demand platforms, EU audiovisual works only constitute one third of works available to consumers on those platforms. Again, this lack of availability partly derives from a complex clearance process. This proposal provides for measures aiming at facilitating the licensing and clearance of rights process. This would ultimately facilitate consumers' cross-border access to copyright-protected content.

Evolution of digital technologies has led to the emergence of new business models and reinforced the role of the Internet as the main marketplace for the distribution and access to copyright-protected content. In this new framework, rightholders face difficulties when seeking to license their rights and be remunerated for the online distribution of their works. This could put at risk the development of European creativity and production of creative content. It is therefore necessary to guarantee that authors and rightholders receive a fair share of the value that is generated by the use of their works and other subject-matter. Against this background, this proposal provides for measures aiming at improving the position of rightholders to negotiate and be remunerated for the exploitation of their content by online services giving access to user-uploaded content. A fair sharing of value is also necessary to ensure the sustainability of the press publications sector. Press publishers are facing difficulties in licensing their publications online and obtaining a fair share of the value they generate. This could ultimately affect citizens' access to information. This proposal provides for a new right for press publishers aiming at facilitating online licensing of their publications, the recoupment of their investment and the enforcement of their rights. It also addresses existing legal uncertainty as regards the possibility for all publishers to receive a share in the compensation for uses of works under an exception. Finally, authors and performers often have a weak bargaining position in their contractual relationships, when licensing their rights. In addition, transparency on the revenues generated by the use of their works or performances often remains limited. This ultimately affects the remuneration of the authors and performers. This proposal includes measures to improve transparency and better balanced contractual relationships between authors and performers and those to whom they assign their rights. Overall, the measures proposed in title IV of the proposal aiming at achieving a well-functioning market place for copyright are expected to have in the medium term a positive impact on the production and availability of content and on media pluralism, to the ultimate benefit of consumers.

- **Consistency with existing policy provisions in the policy area**

The Digital Single Market Strategy puts forward a range of initiatives with the objective of creating an internal market for digital content and services. In December 2015, a first step has been undertaken by the adoption by the Commission of a proposal for a Regulation of the European Parliament and of the Council on ensuring the cross-border portability of online content services in the internal market[1].

The present proposal aims at addressing several of the targeted actions identified in the Communication "Towards a modern, more European copyright framework". Other actions identified in this Communication are covered by the "Proposal for a Regulation of the European Parliament and of the Council laying down rules on the exercise of copyright and related rights applicable to certain online transmissions of broadcasting organisations and retransmissions of television and radio programmes"[2], the "Proposal for a Regulation of the European Parliament and of the Council on the cross-border exchange between the Union and third countries of accessible format copies of certain works and other subject-matter protected by copyright and related

---

[1] COM(2015) 627 final.
[2] COM(2016) 594 final.

rights for the benefit of persons who are blind, visually impaired or otherwise print disabled"[1] and the "Proposal for a Directive of the European Parliament and of the Council on certain permitted uses of works and other subject-matter protected by copyright and related rights for the benefit of persons who are blind, visually impaired or otherwise print disabled and amending Directive 2001/29/EC on the harmonisation of certain aspects of copyright and related rights in the information society"[2], adopted on the same date of this proposal for a Directive.

This proposal is consistent with the existing EU copyright legal framework. This proposal is based upon, and complements the rules laid down in Directive 96/9/EC[3], Directive 2001/29/EC[4], Directive 2006/115/EC[5], Directive 2009/24/EC[6], Directive 2012/28/EU[7] and Directive 2014/26/EU[8]. Those Directives, as well as this proposal, contribute to the functioning of the internal market, ensure a high level of protection for right holders and facilitate the clearance of rights.

This proposal complements Directive 2010/13/EU[9] and the proposal[10] amending it.

• **Consistency with other Union policies**

This proposal would facilitate education and research, improve dissemination of European cultures and positively impact cultural diversity. This Directive is therefore consistent with Articles 165, 167 and 179 of the Treaty on the Functioning of the European Union (TFEU). Furthermore, this proposal contributes to promoting the inter-

---

[1] COM(2016) 595 final.

[2] COM(2016) 596 final.

[3] Directive 96/9/EC of the European Parliament and of the Council of 11 March 1996 on the legal protection of databases (OJ L 077, 27.03.1996, p. 20-28).

[4] Directive 2001/29/EC of the European Parliament and of the Council of 22 May 2001 on the harmonisation of certain aspects of copyright and related rights in the information society (OJ L 167, 22.6.2001, p. 10-19).

[5] Directive 2006/115/EC of the European Parliament and of the Council of 12 December 2006 on rental right and lending right and on certain rights related to copyright in the field of intellectual property (OJ L 376, 27.12.2006, p. 28-35).

[6] Directive 2009/24/EC of the European Parliament and of the Council of 23 April 2009 on the legal protection of computer programs (OJ L 111, 5.5.2009, p. 16-22).

[7] Directive 2012/28/EU of the European Parliament and of the Council of 25 October 2012 on certain permitted uses of orphan works (OJ L 299, 27.10.2012, p. 5-12).

[8] Directive 2014/26/EU of the European Parliament and of the Council of 26 February 2014 on collective management of copyright and related rights and multi-territorial licensing of rights in musical works for online use in the internal market (OJ L 84, 20.3.2014, p. 72-98).

[9] Directive 2010/13/EU of the European Parliament and of the Council of 10 March 2010 on the coordination of certain provisions laid down by law, regulation or administrative action in Member States concerning the provision of audiovisual media services (Audiovisual Media Services Directive) (OJ L 95, 15.4.2010, p. 1-24).

[10] COM(2016) 287 final.

ests of consumers, in accordance with the EU policies in the field of consumer protection and Article 169 TFEU, by allowing a wider access to and use of copyright-protected content.

2. LEGAL BASIS, SUBSIDIARITY AND PROPORTIONALITY

- Legal basis

The proposal is based on Article 114 TFEU. This Article confers on the EU the power to adopt measures which have as their object the establishment and functioning of the internal market.

- Subsidiarity (for non-exclusive competence)

Since exceptions and limitations to copyright and related rights are harmonised at EU level, the margin of manoeuver of Member States in creating or adapting them is limited. In addition, intervention at national level would not be sufficient in view of the cross-border nature of the identified issues. EU intervention is therefore needed to achieve full legal certainty as regards cross-border uses in the fields of research, education and cultural heritage.

Some national initiatives have already been developed to facilitate dissemination of and access to out-of-commerce works. However, these initiatives only exist in some Member States and are only applicable on the national territory. EU intervention is therefore necessary to ensure that licensing mechanisms for the access and dissemination of out-of-commerce works are in place in all Member States and to ensure their cross-border effect. As regards online exploitation of audiovisual works, to foster the availability of European works on video-on-demand platforms across the EU, there is a need to facilitate negotiations of licensing agreements in all Member States.

Online distribution of copyright-protected content is by essence cross-border. Only mechanisms decided at European level could ensure a well-functioning marketplace for the distribution of works and other subject-matter and to ensure the sustainability of the publishing sector in the face of the challenges of the digital environment. Finally, authors and performers should enjoy in all Member States the high level of protection established by EU legislation. In order to do so and to prevent discrepancies across Member States, it is necessary to set an EU common approach to transparency requirements and mechanisms allowing for the adjustment of contracts in certain cases as well as for the resolution of disputes.

- Proportionality

The proposal provides for mandatory exceptions for Member States to implement. These exceptions target key public policy objectives and uses with a cross-border dimension. Exceptions also contain conditions that ensure the preservation of functioning markets and rightholders' interests and incentives to create and invest. When relevant, and while ensuring that the objectives of the Directive are met, room for national decision has been preserved.

The proposal requires Member States to establish mechanisms aiming at facilitating the clearance of copyright and related rights in the fields of out-of-commerce works and online exploitation of audiovisual works. Whereas the proposal aims at ensuring a wider access and dissemination of content, it does so while preserving the rights of authors and other rightholders. Several safeguards are put in place to that effect (e. g. opt-out possibilities, preservation of licensing possibilities, participation in the negotiation forum on a voluntary basis). The proposal does not go further than what is necessary to achieve the intended aim while leaving sufficient room for Member States to make decisions as regards the specifics of these mechanisms and does not impose disproportionate costs.

The proposal imposes obligations on some information society services. However, these obligations remain reasonable in view of the nature of the services covered, the significant impact of these services on the online content market and the large amounts of copyright-protected content stored by these services. The introduction of a related right for press publishers would improve legal certainty and their bargaining position, which is the pursued objective. The proposal is proportionate as it only covers press publications and digital uses. Furthermore, the proposal will not affect retroactively any acts undertaken or rights acquired before the date of transposition. The transparency obligation contained in the proposal only aims at rebalancing contractual relationships between creators and their contractual counterparts while respecting contractual freedom.

- **Choice of the instrument**

The proposal relates to, and in some instances modifies, existing Directives. It also leaves, when appropriate and taking into account the aim to be achieved, margin of manoeuver for Member States while ensuring that the objective of a functioning internal market is met. The choice of a Directive is therefore adequate.

3. RESULTS OF EX-POST EVALUATIONS, STAKEHOLDER CONSULTATIONS AND IMPACT ASSESSMENTS

- **Ex-post evaluations/fitness checks of existing legislation**

The Commission carried out a review of the existing copyright rules between 2013 and 2016 with the objective to "ensure that copyright and copyright-related practices stay fit for purpose in the new digital context"[1]. Even if it started before the adoption of the Commission's Better Regulation Agenda in May 2015[2], this review process was carried out in the spirit of the Better Regulation guidelines. The review process highlighted, in particular, problems with the implementation of certain exceptions and their lack of cross-border effect[3] and pointed out to difficulties in the use of copyright-protected content, notably in the digital and cross-border context that have emerged in recent years.

• **Stakeholder consultations**

Several public consultations were held by the Commission. The consultation on the review of the EU copyright rules carried out between 5 December 2013 and 5 March 2014[4] provided the Commission with an overview of stakeholders' views on the review of the EU copyright rules, including on exceptions and limitations and on the remuneration of authors and performers. The public consultation carried out between 24 September 2015 and 6 January 2016 on the regulatory environment for platforms, online intermediaries, data and cloud computing and the collaborative economy[5] provided evidence and views from all stakeholders on the role of intermediaries in the on-line distribution of works and other subject-matter. Finally, a public consultation was held between the 23 March 2016 and 15 June 2016 on the role of publishers in the copyright value chain and on the "panorama exception". This consultation allowed collecting views notably on the possible introduction in EU law of a new related right for publishers.

In addition, between 2014 and 2016, the Commission had discussions with the relevant stakeholders on the different topics addressed by the proposal.

---

[1] COM(2012) 789 final.

[2] COM(2015) 215 final.

[3] Covering, respectively, the exception on illustration for teaching and research (as it relates to text and data mining) and on specific acts of reproduction (as it relates to preservation).

[4] Reports on the responses to the consultation available on: http://ec.europa.eu/internal_market/consultations/2013/copyright-rules/docs/contributions/consultation-report_en.pdf.

[5] First results available on https://ec.europa.eu/digital-single-market/news/first-brief-results-public-consultation-regulatory-environment-platforms-online-intermediaries.

- Collection and use of expertise

Legal[1] and economic[2] studies have been conducted on the application of Directive 2001/29/EC, on the economic impacts of adapting some exceptions and limitations, on the legal framework of text and data mining and on the remuneration of authors and performers.

- Impact assessment

An impact assessment was carried out for this proposal[3]. On 22 July 2016, the Regulatory Scrutiny Board gave a positive opinion on the understanding that the impact assessment will be further improved.[4] The final Impact Assessment takes into account comments contained in that opinion.

The Impact Assessment examines the baseline scenarios, policy options and their impacts for eight topics regrouped under three chapters, namely (i) ensuring wider access to content, (ii) adapting exceptions to digital and cross-border environment and (iii) achieving a well-functioning marketplace for copyright. The impact on the different stakeholders was analysed for each policy option; taking in particular into account the predominance of SMEs in the creative industries the analysis concludes that introducing a special regime would not be appropriate as it would defeat the purpose of the intervention. The policy options of each topic are shortly presented below.

Access and availability of audiovisual works on video-on-demand platforms: A non-legislative option (Option 1), consisting in the organisation of a stakeholder dialogue on licensing issues, was not retained as it was deemed insufficient to address individual cases of blockages. The chosen option (Option 2) combines the organisati-

---

[1] Study on the application of Directive 2001/29/EC on copyright and related rights in the information society: http://ec.europa.eu/internal_market/copyright/studies/index_en.htm; Study on the legal framework of text and data mining: http://ec.europa.eu/internal_market/copyright/docs/studies/1403_study2_en.pdf; Study on the making available right and its relationship with the reproduction right in cross-border digital transmissions: http://ec.europa.eu/internal_market/copyright/docs/studies/141219-study_en.pdf; Study on the remuneration of authors and performers for the use of their works and the fixation of their performances: https://ec.europa.eu/digital-single-market/en/news/commission-gathers-evidence-remuneration-authors-and-performers-use-their-works-and-fixations; Study on the remuneration of authors of books and scientific journals, translators, journalists and visual artists for the use of their works: [hyperlink to be included—publication pending].

[2] Study "Assessing the economic impacts of adapting certain limitations and exceptions to copyright and related rights in the EU": http://ec.europa.eu/internal_market/copyright/docs/studies/131001-study_en.pdf and "Assessing the economic impacts of adapting certain limitations and exceptions to copyright and related rights in the EU—Analysis of specific policy options": http://ec.europa.eu/internal_market/copyright/docs/studies/140623-limitations-economic-impacts-study_en.pdf.

[3] Add link to IA and Executive Summary.

[4] Add link to RSB opinion.

on of a stakeholder dialogue with the obligation for Member States to set up a negotiation mechanism.

Out-of-commerce works: Option 1 required Member States to put in place legal mechanisms, with cross-border effect, to facilitate licensing agreements for out-of-commerce books and learned journals and to organise a stakeholder dialogue at national level to facilitate the implementation of that mechanism. Option 2 went further since it applied to all types of out-of-commerce works. This extension was deemed necessary to address the licensing of out-of-commerce works in all sectors. Option 2 was therefore chosen.

Use of works and other subject-matter in digital and cross-border teaching activities: Option 1 consisted in providing guidance to Member States on the application of the existing teaching exception in the digital environment and the organisation of a stakeholder dialogue. This was considered not sufficient to ensure legal certainty, in particular as regards cross-border uses. Option 2 required the introduction of a mandatory exception with a cross-border effect covering digital uses. Option 3 is similar to Option 2 but leaves some flexibility to Member States that can decide to apply the exception depending on the availability of licences. This option was deemed to be the most proportionate one.

Text and data mining: Option 1 consisted in self-regulation initiatives from the industry. Other options consisted in the introduction of a mandatory exception covering text and data mining. In Option 2, the exception only covered uses pursuing a non-commercial scientific research purpose. Option 3 allowed uses for commercial scientific research purpose but limited the benefit of the exception to some beneficiaries. Option 4 went further as it did not restrict beneficiaries. Option 3 was deemed to be the most proportionate one.

Preservation of cultural heritage: Option 1 consisted in the provision of guidance to Member States on the implementation of the exception on specific acts of reproduction for preservation purposes. This Option was rejected as it was deemed insufficient to achieve legal certainty in the field. Option 2, consisting in a mandatory exception for preservation purposes by cultural heritage institutions, was chosen.

Use of copyright-protected content by information society services storing and giving access to large amounts of works and other subject-matter uploaded by their users: Option 1 consisted in the organisation of a stakeholder dialogue. This approach was rejected as it would have a limited impact on the possibility for rightholders to determine the conditions of use of their works and other subject-matter. The chosen option (Option 2) goes further and provides for an obligation for certain service providers to put in place appropriate technologies and fosters the conclusion of agreements with rightholders.

Rights in publications: Option 1 consisted in the organisation of a stakeholder dialogue to find solutions for the dissemination of press publishers' content. This option was deemed insufficient to ensure legal certainty across the EU. Option 2 consisted in the introduction of a related right covering digital uses of press publications. In addition to this, Option 3 leaves the option for Member States to enable publishers, to which rights have been transferred or licensed by an author, to claim a share in the compensation for uses under an exception. This last option was the one retained as it addressed all relevant problems.

Fair remuneration in contracts of authors and performers: Option 1 consisted in providing a recommendation to Member States and organising a stakeholder dialogue. This option was rejected since it would not be efficient enough. Option 2 foresaw the introduction of transparency obligations on the contractual counterparts of creators. On top of that, Option 3 proposed the introduction of a remuneration adjustment mechanism and a dispute resolution mechanism. This option was the one retained since Option 2 would not have provided enforcement means to creators to support the transparency obligation.

- **Regulatory fitness and simplification**

For the uses covered by the exceptions, the proposal will allow educational establishments, public-interest research institutions and cultural heritage institutions to reduce transaction costs. This reduction of transaction costs does not necessarily mean that rightholders would suffer a loss of income or licensing revenues: the scope and conditions of the exceptions ensure that rightholders would suffer minimal harm. The impact on SMEs in these fields (in particular scientific and educational publishers) and on their business models should therefore be limited.

Mechanisms aiming to improve licensing practices are likely to reduce transaction costs and increase licensing revenues for rightholders. SMEs in the fields (producers, distributors, publishers, etc.) would be positively affected. Other stakeholders, such as VoD platforms, would also be positively affected. The proposal also includes several measures (transparency obligation on rightholders' counterparts, introduction of a new right for press publishers and obligation on some online services) that would improve the bargaining position of rightholders and the control they have on the use of their works and other subject-matter. It is expected to have a positive impact on rightholders' revenues.

The proposal includes new obligations on some online services and on those to which authors and performers transfer their rights. These obligations may impose additional costs. However, the proposal ensures that the costs will remain proportionate and that, when necessary, some actors would not be subject to the obligation. For instance, the transparency obligation will not apply when the administrative costs it implies are disproportionate in view of the generated revenues. As for the obligation on online services, it only applies to information society services storing and giving access to large amounts of copyright-protected content uploaded by their users.

The proposal foresees the obligation for Member States to implement negotiation and dispute resolution mechanisms. This implies compliance costs for Member States. However, they could rely in most cases on existing structures, which would limit the costs. The teaching exception can also entail some costs for Member States linked to the measures ensuring the availability and visibility of licences for educational establishments.

New technological developments have been carefully examined. The proposal includes several exceptions that aim at facilitating the use of copyright-protected content via new technologies. This proposal also includes measures to facilitate access to content, including via digital networks. Finally, it ensures a balanced bargaining position between all actors in the digital environment.

- **Fundamental rights**

By improving the bargaining position of authors and performers and the control rightholders have on the use of their copyright-protected content, the proposal will have a positive impact on copyright as a property right, protected under Article 17 of the Charter of Fundamental Rights of the European Union ("the Charter"). This positive impact will be reinforced by the measures to improve licensing practices, and ultimately rightholders' revenues. New exceptions that reduce to some extent the rightholders' monopoly are justified by other public interest objectives. These exceptions are likely to have a positive impact on the right to education and on cultural diversity. Finally, the Directive has a limited impact on the freedom to conduct a business and on the freedom of expression and information, as recognised respectively by Articles 16 and 11 of the Charter, due to the mitigation measures put in place and a balanced approach to the obligations set on the relevant stakeholders.

4. BUDGETARY IMPLICATIONS

The proposal has no impact on the European Union budget.

5. OTHER ELEMENTS

- **Implementation plans and monitoring, evaluation and reporting arrangements**

In accordance with Article 22 the Commission shall carry out a review of the Directive no sooner than[five] years after the date of [transposition].

- **Explanatory documents**

In compliance with recital 48 of the proposal, Member States will notify the Commission of their transposition measures with explanatory documents. This is necessary given the complexity of rules laid down by the proposal and the importance to keep a harmonised approach of rules applicable to the digital and cross-border environment.

- **Detailed explanation of the specific provisions of the proposal**

The first title contains general provisions which (i) specify the subject-matter and the scope of the Directive and (ii) provide definitions that will need to be interpreted in a uniform manner in the Union.

The second title concerns measures to adapt exceptions and limitations to the digital and cross-border environment. This title includes three articles which require Member States to provide for mandatory exceptions or a limitation allowing (i) text and data mining carried out by research organisations for the purposes of scientific research (Article 3); (ii) digital uses of works and other subject-matter for the sole purpose of illustration for teaching (Article 4) and (iii) cultural heritage institutions to make copies of works and other subject-matter that are permanently in their collections to the extent necessary for their preservation (Article 5). Article 6 provides for common provisions to the title on exceptions and limitations.

The third title concerns measures to improve licensing practices and ensure wider access to content. Article 7 requires Member States to put in place a legal mechanism to facilitate licensing agreements of out-of-commerce works and other subject-matter. Article 8 guarantees the cross-border effect of such licensing agreements. Article 9 requires Member States to put in place a stakeholder dialogue on issues relating to Articles 7 and 8. Article 10 creates an obligation for Member States to put in place a negotiation mechanism to facilitate negotiations on the online exploitation of audiovisual works.

The fourth title concerns measures to achieve a well-functioning marketplace for copyright. Articles 11 and 12 (i) extend the rights provided for in Articles 2 and 3(2) of Directive 2001/29/EC to publishers of press publications for the digital use of their publications and (ii) provide for the option for Member States to provide all publishers with the possibility to claim a share in the compensation for uses made under an exception. Article 13 creates an obligation on information society service providers storing and giving access to large amounts of works and other subject-matter uploaded by their users to take appropriate and proportionate measures to ensure the functioning of agreements concluded with rightholders and to prevent the availability on their services of content identified by rightholders in cooperation with the service providers. Article 14 requires Member States to include transparency obligations to the benefit of authors and performers. Article 15 requires Member States to establish a contract adjustment mechanism, in support of the obligation provided for in Article 14. Article 16 requires Member States to set up a dispute resolution mechanism for issues arising from the application of Articles 14 and 15.

The fifth title contains final provisions on amendments to other directives, the application in time, transitional provisions, the protection of personal data, the transposition, the review and the entry into force.

2016/0280 (COD)

Proposal for a

DIRECTIVE OF THE EUROPEAN PARLIAMENT AND OF THE COUNCIL

on copyright in the Digital Single Market

(Text with EEA relevance)

THE EUROPEAN PARLIAMENT AND THE COUNCIL OF THE EUROPEAN UNION,

Having regard to the Treaty on the Functioning of the European Union, and in particular Article 114 thereof,

Having regard to the proposal from the European Commission,

After transmission of the draft legislative act to the national parliaments,

Having regard to the opinion of the European Economic and Social Committee[1],

Having regard to the opinion of the Committee of the Regions[2],

Acting in accordance with the ordinary legislative procedure,

Whereas:

(1) The Treaty provides for the establishment of an internal market and the institution of a system ensuring that competition in the internal market is not distorted. Harmonisation of the laws of the Member States on copyright and related rights should contribute further to the achievement of those objectives.

(2) The directives which have been adopted in the area of copyright and related rights provide for a high level of protection for rightholders and create a framework wherein the exploitation of works and other protected subject-matter can take place. This harmonised legal framework contributes to the good functioning of the internal market; it stimulates innovation, creativity, investment and production of new content, also in the digital environment. The protection provided by this legal framework also contributes to the Union's objective of respecting and promoting cultural diversity while at the same time bringing the European common cultural heritage to the fore. Article 167(4) of the Treaty on the Functioning of the European Union requires the Union to take cultural aspects into account in its action.

(3) Rapid technological developments continue to transform the way works and other subject-matter are created, produced, distributed and exploited. New business

---

[1] OJ C , , p. .
[2] OJ C , , p. .

models and new actors continue to emerge. The objectives and the principles laid down by the Union copyright framework remain sound. However, legal uncertainty remains, for both rightholders and users, as regards certain uses, including cross-border uses, of works and other subject-matter in the digital environment. As set out in the Communication of the Commission entitled "Towards a modern, more European copyright framework"[1], in some areas it is necessary to adapt and supplement the current Union copyright framework. This Directive provides for rules to adapt certain exceptions and limitations to digital and cross-border environments, as well as measures to facilitate certain licensing practices as regards the dissemination of out-of-commerce works and the online availability of audiovisual works on video-on-demand platforms with a view to ensuring wider access to content. In order to achieve a well-functioning marketplace for copyright, there should also be rules on rights in publications, on the use of works and other subject-matter by online service providers storing and giving access to user uploaded content and on the transparency of authors' and performers' contracts.

(4) This Directive is based upon, and complements, the rules laid down in the Directives currently in force in this area, in particular Directive 96/9/EC of the European Parliament and of the Council[2], Directive 2001/29/EC of the European Parliament and of the Council[3], Directive 2006/115/EC of the European Parliament and of the Council[4], Directive 2009/24/EC of the European Parliament and of the Council[5], Directive 2012/28/EU of the European Parliament and of the Council[6] and Directive 2014/26/EU of the European Parliament and of the Council[7].

---

[1] COM(2015) 626 final.

[2] Directive 96/9/EC of the European Parliament and of the Council of 11 March 1996 on the legal protection of databases (OJ L 77, 27.3.1996, p. 20–28).

[3] Directive 2001/29/EC of the European Parliament and of the Council of 22 May 2001 on the harmonisation of certain aspects of copyright and related rights in the information society (OJ L 167, 22.6.2001, p. 10–19).

[4] Directive 2006/115/EC of the European Parliament and of the Council of 12 December 2006 on rental right and lending right and on certain rights related to copyright in the field of intellectual property (OJ L 376, 27.12.2006, p. 28–35).

[5] Directive 2009/24/EC of the European Parliament and of the Council of 23 April 2009 on the legal protection of computer programs (OJ L 111, 5.5.2009, p. 16–22).

[6] Directive 2012/28/EU of the European Parliament and of the Council of 25 October 2012 on certain permitted uses of orphan works (OJ L 299, 27.10.2012, p. 5–12).

[7] Directive 2014/26/EU of the European Parliament and of the Council of 26 February 2014 on collective management of copyright and related rights and multi-territorial licensing of rights in musical works for online use in the internal market (OJ L 84, 20.3.2014, p. 72–98).

(5) In the fields of research, education and preservation of cultural heritage, digital technologies permit new types of uses that are not clearly covered by the current Union rules on exceptions and limitations. In addition, the optional nature of exceptions and limitations provided for in Directives 2001/29/EC, 96/9/EC and 2009/24/EC in these fields may negatively impact the functioning of the internal market. This is particularly relevant as regards cross-border uses, which are becoming increasingly important in the digital environment. Therefore, the existing exceptions and limitations in Union law that are relevant for scientific research, teaching and preservation of cultural heritage should be reassessed in the light of those new uses. Mandatory exceptions or limitations for uses of text and data mining technologies in the field of scientific research, illustration for teaching in the digital environment and for preservation of cultural heritage should be introduced. For uses not covered by the exceptions or the limitation provided for in this Directive, the exceptions and limitations existing in Union law should continue to apply. Directives 96/9/EC and 2001/29/EC should be adapted.

(6) The exceptions and the limitation set out in this Directive seek to achieve a fair balance between the rights and interests of authors and other rightholders on the one hand, and of users on the other. They can be applied only in certain special cases which do not conflict with the normal exploitation of the works or other subject-matter and do not unreasonably prejudice the legitimate interests of the rightholders.

(7) The protection of technological measures established in Directive 2001/29/EC remains essential to ensure the protection and the effective exercise of the rights granted to authors and to other rightholders under Union law. This protection should be maintained while ensuring that the use of technological measures does not prevent the enjoyment of the exceptions and the limitation established in this Directive, which are particularly relevant in the online environment. Rightholders should have the opportunity to ensure this through voluntary measures. They should remain free to choose the format and the modalities to provide the beneficiaries of the exceptions and the limitation established in this Directive with the means to benefit from them provided that such means are appropriate. In the absence of voluntary measures, Member States should take appropriate measures in accordance with the first subparagraph of Article 6(4) of Directive 2001/29/EC.

(8) New technologies enable the automated computational analysis of information in digital form, such as text, sounds, images or data, generally known as text and data mining. Those technologies allow researchers to process large amounts of information to gain new knowledge and discover new trends. Whilst text and data mining

technologies are prevalent across the digital economy, there is widespread acknowledgment that text and data mining can in particular benefit the research community and in so doing encourage innovation. However, in the Union, research organisations such as universities and research institutes are confronted with legal uncertainty as to the extent to which they can perform text and data mining of content. In certain instances, text and data mining may involve acts protected by copyright and/or by the *sui generis* database right, notably the reproduction of works or other subject-matter and/or the extraction of contents from a database. Where there is no exception or limitation which applies, an authorisation to undertake such acts would be required from rightholders. Text and data mining may also be carried out in relation to mere facts or data which are not protected by copyright and in such instances no authorisation would be required.

(9) Union law already provides certain exceptions and limitations covering uses for scientific research purposes which may apply to acts of text and data mining. However, those exceptions and limitations are optional and not fully adapted to the use of technologies in scientific research. Moreover, where researchers have lawful access to content, for example through subscriptions to publications or open access licences, the terms of the licences may exclude text and data mining. As research is increasingly carried out with the assistance of digital technology, there is a risk that the Union's competitive position as a research area will suffer unless steps are taken to address the legal uncertainty for text and data mining.

(10) This legal uncertainty should be addressed by providing for a mandatory exception to the right of reproduction and also to the right to prevent extraction from a database. The new exception should be without prejudice to the existing mandatory exception on temporary acts of reproduction laid down in Article 5(1) of Directive 2001/29, which should continue to apply to text and data mining techniques which do not involve the making of copies going beyond the scope of that exception. Research organisations should also benefit from the exception when they engage into public-private partnerships.

(11) Research organisations across the Union encompass a wide variety of entities the primary goal of which is to conduct scientific research or to do so together with the provision of educational services. Due to the diversity of such entities, it is important to have a common understanding of the beneficiaries of the exception. Despite different legal forms and structures, research organisations across Member States generally have in common that they act either on a not for profit basis or in the context of a public-interest mission recognised by the State. Such a public-interest mission may, for

example, be reflected through public funding or through provisions in national laws or public contracts. At the same time, organisations upon which commercial undertakings have a decisive influence allowing them to exercise control because of structural situations such as their quality of shareholders or members, which may result in preferential access to the results of the research, should not be considered research organisations for the purposes of this Directive.

(12) In view of a potentially high number of access requests to and downloads of their works or other subject-matter, rightholders should be allowed to apply measures where there is risk that the security and integrity of the system or databases where the works or other subject-matter are hosted would be jeopardised. Those measures should not exceed what is necessary to pursue the objective of ensuring the security and integrity of the system and should not undermine the effective application of the exception.

(13) There is no need to provide for compensation for rightholders as regards uses under the text and data mining exception introduced by this Directive given that in view of the nature and scope of the exception the harm should be minimal.

(14) Article 5(3)(a) of Directive 2001/29/EC allows Member States to introduce an exception or limitation to the rights of reproduction, communication to the public and making available to the public for the sole purpose of, among others, illustration for teaching. In addition, Articles 6(2)(b) and 9(b) of Directive 96/9/EC permit the use of a database and the extraction or reutilization of a substantial part of its contents for the purpose of illustration for teaching. The scope of those exceptions or limitations as they apply to digital uses is unclear. In addition, there is a lack of clarity as to whether those exceptions or limitations would apply where teaching is provided online and thereby at a distance. Moreover, the existing framework does not provide for a cross-border effect. This situation may hamper the development of digitally-supported teaching activities and distance learning. Therefore, the introduction of a new mandatory exception or limitation is necessary to ensure that educational establishments benefit from full legal certainty when using works or other subject-matter in digital teaching activities, including online and across borders.

(15) While distance learning and cross-border education programmes are mostly developed at higher education level, digital tools and resources are increasingly used at all education levels, in particular to improve and enrich the learning experience. The exception or limitation provided for in this Directive should therefore benefit all educational establishments in primary, secondary, vocational and higher education to the extent they pursue their educational activity for a non-commercial purpose. The

organisational structure and the means of funding of an educational establishment are not the decisive factors to determine the non-commercial nature of the activity.

(16) The exception or limitation should cover digital uses of works and other subject-matter such as the use of parts or extracts of works to support, enrich or complement the teaching, including the related learning activities. The use of the works or other subject-matter under the exception or limitation should be only in the context of teaching and learning activities carried out under the responsibility of educational establishments, including during examinations, and be limited to what is necessary for the purpose of such activities. The exception or limitation should cover both uses through digital means in the classroom and online uses through the educational establishment's secure electronic network, the access to which should be protected, notably by authentication procedures. The exception or limitation should be understood as covering the specific accessibility needs of persons with a disability in the context of illustration for teaching.

(17) Different arrangements, based on the implementation of the exception provided for in Directive 2001/29/EC or on licensing agreements covering further uses, are in place in a number of Member States in order to facilitate educational uses of works and other subject-matter. Such arrangements have usually been developed taking account of the needs of educational establishments and different levels of education. Whereas it is essential to harmonise the scope of the new mandatory exception or limitation in relation to digital uses and cross-border teaching activities, the modalities of implementation may differ from a Member State to another, to the extent they do not hamper the effective application of the exception or limitation or cross-border uses. This should allow Member States to build on the existing arrangements concluded at national level. In particular, Member States could decide to subject the application of the exception or limitation, fully or partially, to the availability of adequate licences, covering at least the same uses as those allowed under the exception. This mechanism would, for example, allow giving precedence to licences for materials which are primarily intended for the educational market. In order to avoid that such mechanism results in legal uncertainty or administrative burden for educational establishments, Member States adopting this approach should take concrete measures to ensure that licensing schemes allowing digital uses of works or other subject-matter for the purpose of illustration for teaching are easily available and that educational establishments are aware of the existence of such licensing schemes.

(18) An act of preservation may require a reproduction of a work or other subject-matter in the collection of a cultural heritage institution and consequently the au-

thorisation of the relevant rightholders. Cultural heritage institutions are engaged in the preservation of their collections for future generations. Digital technologies offer new ways to preserve the heritage contained in those collections but they also create new challenges. In view of these new challenges, it is necessary to adapt the current legal framework by providing a mandatory exception to the right of reproduction in order to allow those acts of preservation.

(19) Different approaches in the Member States for acts of preservation by cultural heritage institutions hamper cross-border cooperation and the sharing of means of preservation by cultural heritage institutions in the internal market, leading to an inefficient use of resources.

(20) Member States should therefore be required to provide for an exception to permit cultural heritage institutions to reproduce works and other subject-matter permanently in their collections for preservation purposes, for example, to address technological obsolescence or the degradation of original supports. Such an exception should allow for the making of copies by the appropriate preservation tool, means or technology, in the required number and at any point in the life of a work or other subject-matter to the extent required in order to produce a copy for preservation purposes only.

(21) For the purposes of this Directive, works and other subject-matter should be considered to be permanently in the collection of a cultural heritage institution when copies are owned or permanently held by the cultural heritage institution, for example as a result of a transfer of ownership or licence agreements.

(22) Cultural heritage institutions should benefit from a clear framework for the digitisation and dissemination, including across borders, of out-of-commerce works or other subject-matter. However, the particular characteristics of the collections of out-of-commerce works mean that obtaining the prior consent of the individual rightholders may be very difficult. This can be due, for example, to the age of the works or other subject-matter, their limited commercial value or the fact that they were never intended for commercial use. It is therefore necessary to provide for measures to facilitate the licensing of rights in out-of-commerce works that are in the collections of cultural heritage institutions and thereby to allow the conclusion of agreements with cross-border effect in the internal market.

(23) Member States should, within the framework provided for in this Directive, have flexibility in choosing the specific type of mechanism allowing for licences for out-of-commerce works to extend to the rights of rightholders that are not represented by the collective management organisation, in accordance to their legal traditions, practices or circumstances. Such mechanisms can include extended collective licen-

sing and presumptions of representation.

(24) For the purpose of those licensing mechanisms, a rigorous and well-functioning collective management system is important. That system includes in particular rules of good governance, transparency and reporting, as well as the regular, diligent and accurate distribution and payment of amounts due to individual rightholders, as provided for by Directive 2014/26/EU. Additional appropriate safeguards should be available for all rightholders, who should be given the opportunity to exclude the application of such mechanisms to their works or other subject-matter. Conditions attached to those mechanisms should not affect their practical relevance for cultural heritage institutions.

(25) Considering the variety of works and other subject-matter in the collections of cultural heritage institutions, it is important that the licensing mechanisms introduced by this Directive are available and can be used in practice for different types of works and other subject-matter, including photographs, sound recordings and audiovisual works. In order to reflect the specificities of different categories of works and other subject-matter as regards modes of publication and distribution and to facilitate the usability of those mechanisms, specific requirements and procedures may have to be established by Member States for the practical application of those licensing mechanisms. It is appropriate that Member States consult rightholders, users and collective management organisations when doing so.

(26) For reasons of international comity, the licensing mechanisms for the digitisation and dissemination of out-of-commerce works provided for in this Directive should not apply to works or other subject-matter that are first published or, in the absence of publication, first broadcast in a third country or, in the case of cinematographic or audiovisual works, to works the producer of which has his headquarters or habitual residence in a third country. Those mechanisms should also not apply to works or other subject-matter of third country nationals except when they are first published or, in the absence of publication, first broadcast in the territory of a Member State or, in the case of cinematographic or audiovisual works, to works of which the producer's headquarters or habitual residence is in a Member State.

(27) As mass digitisation projects can entail significant investments by cultural heritage institutions, any licences granted under the mechanisms provided for in this Directive should not prevent them from generating reasonable revenues in order to cover the costs of the licence and the costs of digitising and disseminating the works and other subject-matter covered by the licence.

(28) Information regarding the future and ongoing use of out-of-commerce works

and other subject-matter by cultural heritage institutions on the basis of the licensing mechanisms provided for in this Directive and the arrangements in place for all rightholders to exclude the application of licences to their works or other subject-matter should be adequately publicised. This is particularly important when uses take place across borders in the internal market. It is therefore appropriate to make provision for the creation of a single publicly accessible online portal for the Union to make such information available to the public for a reasonable period of time before the cross-border use takes place. Under Regulation (EU) No 386/2012 of the European Parliament and of the Council❶, the European Union Intellectual Property Office is entrusted with certain tasks and activities, financed by making use of its own budgetary measures, aiming at facilitating and supporting the activities of national authorities, the private sector and Union institutions in the fight against, including the prevention of, infringement of intellectual property rights. It is therefore appropriate to rely on that Office to establish and manage the European portal making such information available.

(29) On-demand services have the potential to play a decisive role in the dissemination of European works across the European Union. However, agreements on the online exploitation of such works may face difficulties related to the licensing of rights. Such issues may, for instance, appear when the holder of the rights for a given territory is not interested in the online exploitation of the work or where there are issues linked to the windows of exploitation.

(30) To facilitate the licensing of rights in audiovisual works to video-on-demand platforms, this Directive requires Member States to set up a negotiation mechanism allowing parties willing to conclude an agreement to rely on the assistance of an impartial body. The body should meet with the parties and help with the negotiations by providing professional and external advice. Against that background, Member States should decide on the conditions of the functioning of the negotiation mechanism, including the timing and duration of the assistance to negotiations and the bearing of the costs. Member States should ensure that administrative and financial burdens remain proportionate to guarantee the efficiency of the negotiation forum.

(31) A free and pluralist press is essential to ensure quality journalism and

---

❶ Regulation (EU) No 386/2012 of the European Parliament and of the Council of 19 April 2012 on entrusting the Office for Harmonization in the Internal Market (Trade Marks and Designs) with tasks related to the enforcement of intellectual property rights, including the assembling of public and private-sector representatives as a European Observatory on Infringements of Intellectual Property Rights (OJ L 129, 16.5.2012, p.1-6).

citizens' access to information. It provides a fundamental contribution to public debate and the proper functioning of a democratic society. In the transition from print to digital, publishers of press publications are facing problems in licensing the online use of their publications and recouping their investments. In the absence of recognition of publishers of press publications as rightholders, licensing and enforcement in the digital environment is often complex and inefficient.

(32) The organisational and financial contribution of publishers in producing press publications needs to be recognised and further encouraged to ensure the sustainability of the publishing industry. It is therefore necessary to provide at Union level a harmonised legal protection for press publications in respect of digital uses. Such protection should be effectively guaranteed through the introduction, in Union law, of rights related to copyright for the reproduction and making available to the public of press publications in respect of digital uses.

(33) For the purposes of this Directive, it is necessary to define the concept of press publication in a way that embraces only journalistic publications, published by a service provider, periodically or regularly updated in any media, for the purpose of informing or entertaining. Such publications would include, for instance, daily newspapers, weekly or monthly magazines of general or special interest and news websites. Periodical publications which are published for scientific or academic purposes, such as scientific journals, should not be covered by the protection granted to press publications under this Directive. This protection does not extend to acts of hyperlinking which do not constitute communication to the public.

(34) The rights granted to the publishers of press publications under this Directive should have the same scope as the rights of reproduction and making available to the public provided for in Directive 2001/29/EC, insofar as digital uses are concerned. They should also be subject to the same provisions on exceptions and limitations as those applicable to the rights provided for in Directive 2001/29/EC including the exception on quotation for purposes such as criticism or review laid down in Article 5(3)(d) of that Directive.

(35) The protection granted to publishers of press publications under this Directive should not affect the rights of the authors and other rightholders in the works and other subject-matter incorporated therein, including as regards the extent to which authors and other rightholders can exploit their works or other subject-matter independently from the press publication in which they are incorporated. Therefore, publishers of press publications should not be able to invoke the protection granted to them against authors and other rightholders. This is without prejudice to contractual

arrangements concluded between the publishers of press publications, on the one side, and authors and other rightholders, on the other side.

(36) Publishers, including those of press publications, books or scientific publications, often operate on the basis of the transfer of authors' rights by means of contractual agreements or statutory provisions. In this context, publishers make an investment with a view to the exploitation of the works contained in their publications and may in some instances be deprived of revenues where such works are used under exceptions or limitations such as the ones for private copying and reprography. In a number of Member States compensation for uses under those exceptions is shared between authors and publishers. In order to take account of this situation and improve legal certainty for all concerned parties, Member States should be allowed to determine that, when an author has transferred or licensed his rights to a publisher or otherwise contributes with his works to a publication and there are systems in place to compensate for the harm caused by an exception or limitation, publishers are entitled to claim a share of such compensation, whereas the burden on the publisher to substantiate his claim should not exceed what is required under the system in place.

(37) Over the last years, the functioning of the online content marketplace has gained in complexity. Online services providing access to copyright protected content uploaded by their users without the involvement of right holders have flourished and have become main sources of access to content online. This affects rightholders' possibilities to determine whether, and under which conditions, their work and other subject-matter are used as well as their possibilities to get an appropriate remuneration for it.

(38) Where information society service providers store and provide access to the public to copyright protected works or other subject-matter uploaded by their users, thereby going beyond the mere provision of physical facilities and performing an act of communication to the public, they are obliged to conclude licensing agreements with rightholders, unless they are eligible for the liability exemption provided in Article 14 of Directive 2000/31/EC of the European Parliament and of the Council[1].

In respect of Article 14, it is necessary to verify whether the service provider plays an active role, including by optimising the presentation of the uploaded works or subject-matter or promoting them, irrespective of the nature of the means used therefor.

---

[1] Directive 2000/31/EC of the European Parliament and of the Council of 8 June 2000 on certain legal aspects of information society services, in particular electronic commerce, in the Internal Market (OJ L 178, 17.7.2000, p.1-16).

In order to ensure the functioning of any licensing agreement, information society service providers storing and providing access to the public to large amounts of copyright protected works or other subject-matter uploaded by their users should take appropriate and proportionate measures to ensure protection of works or other subject-matter, such as implementing effective technologies. This obligation should also apply when the information society service providers are eligible for the liability exemption provided in Article 14 of Directive 2000/31/EC.

(39) Collaboration between information society service providers storing and providing access to the public to large amounts of copyright protected works or other subject-matter uploaded by their users and rightholders is essential for the functioning of technologies, such as content recognition technologies. In such cases, rightholders should provide the necessary data to allow the services to identify their content and the services should be transparent towards rightholders with regard to the deployed technologies, to allow the assessment of their appropriateness. The services should in particular provide rightholders with information on the type of technologies used, the way they are operated and their success rate for the recognition of rightholders' content. Those technologies should also allow rightholders to get information from the information society service providers on the use of their content covered by an agreement.

(40) Certain rightholders such as authors and performers need information to assess the economic value of their rights which are harmonised under Union law. This is especially the case where such rightholders grant a licence or a transfer of rights in return for remuneration. As authors and performers tend to be in a weaker contractual position when they grant licences or transfer their rights, they need information to assess the continued economic value of their rights, compared to the remuneration received for their licence or transfer, but they often face a lack of transparency. Therefore, the sharing of adequate information by their contractual counterparts or their successors in title is important for the transparency and balance in the system that governs the remuneration of authors and performers.

(41) When implementing transparency obligations, the specificities of different content sectors and of the rights of the authors and performers in each sector should be considered. Member States should consult all relevant stakeholders as that should help determine sector-specific requirements. Collective bargaining should be considered as an option to reach an agreement between the relevant stakeholders regarding transparency. To enable the adaptation of current reporting practices to the transparency obligations, a transitional period should be provided for. The transparency obli-

gations do not need to apply to agreements concluded with collective management organisations as those are already subject to transparency obligations under Directive 2014/26/EU.

(42) Certain contracts for the exploitation of rights harmonised at Union level are of long duration, offering few possibilities for authors and performers to renegotiate them with their contractual counterparts or their successors in title. Therefore, without prejudice to the law applicable to contracts in Member States, there should be a remuneration adjustment mechanism for cases where the remuneration originally agreed under a licence or a transfer of rights is disproportionately low compared to the relevant revenues and the benefits derived from the exploitation of the work or the fixation of the performance, including in light of the transparency ensured by this Directive. The assessment of the situation should take account of the specific circumstances of each case as well as of the specificities and practices of the different content sectors. Where the parties do not agree on the adjustment of the remuneration, the author or performer should be entitled to bring a claim before a court or other competent authority.

(43) Authors and performers are often reluctant to enforce their rights against their contractual partners before a court or tribunal. Member States should therefore provide for an alternative dispute resolution procedure that addresses claims related to obligations of transparency and the contract adjustment mechanism.

(44) The objectives of this Directive, namely the modernisation of certain aspects of the Union copyright framework to take account of technological developments and new channels of distribution of protected content in the internal market, cannot be sufficiently achieved by Member States but can rather, by reason of their scale, effects and cross-border dimension, be better achieved at Union level. Therefore, the Union may adopt measures in accordance with the principle of subsidiarity as set out in Article 5 of the Treaty on European Union. In accordance with the principle of proportionality, as set out in that Article, this Directive does not go beyond what is necessary in order to achieve those objectives.

(45) This Directive respects the fundamental rights and observes the principles recognised in particular by the Charter of Fundamental Rights of the European Union. Accordingly, this Directive should be interpreted and applied in accordance with those rights and principles.

(46) Any processing of personal data under this Directive should respect fundamental rights, including the right to respect for private and family life and the right to protection of personal data under Articles 7 and 8 of the Charter of Fundamental Rights of the European Union and must be in compliance with Directive 95/46/EC of

the European Parliament and of the Council[1] and Directive 2002/58/EC of the European Parliament and of the Council[2].

(47) In accordance with the Joint Political Declaration of 28 September 2011 of Member States and the Commission on explanatory documents[3], Member States have undertaken to accompany, in justified cases, the notification of their transposition measures with one or more documents explaining the relationship between the components of a directive and the corresponding parts of national transposition instruments. With regard to this Directive, the legislator considers the transmission of such documents to be justified,

HAVE ADOPTED THIS DIRECTIVE:

---

[1] Directive 95/46/EC of the European Parliament and of the Council of 24 October 1995 on the protection of individuals with regard to the processing of personal data and on the free movement of such data (OJ L 281, 23.11.1995, p. 31–50). This Directive is repealed with effect from 25 May 2018 and shall be replaced by Regulation (EU) 2016/679 of the European Parliament and of the Council of 27 April 2016 on the protection of natural persons with regard to the processing of personal data and on the free movement of such data, and repealing Directive 95/46/EC (General Data Protection Regulation) (OJ L 119, 4.5.2016, p. 1–88).

[2] Directive 2002/58/EC of the European Parliament and of the Council of 12 July 2002 concerning the processing of personal data and the protection of privacy in the electronic communications sector (Directive on privacy and electronic communications) (OJ L 201, 31.7.2002, p. 37–47), called, as amended by Directives 2006/24/EC and 2009/136/EC, the "e-Privacy Directive".

[3] OJ C 369, 17.12.2011, p. 14.

TITLE I
GENERAL PROVISIONS

Article 1

Subject matter and scope

1. This Directive lays down rules which aim at further harmonising the Union law applicable to copyright and related rights in the framework of the internal market, taking into account in particular digital and cross-border uses of protected content. It also lays down rules on exceptions and limitations, on the facilitation of licences as well as rules aiming at ensuring a well-functioning marketplace for the exploitation of works and other subject-matter.

2. Except in the cases referred to in Article 6, this Directive shall leave intact and shall in no way affect existing rules laid down in the Directives currently in force in this area, in particular Directives 96/9/EC, 2001/29/EC, 2006/115/EC, 2009/24/EC, 2012/28/EU and 2014/26/EU.

Article 2

Definitions

For the purposes of this Directive, the following definitions shall apply:

"research organisation" means a university, a research institute or any other organisation the primary goal of which is to conduct scientific research or to conduct scientific research and provide educational services:

on a non-for-profit basis or by reinvesting all the profits in its scientific research; or

pursuant to a public interest mission recognised by a Member State;

in such a way that the access to the results generated by the scientific research cannot be enjoyed on a preferential basis by an undertaking exercising a decisive influence upon such organisation;

"text and data mining" means any automated analytical technique aiming to analyse text and data in digital form in order to generate information such as patterns, trends and correlations;

"cultural heritage institution" means a publicly accessible library or museum, an archive or a film or audio heritage institution;

"press publication" means a fixation of a collection of literary works of a journalistic nature, which may also comprise other works or subject-matter and constitutes an individual item within a periodical or regularly-updated publication under a single title, such as a newspaper or a general or special interest magazine, having the purpose of providing information related to news or other topics and published in any media under the initiative, editorial responsibility and control of a service provider.

TITLE II
MEASURES TO ADAPT EXCEPTIONS AND LIMITATIONS TO THE DIGITAL AND CROSS-BORDER ENVIRONMENT

Article 3

Text and data mining

1. Member States shall provide for an exception to the rights provided for in Article 2 of Directive 2001/29/EC, Articles 5(a) and 7(1) of Directive 96/9/EC and Article 11(1) of this Directive for reproductions and extractions made by research organisations in order to carry out text and data mining of works or other subject-matter to which they have lawful access for the purposes of scientific research.

2. Any contractual provision contrary to the exception provided for in paragraph 1 shall be unenforceable.

3. Rightholders shall be allowed to apply measures to ensure the security and integrity of the networks and databases where the works or other subject-matter are hosted. Such measures shall not go beyond what is necessary to achieve that objective.

4. Member States shall encourage rightholders and research organisations to define commonly-agreed best practices concerning the application of the measures referred to in paragraph 3.

Article 4

Use of works and other subject-matter in digital and cross-border teaching activities

1. Member States shall provide for an exception or limitation to the rights provided for in Articles 2 and 3 of Directive 2001/29/EC, Articles 5(a) and 7(1) of Directive 96/9/EC, Article 4(1) of Directive 2009/24/EC and Article 11(1) of this Directive in order to allow for the digital use of works and other subject-matter for the sole purpose of illustration for teaching, to the extent justified by the non-commercial purpose to be achieved, provided that the use:

takes place on the premises of an educational establishment or through a secure electronic network accessible only by the educational establishment's pupils or students and teaching staff; is accompanied by the indication of the source, including the author's name, unless this turns out to be impossible.

2. Member States may provide that the exception adopted pursuant to paragraph 1 does not apply generally or as regards specific types of works or other subject-matter, to the extent that adequate licences authorising the acts described in paragraph 1 are easily available in the market.

Member States availing themselves of the provision of the first subparagraph shall take the necessary measures to ensure appropriate availability and visibility of the licences authorising the acts described in paragraph 1 for educational establishments.

3. The use of works and other subject-matter for the sole purpose of illustration for

teaching through secure electronic networks undertaken in compliance with the provisions of national law adopted pursuant to this Article shall be deemed to occur solely in the Member State where the educational establishment is established.

4. Member States may provide for fair compensation for the harm incurred by the rightholders due to the use of their works or other subject-matter pursuant to paragraph 1.

Article 5

Preservation of cultural heritage

Member States shall provide for an exception to the rights provided for in Article 2 of Directive 2001/29/EC, Articles 5(a) and 7(1) of Directive 96/9/EC, Article 4(1)(a) of Directive 2009/24/EC and Article 11(1) of this Directive, permitting cultural heritage institutions, to make copies of any works or other subject-matter that are permanently in their collections, in any format or medium, for the sole purpose of the preservation of such works or other subject-matter and to the extent necessary for such preservation.

Article 6

Common provisions

Article 5(5) and the first, third and fifth subparagraphs of Article 6(4) of Directive 2001/29/EC shall apply to the exceptions and the limitation provided for under this Title.

TITLE III
MEASURES TO IMPROVE LICENSING PRACTICES AND ENSURE WIDER ACCESS TO CONTENT

CHAPTER 1
Out-of-commerce works
Article 7
Use of out-of-commerce works by cultural heritage institutions

1. Member States shall provide that when a collective management organisation, on behalf of its members, concludes a non-exclusive licence for non-commercial purposes with a cultural heritage institution for the digitisation, distribution, communication to the public or making available of out-of-commerce works or other subject-matter permanently in the collection of the institution, such a non-exclusive licence may be extended or presumed to apply to rightholders of the same category as those covered by the licence who are not represented by the collective management organisation, provided that:

the collective management organisation is, on the basis of mandates from rightholders, broadly representative of rightholders in the category of works or other subject-matter and of the rights which are the subject of the licence;

equal treatment is guaranteed to all rightholders in relation to the terms of the licence;

all rightholders may at any time object to their works or other subject-matter being deemed to be out of commerce and exclude the application of the licence to their works or other subject-matter.

2. A work or other subject-matter shall be deemed to be out of commerce when the whole work or other subject-matter, in all its translations, versions and manifestations, is not available to the public through customary channels of commerce and cannot be reasonably expected to become so.

Member States shall, in consultation with rightholders, collective management organisations and cultural heritage institutions, ensure that the requirements used to determine whether works and other subject-matter can be licensed in accordance with paragraph 1 do not extend beyond what is necessary and reasonable and do not preclude the possibility to determine the out-of-commerce status of a collection as a whole, when it is reasonable to presume that all works or other subject-matter in the collection are out of commerce.

3. Member States shall provide that appropriate publicity measures are taken regarding:

the deeming of works or other subject-matter as out of commerce;

the licence, and in particular its application to unrepresented rightholders;

the possibility of rightholders to object, referred to in point (c) of paragraph 1;

including during a reasonable period of time before the works or other subject-matter are digitised, distributed, communicated to the public or made available.

4. Member States shall ensure that the licences referred to in paragraph 1 are sought from a collective management organisation that is representative for the Member State where:

the works or phonograms were first published or, in the absence of publication, where they were first broadcast, except for cinematographic and audiovisual works;

the producers of the works have their headquarters or habitual residence, for cinematographic and audiovisual works; or

the cultural heritage institution is established, when a Member State or a third country could not be determined, after reasonable efforts, according to points (a) and (b).

5. Paragraphs 1, 2 and 3 shall not apply to the works or other subject-matter of third country nationals except where points (a) and (b) of paragraph 4 apply.

Article 8
Cross-border uses

1. Works or other subject-matter covered by a licence granted in accordance with Article 7 may be used by the cultural heritage institution in accordance with the terms of the licence in all Member States.

2. Member States shall ensure that information that allows the identification of the works or other subject-matter covered by a licence granted in accordance with Article 7 and information about the possibility of rightholders to object referred to in Article 7(1)(c) are made publicly accessible in a single online portal for at least six months before the works or other subject-matter are digitised, distributed, communicated to the public or made available in Member States other than the one where the licence is granted, and for the whole duration of the licence.

3. The portal referred to in paragraph 2 shall be established and managed by the European Union Intellectual Property Office in accordance with Regulation (EU) No 386/2012.

Article 9
Stakeholder dialogue

Member States shall ensure a regular dialogue between representative users' and rightholders' organisations, and any other relevant stakeholder organisations, to, on a sector-specific basis, foster the relevance and usability of the licensing mechanisms referred to in Article 7(1), ensure the effectiveness of the safeguards for rightholders referred to in this Chapter, notably as regards publicity measures, and, where applicable, assist in the establishment of the requirements referred to in the second subparagraph of Article 7(2).

CHAPTER 2
Access to and availability of audiovisual works on video-on-demand platforms

Article 10
Negotiation mechanism

Member States shall ensure that where parties wishing to conclude an agreement for the purpose of making available audiovisual works on video-on-demand platforms face difficulties relating to the licensing of rights, they may rely on the assistance of an impartial body with relevant experience. That body shall provide assistance with negotiation and help reach agreements.

No later than[date mentioned in Article 21(1)] Member States shall notify to the Commission the body referred to in paragraph 1.

TITLE IV
MEASURES TO ACHIEVE A WELL-FUNCTIONING MARKETPLACE FOR COPYRIGHT
CHAPTER 1
Rights in publications

Article 11

Protection of press publications concerning digital uses

1. Member States shall provide publishers of press publications with the rights provided for in Article 2 and Article 3(2) of Directive 2001/29/EC for the digital use of their press publications.

2. The rights referred to in paragraph 1 shall leave intact and shall in no way affect any rights provided for in Union law to authors and other rightholders, in respect of the works and other subject-matter incorporated in a press publication. Such rights may not be invoked against those authors and other rightholders and, in particular, may not deprive them of their right to exploit their works and other subject-matter independently from the press publication in which they are incorporated.

3. Articles 5 to 8 of Directive 2001/29/EC and Directive 2012/28/EU shall apply *mutatis mutandis* in respect of the rights referred to in paragraph 1.

4. The rights referred to in paragraph 1 shall expire 20 years after the publication of the press publication. This term shall be calculated from the first day of January of the year following the date of publication.

Article 12

Claims to fair compensation

Member States may provide that where an author has transferred or licensed a right to a publisher, such a transfer or a licence constitutes a sufficient legal basis for the publisher to claim a share of the compensation for the uses of the work made under an exception or limitation to the transferred or licensed right.

CHAPTER 2
Certain uses of protected content by online services

Article 13

Use of protected content by information society service providers storing and giving access to large amounts of works and other subject-matter uploaded by their users

1. Information society service providers that store and provide to the public access to large amounts of works or other subject-matter uploaded by their users shall, in cooperation with rightholders, take measures to ensure the functioning of agreements concluded with rightholders for the use of their works or other subject-matter or to prevent the availability on their services of works or other subject-matter identified by rightholders through the coopera-

tion with the service providers. Those measures, such as the use of effective content recognition technologies, shall be appropriate and proportionate. The service providers shall provide rightholders with adequate information on the functioning and the deployment of the measures, as well as, when relevant, adequate reporting on the recognition and use of the works and other subject-matter.

2. Member States shall ensure that the service providers referred to in paragraph 1 put in place complaints and redress mechanisms that are available to users in case of disputes over the application of the measures referred to in paragraph 1.

3. Member States shall facilitate, where appropriate, the cooperation between the information society service providers and rightholders through stakeholder dialogues to define best practices, such as appropriate and proportionate content recognition technologies, taking into account, among others, the nature of the services, the availability of the technologies and their effectiveness in light of technological developments.

CHAPTER 3
Fair remuneration in contracts of authors and performers
Article 14
Transparency obligation

1. Member States shall ensure that authors and performers receive on a regular basis and taking into account the specificities of each sector, timely, adequate and sufficient information on the exploitation of their works and performances from those to whom they have licensed or transferred their rights, notably as regards modes of exploitation, revenues generated and remuneration due.

2. The obligation in paragraph 1 shall be proportionate and effective and shall ensure an appropriate level of transparency in every sector. However, in those cases where the administrative burden resulting from the obligation would be disproportionate in view of the revenues generated by the exploitation of the work or performance, Member States may adjust the obligation in paragraph 1, provided that the obligation remains effective and ensures an appropriate level of transparency.

3. Member States may decide that the obligation in paragraph 1 does not apply when the contribution of the author or performer is not significant having regard to the overall work or performance.

4. Paragraph 1 shall not be applicable to entities subject to the transparency obligations established by Directive 2014/26/EU.

Article 15
Contract adjustment mechanism

Member States shall ensure that authors and performers are entitled to request additional, appropriate remuneration from the party with whom they entered into a contract for the exploitation of the rights when the remuneration originally agreed is disproportionately low compared to the subsequent relevant revenues and benefits derived from the exploitation of the works or performances.

Article 16

Dispute resolution mechanism

Member States shall provide that disputes concerning the transparency obligation under Article 14 and the contract adjustment mechanism under Article 15 may be submitted to a voluntary, alternative dispute resolution procedure.

TITLE V
FINAL PROVISIONS

Article 17

Amendments to other directives

1. Directive 96/9/EC is amended as follows:

In Article 6(2), point (b) is replaced by the following:

"(b) where there is use for the sole purpose of illustration for teaching or scientific research, as long as the source is indicated and to the extent justified by the non-commercial purpose to be achieved, without prejudice to the exceptions and the limitation provided for in Directive [this Directive];"

In Article 9, point (b) is replaced by the following:

"(b) in the case of extraction for the purposes of illustration for teaching or scientific research, as long as the source is indicated and to the extent justified by the non-commercial purpose to be achieved, without prejudice to the exceptions and the limitation provided for in Directive [this Directive];"

2. Directive 2001/29/EC is amended as follows:

In Article 5(2), point (c) is replaced by the following:

"(c) in respect of specific acts of reproduction made by publicly accessible libraries, educational establishments or museums, or by archives, which are not for direct or indirect economic or commercial advantage, without prejudice to the exceptions and the limitation provided for in Directive [this Directive];"

In Article 5(3), point (a) is replaced by the following:

"(a) use for the sole purpose of illustration for teaching or scientific research, as long as the source, including the author's name, is indicated, unless this turns out to be impossible and to the extent justified by the non-commercial purpose to be achieved, without prejudice to the exceptions and the limitation provided for in Directive [this Directive];"

In Article 12(4), the following points are added:

"(e) to examine the impact of the transposition of Directive [this Directive] on the functioning of the internal market and to highlight any transposition difficulties;

(f) to facilitate the exchange of information on the relevant developments in legislation and case law as well as on the practical application of the measures taken by Member States to implement Directive [this Directive];

(g) to discuss any other questions arising from the application of Directive [this Directive]."

Article 18

Application in time

1. This Directive shall apply in respect of all works and other subject-matter which are

protected by the Member States' legislation in the field of copyright on or after [the date mentioned in Article 21(1)].

2. The provisions of Article 11 shall also apply to press publications published before [the date mentioned in Article 21(1)].

3. This Directive shall apply without prejudice to any acts concluded and rights acquired before [the date mentioned in Article 21(1)].

Article 19
Transitional provision

Agreements for the licence or transfer of rights of authors and performers shall be subject to the transparency obligation in Article 14 as from [one year after the date mentioned in Article 21(1)].

Article 20
Protection of personal data

The processing of personal data carried out within the framework of this Directive shall be carried out in compliance with Directives 95/46/EC and 2002/58/EC.

Article 21
Transposition

1. Member States shall bring into force the laws, regulations and administrative provisions necessary to comply with this Directive by [12 months after entry into force] at the latest. They shall forthwith communicate to the Commission the text of those provisions.

When Member States adopt those provisions, they shall contain a reference to this Directive or be accompanied by such a reference on the occasion of their official publication. Member States shall determine how such reference is to be made.

2. Member States shall communicate to the Commission the text of the main provisions of national law which they adopt in the field covered by this Directive.

Article 22
Review

1. No sooner than [five years after the date mentioned in Article 21(1)], the Commission shall carry out a review of this Directive and present a report on the main findings to the European Parliament, the Council and the European Economic and Social Committee.

2. Member States shall provide the Commission with the necessary information for the preparation of the report referred to in paragraph 1.

Article 23
Entry into force

This Directive shall enter into force on the twentieth day following that of its publication in the *Official Journal of the European Union*.

Article 24

Addressees

This Directive is addressed to the Member States.

Done at Brussels,

For the European Parliament *For the Council*
The President *The President*